SCHOOL
BULLYING

Violence entered my life, destroying that which I loved. Because I was a victim of hatred, I dedicated my life to turn this hatred into understanding, into tolerance, and, why not say it, into love . . . You can love justice and be generous at the same time.

—Michelle Bachelet, President of Chile (2006)

To my daughters, Adrianne and Cindy, who transported me to a life full of possibility

SCHOOL BULLYING

Tools for Avoiding Harm and Liability

MARY JO McGRATH

CORWIN PRESS
A SAGE Publications Company
Thousand Oaks, CA 91320

For information:

Corwin Press
A Sage Publications Company
2455 Teller Road
Thousand Oaks, California 91320
www.corwinpress.com

Sage Publications Ltd.
1 Oliver's Yard
55 City Road
London EC1Y 1SP
United Kingdom

Sage Publications India Pvt. Ltd.
B-42 Panchsheel Enclave
Post Box 4109
New Delhi 110 017   India

Printed in the United States of America.

Library of Congress Cataloging-in-Publication Data

McGrath, Mary Jo.
School bullying: Tools for avoiding harm and liability / Mary Jo McGrath.
     p. cm. Includes bibliographical references and index.
ISBN 1-4129-1571-6 (cloth) — ISBN 1-4129-1572-4 (pbk.)
    1. Bullying in schools—Prevention. 2. School violence. I. Title.
LB3013.3.M355 2007
371.5'8—dc22   2006014861

This book is printed on acid-free paper.

06   07   08   09   10   10 9   8   7   6   5   4   3   2   1

Acquisitions Editor:	Elizabeth Brenkus
Editorial Assistant:	Desirée Enayati
Production Editor:	Diane S. Foster
Copy Editor:	Diana Breti
Typesetter:	C&M Digitals (P) Ltd.
Proofreader:	Annette Pagliaro
Cover Designer:	Monique Hahn
Graphic Designer:	Scott Van Atta

Contents

Figures

Preface

Many of the teachers and parents who grumble that kids "just don't take responsibility" spend their days ordering kids around as though children could learn how to make good decisions by following directions.

—Alfie Kohn, Educational Theorist
(Kohl, 2000, p. 57)

A ll day the phone kept ringing off the hook. And, of course, I was behind on everything. Again the phone rang. I couldn't possibly take another call! I glanced at the caller ID and saw that it was one of my key employees who lives in another city. Hoping to handle the matter quickly, I answered, "Hey Susan, what can I do for you?"

"I'm having a really bad day," Susan responded. Oh, no! I thought. So much for handling this quickly. "What's happening?" I asked.

"Johnny got sent home from school for fighting and I don't know what to do. My child is a bully and I am a terrible mother," Susan sobbed.

"I understand your feelings. Having your seven-year-old sent home from school for fighting would upset any parent. Let's see if we can sort the problem out in a way that allows both you and Johnny to grow even closer."

FOUR POWERFUL QUESTIONS

I had no ready-made answer for Susan, but I had a set of four questions that I knew could guide Susan and Johnny to resolution. I had the same four questions for this mother and son that I give to school leaders all over the world while training them to deal fairly and justly with misconduct issues.

"OK, Susan, let's use the McGrath SUCCEED System approach on this situation. The approach will guide you in using constructive thinking, listening, and speaking and help you to decide what effective action to take to handle the situation. Now, go ask Johnny these four questions:

- What happened at school today that you got sent home for?
- How did those things hurt somebody else or even you?
- Was there something else happening that we need to know about to understand what's going on?
- What should we do now that we know all of the things we just looked at?"

Then I hung up and waited for Susan to call me back.

I have developed and refined these four questions over the span of the last 25 years. One wouldn't think it would take 25 years to sort out four questions, but these are very special questions. They synthesize a great deal of knowledge in various fields, including law, science, philosophy, and ontology (the study of being). These questions are also used to put into action the fundamental human principles of trust, respect, understanding, and growth, while at the same time being legally sound.

Since I am a lawyer, mother, and grandmother, it was natural that I turned to the law to discover the fundamentals of justice and fairness and then combined them with caring. The legal cases from which these questions derive address all kinds of people issues in schools, from employee terminations to student expulsions. These questions capture the essence of how the judges weigh, balance, and decide a fair and just resolution of any particular situation.

The four questions are also the heart of the McGrath SUCCEED System, an approach specifically designed to address the complex and painful people issues within our schools, of which bullying is just one. The McGrath SUCCEED System is a comprehensive approach to complaint intake, management, and investigation that emphasizes due process and just cause rights of the individual. Said in plain English, the McGrath SUCCEED System is about both the skill to handle bullying issues well and the will to transform the culture and climate in which the bullying occurs.

WHY ADDRESS BULLYING?

Every hour of every day, in every schoolhouse around the world, children experience bullying and harassment by their peers (and sometimes even by the adults in their lives, but that is beyond the scope of this book). Peer-to-peer bullying is so pervasive in our schools that it's almost transparent, invisible to the adult eye. The prevailing sentiment often is that "it is simply part of growing up." Yet both the immediate and long-term impacts on the victims' ability to study and learn, their emotional health, and their self-esteem are staggering.

In a 2002 address to the American Medical Association, Dr. Joseph L. Wright, Medical Director of Advocacy and Community Affairs of Children's National Medical Center in Washington, DC, remarked on the 30% prevalence rate of bullying reported by researchers:

> These are remarkable rates of bullying. If this were a medical issue, for example, an infectious disease in my pediatrics practice, we would have the Epidemic Intelligence Service people from the Centers for Disease Control and Prevention investigate it. (Wright, 2002, p. 23)

In addition, our federal and state legislative bodies and various courts of law are holding school personnel more and more accountable for preventing and intervening in these matters. Parents, student advocates, and even the students themselves are calling for a new world order. One family in Canada recently filed suit against a school district, alleging that the district had not fulfilled its duty to create a school climate that supports student learning (Egale Canada, 2005). In December 2005, a Kansas City teen received a $440,000 settlement from the Tonganoxie School District for the incessant bullying he experienced from his seventh-grade year through the eleventh grade, when he left school (Associated Press, 2005). Parents and students want school environments that are free from bullying and harassment, and they are willing to fight for those environments as a fundamental educational right.

This is where I come in. I am a school law attorney. My focus is employee and student misconduct, with an emphasis on illegal harassment and bullying. I have been representing school boards and training students and staff on these matters for nearly 30 years. I was a pioneer in peer-to-peer sexual harassment training and am at the top of the field on bullying, sexual harassment, and abuse investigation pertaining to schools.

In addition, over the course of my 30-year practice, I have been training the adults in schools to deal effectively with delicate and extremely complex employee issues. Implementing the philosophy "lead from the heart while using your head" through the McGrath SUCCEED System, I have trained school district leaders to successfully transform the culture of administrator-employee-student relations so that true partnerships and systemic change are possible.

WHAT IS THE McGRATH SUCCEED SYSTEM?

The McGrath SUCCEED System organizes fundamental legal and human principles into a powerful methodology for resolving and transforming complex human situations. On the one hand, the McGrath SUCCEED System provides step-by-step, legally sound procedures and practices for identification of bullying and for complaint intake, management, and investigation of these matters. On the other hand, the McGrath SUCCEED System provides practical transformational tools for analyzing bullying situations and for listening to and communicating with all of the constituents involved—students, parents, teachers, staff, community members, and others. The intended outcome of the McGrath SUCCEED System is the creation of a school environment of safety, caring, and excellence.

WHAT SPECIFICALLY DOES THE McGRATH SUCCEED SYSTEM ADDRESS?

The McGrath SUCCEED System addresses both the *content* and the *context* of bullying. Content means "Who did what to whom?" and "What are we going to do about it?" Provided in the system are practical action steps that respect the due process and just cause rights of those involved, and include:

- distinguishing actionable bullying from acceptable student behavior;
- having a uniform, three-tiered systemwide approach for complaint intake and management;
- applying legally fit procedures throughout the process;
- creating quality records of the actions taken; and
- maintaining step-by-step documentation of the investigation.

When dealing with the context of bullying, the environment is addressed from two views: (1) the environment in which the behavior arose, and (2) the future environment that the school community is committed to having in school. For this purpose, included in the McGrath SUCCEED System are practices that bring out qualities such as:

- acting with honesty, compassion, and accountability;
- fostering trust, respect, understanding, and a commitment to growth;
- honoring the whole human being;
- addressing the varying needs of that whole human being; and
- providing a basic format to integrate these qualities into daily life.

The McGrath SUCCEED System offers practices that put fundamental ethical principles into action. Each interaction flows from an application of the McGrath SUCCEED System's ultimate purpose—to develop people and the culture and climate in which they work and study. While accomplishing the appropriate result with each individual, the McGrath SUCCEED System provides the means to alter the culture and climate of the school.

FACTS-IMPACT-CONTEXT

The phone rang and it was Susan again. "OK, this has been going really well. I have been talking with Johnny and have learned a lot. I asked Johnny what happened and he told me that he and his friend Tim were tackling each other. The tackling got out of hand and Johnny hurt Tim, who responded by biting him. Johnny went to the yard duty monitor and told her that they had been wrestling and Tim had bitten him. He knew that things had gotten out of hand and wanted some help. The yard duty monitor simply told Johnny and Tim to go play somewhere else. Tim picked up a stick and was poking Johnny with it. Johnny hit Tim. The assistant principal sent both boys home.

"When I asked Johnny how this had hurt someone else or even himself, he said, 'When I hit Tim I was angry, then he bit me and I pushed him. After I pushed him I was still angry, and I was also sad. I didn't know how to be friends again. It was hopeless. That's why I got the yard duty lady.'

"Johnny also acknowledged that he had worried his teacher, his classmates, and his friends, and that he felt I was disappointed in him. I did not know that Johnny was so insightful. I have a whole new respect for my child out of this conversation.

"I asked him about the context. It turns out this is the first time he has ever been in trouble for fighting. He also tried to get help and was frustrated by the yard duty monitor's response.

"I realize that I was about to label my child a 'bully' rather than deal objectively with the behavior and its impact. Johnny is not a bully. He is learning a lot from this incident. We both are."

ACTION

Susan and I reviewed the facts and impact of the situation and considered them in light of the context that this was Johnny's first time in trouble at school. Then we came up with actions to take:

1. Johnny's consequence would be formative—something that would develop him as a good citizen and restore his relationship with himself as a caring person. Johnny himself came up with the idea that he would do 10 acts of kindness that night and the following day at school.

2. Johnny would be warned that any future fighting at school would result in lost television privileges.

3. Susan would speak to the teacher to let her know the facts—including what had transpired with the yard duty monitor. She would request that the teacher speak to the yard duty monitor about what else she could have done when Johnny came to her for help.

4. Susan would follow up with Johnny after school the next day regarding the 10 acts of kindness and talk about what he had learned.

When I next spoke with Susan, she was ecstatic. Johnny had remarked that his mother was his "guardian angel." He was already in action on the acts of kindness and had started setting the table for dinner—without being asked! Susan spoke to Johnny's teacher, who was enthralled with the outcome. She said, "I know I shouldn't be happy about this, but I have to say that we have all learned so much from it that I am really glad that it happened."

FOUR GUIDING QUESTIONS

Four questions, linked by a simple logic formula and housed inside four fundamental human principles, provide a clear path for the way human beings can and should treat each other—fairly and justly, in a legally sound manner. This whole approach, its component parts, and how it applies to bullying in schools will be addressed as we go forward through this book. The organization of the book will be guided by the McGrath SUCCEED System and its Facts-Impact-Context-Action structure.

INTENDED AUDIENCE

School Bullying: Tools for Avoiding Harm and Liability is intended to be a practical resource for the extraordinary men and women who administer the daily operations of K–12 school sites—superintendents, school principals, assistant principals, deans, student services directors, risk managers, directors of curriculum and instruction, Title IX officers, complaint managers, and others who create and oversee the culture and climate of our schools. While they may not use the final chapters on Level III investigation procedures and techniques, it is also critical that school counselors, nurses, teachers, and others in whom students confide their concerns and complaints read and understand Chapters 1 through 7 so that their actions are consistent with the legal duties and responsibilities entrusted to the school district.

Acknowledgments

I t is with great gratitude that I strive to acknowledge all of the people who have contributed to the birth of this book. As I begin, I find it a daunting task because, in truth, this book reflects a life's journey. So many people and so many places are part of the mosaic of my life that it seems capricious to acknowledge only a few. That being said, a few I will mention, and to all I am boundlessly grateful.

I am awed by those who came before me and from whom I have learned about bullying and harassment in our schools. In their pioneering struggles to bring this issue to the forefront, they braved the dismissiveness of people who claimed that bullying didn't really hurt anyone and that it was just a part of growing up. But they persisted and would not be ignored. Many of their names are listed in the Bibliography of this book; many more are not. All have made a huge difference to our world based on their love and tireless commitment and a huge difference in my life. Particular thanks to Nan Stein and her relentless commitment to bullyproofing our schools and making our school hallways safe from violence and sexual harassment.

I also want to thank the people who work in our school districts. These men and women are unstoppable in their love for and service of children. They teach me what commitment is all about—day in and day out. Particularly, I want to acknowledge the administrators. You are the unsung heroes of our schools, making everything work no matter what! A special thank you to Kathie Crume who "started it all" and to Mike Bond, Greg Firn, Larry Galli, Darcy Lees, Steve Lyng, Larry Reznicek, Jennifer Terrazas, and Steve Young for contributing their stories to this book.

To my friends at AGELE (Association of Gender Equity Leadership in Education), AASPA (American Association of School Personnel Administrators), AGRIP (Association of Government Risk Management Pools), and PASPA (Pennsylvania Association of School Personnel Administrators), a huge thanks to you, particularly Mary Sue Linville, Cindy Hoogasian, and Harold Pumford. I am grateful for all that I have learned from you, and the great times we always have together.

I am the luckiest woman in the world to be part of the team that is called McGrath Training Systems. McGrath Trainers Bill Berard, Grant House, Deborah Washington, Bob Poffenbarger, and (in the early years) Peggy Weeks:

You go out on the front lines into schools throughout the United States and Canada, sharing what "McGrath" has to offer. You have boarded more than your share of airplanes—dealing with the inevitable lost luggage, delayed flights, and wrong directions—and always you go forth with love and enthusiasm, giving your all. You learn from educators far and wide and bring it back home as a contribution to the future we are building. Thank you for your love, loyalty, and friendship.

Doris Scott, you are the voice of McGrath Training Systems. You bring your huge heart and your love for people to everything you do. Your respect for educators and your passion for what is possible in the field of education know no bounds. We cannot imagine doing this without you.

I thank our staff, past and present, for their amazing contributions to what we do: Honor Simpson and Kelly McIntyre Knight, Gail Kennedy and Lynne Hannay, for your stewardship of the company; Cecilia Burch; Diane Calderon; Katherine Lash; Mark Todd; Coleen Martin; Theodora Sims; and Marcy Luikart. You saw to the powerful delivery of every training session on which this book was built. You worked tirelessly on every edition of every manual, often proofreading far into the night. Your dedication lives in every line of this book.

To my mentors Herb Gravitz and Gloria Arenson, and my beautiful friends on the mountain in Tibet: You have always believed in me and told me so. No words can fully express what is in my heart. I love you. Thank you to my dear friends Judy Maloy, Tom Stone, and Jane Downes for always bringing your integrity and "straightness" to coach me forward. To Jon Charles for loving Maureen Charles like she is Empress of the Universe.

To my Acquisitions Editor at Corwin Press, Lizzie Brenkus, who kept saying, "Trust the process," a great big thank you for believing in this book.

A beyond words thank you to Jill Proudfoot who has stood by my side through this process, taking everything we do to the next level of greatness. Ms. Jill is beyond amazing! Every illustration in this book comes from her genius.

A most special thank you to Maureen Charles. But for her this book would not be. When I would say, "Oh, I don't know about that bullying stuff," she would say, "Yes, you do; in fact, you know way more than you think." When I would say, "But I don't know how to write a book," she would say, "I do, and I will." Maureen's research on the definition and prevalence of bullying, her digging out the new technobullying phenomenon, and presenting interesting and innovative ideas on "girl bullying" and social aggression add immediacy to the book. Mo, as she is called, is also the artiste of writing in the McGrath family, so whatever gracefulness this book enjoys is thanks to her. The heart and love that Maureen Charles is knows no measure, and she has given it all to you in this book.

Last, I want to thank my daughters for inspiring me throughout my whole adult life. What awesome women you are and I love you beyond belief! I wouldn't be who I am today but for loving and being loved by you.

And kisses to my grandchildren, who light up my life.

Mary Jo McGrath
Santa Barbara, California

Corwin Press gratefully acknowledges the contributions of the following individuals:

Judy Brunner, Co-Owner
Edu-Safe LLC, School Safety Consulting Firm
Springfield, MO

Lyman Goding
Retired Principal, Plymouth Community Intermediate School
Plymouth, MA
Visiting Lecturer, Bridgewater State College
Bridgewater, MA

Gwen Gross
Superintendent, Manhattan Beach Unified School District
Manhattan Beach, CA
Adjunct Professor, Pepperdine University
Malibu, CA

Steve Hutton, Professional Development Specialist
Mayerson Academy
Cincinnati, OH

Cynthia Knowles, Prevention Specialist
Livonia Central School
Livonia, NY

Matthew Jennings, Assistant Superintendent
Berkeley Heights Public Schools
Berkeley Heights, NJ

Diana Joyce, School Psychologist
University of Florida
Gainesville, FL

Dennis Lewis, Director School Public Safety
Springfield, MO

Jamie Ostrov, Assistant Professor
University of Buffalo
Buffalo, NY

About the Author

 **Mary Jo McGrath** is an education and personnel law attorney and professional development specialist. She graduated magna cum laude in 1974 from the University of California Los Angeles, and from Loyola University School of Law cum laude in 1977. She has been a practicing attorney for nearly 30 years, specializing in performance issues and legal mandates in the school and workplace.

Ms. McGrath's unique practice involves cases dealing with termination, suspension, and layoffs, as well as labor relation matters such as negotiations, arbitrations, unfair practice proceedings, and employment discrimination issues, with an emphasis on sexual harassment, sexual abuse, and bullying in schools.

Ms. McGrath is founder and CEO of McGrath Training Systems, which produces two highly acclaimed educational video series for schools, *Student Sexual Harassment and Abuse: Minimize the Risk* and *The Early Faces of Violence: From Schoolyard Bullying and Ridicule to Sexual Harassment.* McGrath Training has delivered workshops and provided materials on topics ranging from bullying, harassment awareness, and investigation to employee supervision, evaluation, and leadership to more than 3,500 school districts and 250,000 school administrators, teachers, staff, students, parents, and community members throughout the United States and Canada.

Ms. McGrath is acknowledged internationally for her work in sexual harassment and child sexual abuse law, bullying, and performance quality and discipline law. She served as an expert consultant to the office of the California Governor on teacher tenure reform and has been the featured legal expert on CBS's *Eye to Eye With Connie Chung, The CBS Evening News With Dan Rather,* and *48 Hours With Paula Zahn* programs on the issue of sexual harassment and abuse, and on ABC's *20/20* on the issue of teacher quality and performance. She has been featured in the *Los Angeles Times, The New York Times, Christian Science Monitor, Trial Magazine, Redbook, Reader's Digest, Seventeen,* and several nationally circulated professional journals. Ms. McGrath served as Chair of the U.S. Department of Education Safe, Disciplined, and Drug-Free Schools Expert Panel from 2000 to 2002.

PART I

Fact, Myth, and Impact

1

What Bullying Is and What It Is Not

*What is most surprising of all is how much **fear** there is in school . . . Like good soldiers, [students] control their fears, live with them, and adjust themselves to them. But the trouble is, and here is a vital difference between school and war, that the adjustments children make to their fears are almost wholly bad, destructive of their intelligence and capacity. The scared fighter may be the best fighter, but the scared learner is always a poor learner.*

—John Holt, *How Children Fail* (1982, p. 49)

Joan (not her real name) is the mother of 12-year-old Theresa (also not her real name), a student at a small, private K–8 school who was bullied persistently by her peers. In a videotaped interview, Joan was remarkably candid about her daughter's ordeal:

I have a 12-year-old daughter, Theresa. She had always been kind of a clown because that was what was working for her socially. In sixth grade, the kids started changing . . . from laughing and pointing when she would clown around to something that was far more negative. They started calling her names: fatso, stupid idiot. It just kept getting worse and worse. On the school grounds, Theresa would trip and fall. She'd try to get up and they'd shove her back down again. I saw footprints on her backside. It just kept escalating. When it got to that point, the children were entrenched in this behavior.

Out of a class of 28, I'd have to say that 20 of them were participating in this. There were just one or two that had that bully behavior all the time, and not just with my daughter but with others also. But there were far more of the children that would let that bully come out when it suited them, when they felt like it. . . . There was no respite for her. The teacher would try and talk to the students as a group. That would be helpful for perhaps a day or two, but by the third or the fourth day, the behavior was back.

Theresa started that sixth-grade year quite well. Then, as the bullying escalated, her grades took a nosedive. . . . She was acting out at home. She was yelling at me, calling me names, making me feel bad, and trying to insult me. . . . She started eating disorder behaviors that were very scary . . . bingeing. It affected her grades. It affected her emotionally. And it affected how she behaved and the kind of person that she was. Her sense of self tanked. She ended up being a very depressed, disappointed, and angry little girl. (McGrath, 1998e)

There is no doubt that what Theresa experienced was bullying. Unfortunately, her experience is all too prevalent in today's K–12 schoolyards. Large schools, small schools, private schools, and public schools—no school or child is immune. This chapter will provide an overview of the behaviors that constitute bullying, their prevalence in schools, and ways to recognize bullying in both its overt and covert manifestations.

SPOTTING THE BULLY

In *The Bully, the Bullied and the Bystander,* Barbara Coloroso (2003) writes,

Bullies come in all different sizes and shapes: some are big, some are small; some bright; some attractive and some not so attractive; some popular and some absolutely disliked by almost everybody. You can't always identify bullies by what they *look* like, but you can pick them out by what they *act* like. (p. 11)

The term "bully" is used here to describe anyone who engages in bullying behavior. This usage is a step into reality and away from the classic paradigm of the "class bully," usually viewed as the big bruiser boy. Bullying behavior pervades our classrooms, hallways, playgrounds, and school buses. We want to capture and understand the cultural and behavioral phenomenon that resulted in over 70% of the children in a sixth-grade class tormenting a 12-year-old girl until her very sense of self shattered.

How Bullies Act

There are many different definitions of bullying and peer victimization in the literature. Among the various definitions, there are certain patterns of behavior typically identified as bullying:

🌊   **Figure 1.1** How Bullies Act 🌊

- Harm or hurt is intended, rather than the result of a mistake or negligence.
- A power imbalance exists between the target and the perpetrator.
- The perpetrator enjoys carrying out the action.
- The perpetrator repeats the behavior, often in a systematic way.
- The victim is hurt physically or psychologically and has a sense of being persecuted or oppressed.

SOURCE: Olweus (1993), Davis (2004), Sullivan (2000), Coloroso (2003).

Intent to Harm

According to Stan Davis (2004), author of *Schools Where Everyone Belongs*, "bullies experience a wish for power that is stronger than their empathetic sense, so they are willing to hurt others in order to feel powerful. As Dorothea Ross (1996) points out, young people who bully enjoy the power they have over their victims and do not bully in order to receive tangible rewards such as lunch money. Instead, bullies focus on behaviors that will hurt or embarrass their targets" (p. 10).

The intent of the perpetrator is critical to the present discussion. Most anti-bullying laws include intent to harm in their definitions of bullying. It is this criterion that sets bullying apart from illegal harassment, which is defined (in part) by how the victim perceives the situation rather than by the intent of the perpetrator to harm. We will be discussing this distinction in depth in Chapter 5.

An Imbalance of Power

In bullying incidents, there is an imbalance of physical, psychological, and/or social power. The perpetrator has (or at least seems to have) more power than the target of the bullying. This abuse of power makes bullying just that—a form of abuse. Bullying is not a conflict between equals; it is a power play. It instills fear and, over time, terror in the mind of the recipient. Of equal importance, as John Holt (1982) points out in the opening quote in this chapter, fear negatively impacts learning.

The Perpetrator Enjoys Bullying

Those who typically enjoy bullying are called *confident bullies*. The characteristic "that the bully enjoys bullying" is not present all of the time, but it is a predominant feature for the majority of bullies, girls and boys alike.

Most bullying experts concur with the notion of multiple types of bullies. Let's look at the three types of bullies identified in the literature. See whether you can come up with examples of each from your experience with students.

Types of Bullies

1. Confident (or Clever) Bullies—enjoy aggression, feel secure, are of average popularity, and are physically strong;*

2. Anxious (or Not-So-Clever) Bullies—are weak academically, have poor concentration, overreact to perceived threats and insults, are less popular, and are less secure; and

3. Bully/Victims—are bullies in some situations and are bullied in others, are very unpopular, and tend to have behavioral problems.

(Sullivan, 2000, Sullivan, Cleary, & Sullivan, 2004)

*Note: Physical strength does not apply with social scheming or "technobullying."

Repeated, Systematic Behavior

Unless the behavior is severe in its harm, a single incident does not typically constitute bullying. Most bullying is either persistent (happening frequently and relentlessly) or pervasive (happening everywhere) in the school environment. Often bullying is both persistent and pervasive. Bullying behavior also tends to be covert in nature, making it difficult for adults to spot patterns.

Adults in the school setting should pay attention to incidents even if they do not appear to be part of an apparent pattern. In fact, one of the deciding factors in current bullying litigation (leading to substantial awards to plaintiffs) is that school officials either missed an obvious pattern of bullying or ignored a pattern of systematic peer victimization over time. In later chapters, I will review some of these cases and discuss how to document incidents and identify patterns in a legally sound manner.

BULLYING HURTS

In 2005, Nishina, Juvonen, and Witkow of the University of California at Los Angeles (UCLA) were in their fifth year of a long-term study of more than 1,900 sixth-grade students—predominantly minority and low-income students in two Los Angeles-area public schools. In "Sticks and Stones May Break My Bones, but Names Will Make Me Feel Sick" (2005), they report on their findings so far regarding the effects of bullying on these middle school children. In the study, students provided confidential reports and their teachers rated students' behavior. The research supported what many have long suspected: There is a correlation between perceived psychological and physical vulnerability and student achievement.

In a press release about their report, Juvonen said,

Now we have evidence that the school environment, psychological health, physical health, and school achievement are all interrelated. . . . If kids continue to get harassed, over time they become more psychologically vulnerable. Those who get repeatedly victimized are most at risk for developing psychological problems. (Nishina & Juvonen, 2005a, p. 1)

The UCLA research shows that middle school students who are bullied are "more likely to feel depressed, lonely, and miserable, which in turn makes them more vulnerable to further bullying incidents" (Nishina & Juvonen, 2005a, p. 2).

The damage to victims of bullying may be physical, emotional, and/or psychological, and the resulting trauma can last a lifetime. The impact of bullying on the victim will be explored more fully in the next chapter.

Educator responsibility to provide a safe school environment for students has been upheld by the courts in numerous illegal harassment cases and is now shaping the courts' response to bullying litigation. Protecting yourself and your school district from liability means proactively protecting students. The first steps are to increase staff, student, and parent awareness of bullying and its harm and to establish channels for everyone on campus to report alleged or suspected bullying behavior. Action steps will be presented later for increasing awareness, encouraging reports, and following up on complaints and rumors.

THREE TYPES OF BULLYING

Bullying is classified in a variety of ways in the literature. For the purposes of this book, three types of bullying are distinguished:

> - **Physical Bullying:** *Harm to another's person or property*
> - **Emotional Bullying:** *Harm to another's self-concept*
> - **Relational Bullying:** *Harm to another through damage (or the threat of damage) to relationships or to feelings of acceptance, friendship, or group inclusion*

Included in these types of bullying are nonverbal, verbal, and physical behaviors. These behaviors may be perpetrated by an individual or by a group, and there may be multiple victims.

Some researchers exclude criminal or illegal behaviors from their classifications. However, given that we are looking through a legal lens, it is imperative to consider the entire range of harmful behavior in the discussion of bullying. When bullying behaviors are directed at a legally protected classification of people (because of race, ethnicity, national origin, sex, or other identified characteristics), the victim's civil rights may be violated. The bullying then constitutes illegal harassment, actionable under antidiscrimination laws. When the bullying behaviors violate the penal code, the perpetrator(s) may face criminal prosecution. Illegal harassment and criminal prosecution will be further discussed in Chapter 4, along with other categories of legal infractions.

Regardless of legal classification, bullying is typically made up of certain identified behaviors. The following chart displays the three types of bullying and the behaviors included in each category.

Figure 1.2 Three Types of Bullying

Physical Bullying   *Harm to another's body or property*

- Threatening physical harm
- Making threatening gestures
- Starting a fight
- Cornering or blocking movement

- Pushing, Shoving
- Pinching, Scratching
- Hair pulling
- Spitting

- Slapping
- Kicking, Tripping
- Biting
- Punching

- Destroying or defacing property
- Extortion
- Theft
- Sexual assault

- Rape
- Child sexual abuse
- Assault with a weapon
- Arson
- Homicide

Emotional Bullying   *Harm to another's self-concept*

- Insulting gestures
- Dirty looks
- Insulting remarks
- Name calling
- Taunting

- Racial, ethnic, or religious slurs or epithets
- Insulting remarks related to disability, gender, or sexual orientation

- Defacing or falsifying schoolwork
- Insulting/degrading graffiti
- Harassing and/or frightening phone calls, e-mail, text or phone messages

- Unwanted sexually suggestive remarks, images, or gestures
- Challenging in public
- Threatening another to secure silence

Relational Bullying   *Harm to another through damage (or threat of damage) to relationships or to feelings of acceptance, friendship, or group inclusion*

- Using negative body language or facial expressions
- Gossiping
- Starting/spreading rumors

- Playing mean tricks
- Insulting publicly
- Ruining a reputation
- Ignoring someone to punish or coerce

- Threatening to end a relationship
- Undermining other relationships
- Passively not including in group

- Exclusion
- Ostracizing/total group rejection
- Arranging public humiliation

Range of Severity

7

PIERCING THE MYTHS ABOUT BULLIES AND BULLYING

Having looked at what bullying is, let's look at what it is not. Bullying in schools has become a national focus, with the likes of Dr. Phil, Oprah Winfrey, and television's "Super Nanny" chiming in. Yet almost every day, school personnel reveal fundamental misunderstandings about the nature and prevalence of bullying with comments such as "Bullies are few" and "We don't have bullying in our school." They will even say, "We have that issue under control" or "We handled bullying last year." If we are to make any real difference, we must dispel the myths and misunderstandings that pervade the school culture and justify complacency.

Myth #1: Our School Doesn't Have Bullies

Studies show that school bullying is widespread in the United States and internationally. The bullying behavior may be hidden from the view of adults, but it is there nonetheless. Estimates of the incidence and prevalence of bullying among students vary widely. Recent evidence indicates, however, that bullying is much more prevalent than the 5% to 10% reported by researchers in the 1980s and 1990s. These older studies primarily looked for overt or physical acts. Most relied on self-reporting of past events by research subjects, sometimes years after the events took place. As understanding of the nature of bullying continues to change and grow, new research methodologies are emerging, revealing startling results.

A 2001 study of 15,600 students in Grades 6 to 10 revealed that almost 16% of U.S. students are bullied regularly and 13% are initiators of bullying behavior; 6% of all these students reported both bullying and being bullied by others (Nansel, Overpeck, Pilla, Ruan, Simmons-Morton, & Scheidt, 2001).

A 2004 UCLA study paints a graphic picture of the extent of bullying. The field part of the study was conducted over a two-week span with a socioeconomically and ethnically diverse group of 192 sixth graders from two urban Los Angeles schools. In school #1, 46% of the sixth graders reported that they experienced peer harassment on at least one day of the survey cycle; in school #2, the incidence was 47%. In school #1, 42% reported witnessing peer harassment at least once; in school #2, 66% reported witnessing this behavior (Nishina & Juvonen, 2005b).

In a press release about the study, Juvonen remarked, "Bullying is a problem that large numbers of kids confront on a daily basis at school; it's not just an issue of the few unfortunate ones. We knew a small group gets picked on regularly, but we were surprised how many kids reported at least one incident" (Nishina & Juvonen, 2005a).

Researchers have also concluded that school size and class size are irrelevant. So far, no one has proven the theory that smaller schools have less bullying (Olweus, 1993, pp. 24–25). Remember the story at the beginning of this chapter about "Theresa," a student at a small private school? No school is immune.

Myth #2: Other Safety Issues Are a Bigger Concern for Kids

The findings from the 2001 *Talking With Kids* survey, a joint project of the Kaiser Family Foundation, Nickelodeon, and Children Now, reveal that bullying is a serious concern for students. In the study, a national sample of 863 children between the ages of 8 and 15 were interviewed. Fifty-five percent of 8- to 11-year-olds and 68% of 12- to 15-year-olds said that bullying is a "big problem" at school. In the study, bullying outranked discrimination, violence, pressure to have sex, alcohol and drugs, racism, and HIV/AIDS as a concern among these students (Nickelodeon & Kaiser Family Foundation, 2001). This is not to say that the other issues are not important, or perhaps more severe or life threatening. Rather, the results emphasize that bullying directly affects the majority of students and it is foremost on their minds.

Results of the 1997 Youth Risk Behavior Surveillance (YRBS) conducted by the U.S. Department of Health and Human Services Centers for Disease Control and Prevention showed that 4% to 7% of students missed at least one day of school during the 30 days preceding the survey because they felt unsafe at school or traveling to and from school. Extrapolated, that's as many as 160,000 children a day who miss school out of fear for their personal safety (Centers for Disease Control and Prevention, 1998, p. 8).

The National Center for Education Statistics Indicators of School Crime and Safety 2005 reports similar findings regarding students' perceptions of personal safety at school and away from school: In 2003, 6% of students aged 12–18 reported that they had been afraid of attack at school or on the way to and from school during the previous six months. Ten percent of urban students reported being fearful, compared to 5% each of suburban and rural students (National Center for Education Statistics, 2005b).

Myth #3: Schools Should Not Encourage Complaints

Over the years, my colleagues and I have found that when bullying-awareness training is conducted with staff and students, there is usually a rise in student complaints. That may sound like bad news, but actually it is not. If implementation of an anti-bullying policy is conducted in a thorough, consistent manner, school districts often report to us that over time, there are fewer incidents and complaints in which to intervene. Even more important, as students see that adults in the school can be trusted to intervene fairly and effectively, incidents are likely to be reported at earlier stages, and the severity of the incidents at the time of first report is likely to decrease (McGrath, 2006b).

Myth #4: Teachers See Everything and Respond When Bullying Takes Place

When asked whether they are aware of the bullying incidents that occur in their classrooms, teachers will generally say "yes." They think that they are in tune with their students and that they don't miss much. Studies show, however, that the mythical "teacher with eyes in the back of her head" is just that—a myth—and that most teachers are not as aware of what is happening as they could be. In a Toronto survey, Ziegler and Pepler (1993) found that although 71% of teachers indicated that they almost always intervene in incidents of bullying, only 25% of students surveyed indicated this to be the case (p. 30).

Dr. Pepler and her associates, who study bullying by direct observation, report that teachers intervene in 18% of classroom episodes and only 4% of playground episodes of bullying. Pepler speculates that low teacher intervention may occur because (1) the majority of episodes are verbal, (2) episodes are brief (in a 1998 study of bullying in classrooms, the average incident lasted 26 seconds), (3) bullying occurs when monitoring is low, and (4) the behavior is covert (Atlas & Pepler, 1998; Pepler & Craig, 2000). If we are going to protect children, we must close the gap between what children experience and what adults in our schools perceive.

Myth #5: It's the Outcasts Who Bully Others

Studies indicate that bullies' popularity among peers ranges from above average to slightly below average. Earlier in this chapter, the three types of bullies were reviewed. The work of Dan Olweus (1993) appears to focus mainly on the confident bullies.

> They are often surrounded by a small group of two or three friends who support them and who seem to like them. . . . The popularity of the bullies decreases in Grade 9. . . . Nevertheless, the bullies do not seem to reach the low level of popularity that characterizes the victims. (p. 35)

Coloroso (2003) identifies two types of bullies who may be popular with adults: the *confident bully*, often admired for his or her powerful personality; and the *social bully*, typically a popular girl who manipulates and ostracizes her targets while charming others (p. 18). Some of the most malicious and covert bullies are students who are popular with adults. They will encourage other children to taunt the victim and then "play innocent." When a victim reports being bullied by a popular student, adults in authority often respond with disbelief, inaction, or even retaliatory behavior toward the complainant (McGrath, 2006g). Being popular, likeable, athletic, or academically gifted does not automatically indicate that a child is a bully, but it also does not mean that the child is *not* capable of such behavior.

Myth #6: Bullies Appear Tough, but They Are All Actually Anxious and Insecure

The commonly held assumption that bullies only appear tough but are really anxious and insecure is incorrect. Studies of bullies as a group indicate the opposite: Most bullies have little anxiety and insecurity or are average in this area, and they do not have poor self-esteem. In fact, bullies often have a very positive self-image (Olweus, 1993).

If insecurity isn't the source of most bullying, then what is? Olweus's (1993) research indicates four possible psychological sources underlying bullying:

- a strong need for power and dominance,
- family conditions,
- benefits and rewards (extorting victim's money, cigarettes, or other valuables), and
- prestige.

Does that mean that bullies are never insecure? No. Anxious bullies tend to struggle academically, have poor social skills and low self-esteem, and do not read social cues accurately. According to Coloroso (2003), this type of bully "often reads hostile intent into other kids' innocent actions, reacts aggressively to even slight provocation, and justifies his aggressive response by placing blame outside himself" (p. 19). However, this is just one type of bully. If you are looking for insecurity or anxiety to identify all bullies, you will miss the confident, secure students who are engaging in bullying behavior.

Figure 1.3 Distinctive Characteristics of Bullies

- Aggressive toward peers (and sometimes adults)
- Lack empathy for their victims
- Have an atypical positive attitude toward violence
- Are impulsive, lack foresight
- Have a sense of entitlement
- Are self-absorbed
- Crave attention
- Are manipulative, use others
- Are predatory (view weaker peers as "prey")
- Tend to hurt other children when adults are not around
- Refuse to take responsibility, blame others
- Are intolerant of differences
- Have a strong need to dominate others

SOURCE: Olweus (1993), Coloroso (2003).

Myth #7: The "Class Bully" Is Easy to Identify

The misconception that bullying is limited to a few, obvious "class bullies" is dispelled by the four findings addressed earlier: (1) the high percentage of children who report in anonymous research studies that they have been bullied or have bullied others, (2) the tendency of bullies to operate "behind the backs" of teachers, (3) reports by children that their teachers did not intervene in incidents of bullying when they were present during the incident, and (4) teachers studied who consistently underestimated the level of bullying that students identified as occurring. Like other forms of abuse, bullying often remains hidden and goes unreported by the victim. Identifying persistent, repetitive patterns of bullying in the school setting is not easy, but it can be done. Later in this book, practical tools and techniques for identifying and investigating bullying behavior will be discussed.

Myth #8: It Is Impossible to Catch the Early Warning Signs

Bullying occurs in stages and there are warning signs. In *The Anti-Bullying Handbook,* Keith Sullivan identifies what he terms the "downward spiral of bullying" and presents stages of that spiral (Sullivan, 2000). Bullying is a power imbalance. As such, it is similar to other types of abuse. Over the course of my 30 years of law practice, investigating complaints of both employee and student-to-student misconduct and abuse of power, I have identified three fundamental stages of abuse (McGrath, 1994).

Phase One Is *Trolling.* In this stage, the perpetrator is looking for a victim. Trolling behavior is characterized by single, subtle acts of bullying behavior aimed at different individuals. The perpetrator is looking for easy targets, kids with low self-esteem and low physical strength, kids who are easily intimidated, and kids who don't resist or fight back. The perpetrator will test potential victims' boundaries by invading their personal space and test their reactions with quick comments, threats, or taunts.

Phase Two Is the *Campaign Phase.* In this phase, the perpetrator escalates the behavior. The victim is still hoping for relief and trying to fit in. He experiences guilt, self-blame, and shame at not being able to stop the behavior or stand up for himself. Bullying becomes more frequent and more pervasive. The bully will often enlist the cooperation of bystanders. This phase includes threats and intimidation should the victim "tattle."

Phase Three Is the *Bully-Victim Relationship.* The victim sees no way out. What started on the school bus every morning is now occurring in the classroom, in the cafeteria, on the playground, to and from school every day, and even on the telephone or via e-mail at home. The victim experiences a growing sense of despair. Without intervention, the victim may even attempt suicide or turn violent in response. Without intervention, the bully gets an unrealistic sense of his power and may take greater risks (McGrath, 2006e).

In fact, the bully may extend the antisocial behavior into other arenas, often committing criminal offenses that result in incarceration (Sullivan, 2000). Because this escalation is predictable, it is imperative to recognize the warning signs and intervene early.

Myth #9: There Is No Correlation Between Bullying and Cases of Extreme Violence

At its most extreme, the impact of bullying can be deadly. In England they call it *Bullycide.* The term was coined by the media to describe children who commit suicide in reaction to severe, persistent, or pervasive acts of bullying at school.

In 2004, the Anchorage Alaska School District paid out $4.5 million to settle a lawsuit with the family of Tom, an eighth-grade boy who attempted suicide after being bullied at school. According to court documents and depositions in the case, Tom was gifted in math and science but socially awkward. According to an article in the Anchorage Daily News, "On November 6, 1998, Tom tried to hang himself at home. He had no pulse when paramedics arrived, and they started CPR. Fifteen minutes later they got his heart going. He had already suffered extensive, irreversible brain damage. Tom's condition today is unchanged. He wears diapers, is fed through a tube, and knows only a few words" (Pesznecker, 2004). It may not seem logical to a fully functioning adult, but to a 13-year-old, suicide may seem like the only way out. Then there are the ones who are determined to take others with them.

The 1999 tragedy at Columbine High School left 15 people dead, including the two perpetrators, and 21 more wounded. Oddly enough, this murderous horror was a wake-up call for America, forcing us to pay attention to the plight of bullied children in U.S. schools. In the wake of the Columbine massacre, classmates and other teens across the nation suggested that Eric Harris and Dylan Klebold were reacting to years of bullying, rejection, and abuse by their peers. These theories were soon borne out in the journals, videos, and Web logs the two student gunmen left behind. An anonymous teen posted the following message to the *Seventeen* magazine Web site: "Because of my own experiences with vicious in-crowd members, my sympathies lay with Eric Harris and Dylan Klebold. I know that what they did was wrong, but in my gut I know I'm more like them than the jocks and cheerleaders they targeted."

On March 5, 2001, 15-year-old Charles Andrew Williams of Santee, California told at least 12 people that he was going "to do a Columbine." No one reported what he or she had been told. Andy took his 22-caliber handgun to school and fired over 30 shots, killing two students and wounding 13 others. It would later be revealed that Andy had been the subject of extreme cruelty at the hands of his peers, including being burned on the neck with a cigarette lighter, having his head dunked in a toilet containing human waste, being punched in the face, being called derogatory names, and even being subjected to an unsuccessful attempt by students to set him on fire. He was sentenced to 50 years to life for his actions (Moran, 2002; Roth, 2001).

Two days later and across country, in Williamsport, PA, Elizabeth Catherine Bush, 14, took her father's revolver into the school cafeteria and shot head cheerleader Kimberly Marchese in the shoulder, wounding her. Bush was the first female in over three decades to become a school shooter. In a *Time* magazine article, Jodie Morse (Morse, Barnes, & Rivera, 2001) describes Bush:

> Elizabeth Catherine Bush was no Charles Andrew Williams. She didn't shoplift, booze or boast of pulling a Columbine. Bush was a quiet eighth-grader. . . . A stickler for safety, Bush lectured the school bus driver for speeding through railroad crossings. She tacked posters of Mother Teresa and Martin Luther King Jr. to her bedroom walls and affixed pictures of the Columbine victims to the bulletin board over her desk. Her parents say she wanted to be a human rights activist— or a nun.

Bush was reportedly threatened and teased mercilessly at her old school in Jersey Shore and had transferred to a smaller Roman Catholic school, hoping for a fresh start, but the teasing did not stop and she reacted with violence.

A 2001 study by Anderson and associates, published in the *Journal of the American Medical Association*, examined "all known school-associated violent deaths from 1994 to 1999." During this period, there were 220 reported cases resulting in 253 deaths in U.S. elementary and secondary schools (private and public), occurring either on campus, while the victim was traveling to or from school, or while the victim was traveling to or from or attending a school-sponsored event (172 homicides, 30 suicides, 11 homicide-suicides, 5 legal intervention deaths, 2 unintentional firearm-related deaths). The intent of the study was to distinguish the common features of these events and the students involved and compare homicide perpetrators to homicide victims.

While the rate of single-student homicides declined over this period, the number of multiple-victim homicides increased. Fifty percent of these events took place during school activities, most often during class or afterschool activities. The authors emphasized that these are "rare but complex events" with "no simple solutions." They found that homicide perpetrators at school were twice as likely as homicide victims to have been bullied by peers. Perpetrators were also more likely than homicide victims to be reported to the principal's office for disobeying an authority figure or fighting with peers, and they were less likely to have participated in extracurricular activities. In addition, perpetrators were "far more likely than homicide victims to have expressed suicidal behaviors" (Anderson, Kaufman, Simon, Barrios, Paulozzi, Ryan, Hammond, Modzeleski, Feucht, Potter, & School-Associated Violent Deaths Study Group, 2001).

An investigation by the U.S. Secret Service of 37 school shootings from 1974 to 2000 revealed that 71% of the attackers "felt persecuted, bullied, threatened, attacked or injured by others prior to the incident. In several cases individual attackers had experienced bullying and harassment that was long-standing and severe. In some of these cases, the experience of bullying seemed to have [had] a significant impact on the attacker and appeared to have been a factor in his decision to mount an attack at the school" (Vossekull, Fein, Reddy, Borum, & Modzelski, 2002).

The implications of the U.S. Secret Service report are clear: While not all children who bully will become school shooters, the report's findings underscore the need to combat bullying in our schools. "Educators can play an important role in ensuring that students are not bullied in schools and that schools not only do not permit bullying but also empower other students to let adults in the school know if students are being bullied" (Vossekull et al., 2002, p. 36).

While the U.S. Secret Service study also found that there is "no accurate or useful 'profile' of students who engage in targeted school violence," their findings suggest "some future attacks may be preventable" (Vossekull et al., 2002, pp. 21, 41). One approach that they consider highly promising is threat assessment—"a fact-based investigative and analytical approach that focuses on what a particular student is doing or saying" (p. 41). The U.S. Secret Service has compiled *Threat Assessment in Schools: A Guide to Managing Threatening Situations and to Creating Safe School Climates*. The guide includes procedures for implementing, conducting, and managing threat assessment and threatening situations in the school setting and can be downloaded along with the aforementioned report from their Web site (Fein, Vossekull, Pollack, Borum, Modzelski, & Reddy, 2002).

Myth #10: Bullying Is Not a Legal Issue, It's a Character Issue

Bullying often crosses the line into illegal harassment or criminal behavior. In addition, more and more states are enacting statutes that prohibit bullying in schools and hold educators accountable for prevention and intervention in regard to bullying behavior. While there are many programs, books, and resources that deal with the socioemotional aspects of bullying and encourage character education, a comprehensive anti-bullying campaign must include training for staff, educators, and administrators that combines legal fitness with human dynamics.

SUMMARY

This chapter included a survey of bullying behavior, highlighting both what it is and what it is not. The five common characteristics of bullying behavior and the legal implications of each were examined. The types of bullying and the behaviors that constitute each type were looked at and 10 myths were debunked. The impact on the victim is next.

2

Through the Eyes of the Victim

The schoolyard is not a playful place. The schoolyard is a danger zone.

—Grant House, City Councilman, Santa Barbara, CA

I remember being bullied. They'd just pile on. I remember it was really rough. How to preserve some dignity in that experience? There's no way. I was hurt and scared. I remember running home from school fearful, very scared. I was beginning to develop a self-identity of being fleet, being able to hide really well, and feeling like being crafty was a way to be safe. But the fear ... I always remember hoping that the next level of school would get me out of the environment where I was being tormented. So when I went from elementary to junior high, now I would be taken seriously. Now we would do some important work and none of that would be there any more. But it wasn't true. ... And going to high school. ... [It] was supposed to be an academic place, but it was even worse. That'll stay with me forever. (Grant House, cited in McGrath, 1998e)

Bullying can be emotionally devastating to the victim, and scars to the psyche can last a lifetime. In this chapter, the signs, symptoms, and profound effects of bullying will be discussed.

THE IMPACT OF BULLYING ON VICTIMS

Victims of bullying respond in many ways: some suffer self-doubt and a drop in self-esteem and confidence, others become bullies themselves in an attempt

16

Figure 2.1 Common Effects of Bullying on Victims

Physical Effects	• Increased illnesses, particularly stress-related disorders
	• Physical injuries that are the result of bullying incidents
	• Attempted and completed suicides
Emotional Effects	• Feelings of isolation, exclusion, and/or alienation
	• Difficulty in forming deep friendships
	• Increased fear and anxiety
	• Depression
	• Feelings of incompetence and powerlessness
Academic Effects	• Truancy as the victim seeks to avoid the bully
	• Increased absences due to illness, particularly stress-related disorders
	• Lower academic achievement, including decreased in-class participation and lower grades
	• Difficulty in concentrating on schoolwork

SOURCE: Olweus (1993), Sullivan (2000).

to compensate for their suffering (Graham & Juvonen, 2001). Some victims are resilient in the face of the behaviors perpetrated against them; others are not.

Bullying is particularly harmful because it is a series of repeated acts. The effects are cumulative, and in extreme cases bullying is life threatening, driving the victim to suicide.

Karen, A Parent

I had a very nasty skin disorder when I was going through school in England. Most of my whole school life I was completely ostracized. I was called "scabby knees" and "leper." I was put out of swimming pools. It was a very innocent skin trouble. I feel now, looking back at it, that I could cry because I didn't get a whole lot of sympathy from the teachers. It was very, very difficult to have friends. I think it really affected my self-esteem. It took me way into my teenage years to even start to build some self-confidence. (McGrath, 1998e)

Impacted for Life

The majority of children who are bullied at school do not commit homicide or suicide. They internalize their suffering, which can and often does lead to traumatic stress. Dr. Herbert Gravitz, Ph.D., is a clinical psychologist, a Diplomate of the American Academy of Experts in Traumatic Stress and of the American Board of Forensic Examiners, and a cofounder of Adult Children of Alcoholics. In *Unlocking the Doors to Triumph,* he writes, "Trauma is learning to have so few wants and needs that you can't possibly be disappointed. Trauma is praying every night to a god who never answers and feeling abandoned and disconnected from life's beauty and mystery. Trauma is the constantly breaking heart" (Gravitz, 2004, p. 135).

Psychological trauma is caused by an overpowering life event that breaches the protective barriers of the self. For an event to be traumatic, it must be considered life threatening and dangerous, invoking intense fear, helplessness, or horror. Studies of traumatized people show that it matters little whether the person actually experiences the event(s) directly or bears witness to it. Either way, the trauma can be substantial and lasting (Gravitz, 2004, pp. 134–135).

The Effects of Chronic Trauma

Experts classify bullying as *chronic trauma*. This is distinct from time-limited events that result in trauma, such as rape, natural disasters, and car accidents. Chronic trauma is a repetitive and insidious accumulation of everyday insults to one's integrity and sense of safety as a human being. The more a person is bullied and threatened, the more he or she is traumatized.

According to Dr. Gravitz, one of the most pernicious parts of being bullied is the inculcation of shame, which may show up later in addictions, compulsive behaviors, depression, and anxieties. Trauma causes the victim to view life through a distorted lens, resulting in a loss of self-esteem, misdirection in life, lack of a purpose, an inability to adapt to stress, and/or a disconnection from other people. The eventual cost of cumulative trauma can be a loss of self (McGrath, 1998e).

Post-Traumatic Stress

Dr. Stephen Joseph, a psychologist at Warwick University in England, studied 331 English secondary school children. Surveys revealed that 40% of the students had been bullied at some time in their school careers. Dr. Joseph used an Impact of Event Scale (IES) to measure subjective stress in the students. Thirty-seven percent of those studied had IES scores that indicated "clinically significant levels of post-traumatic stress." According to Dr. Joseph, "This study reveals that bullying and particularly name calling can be degrading for adolescents. . . . Research clearly suggests that [post-traumatic stress] can be caused by bullying" (Mynard, Joseph, & Alexander, 2000; Science Daily, 2003).

The study assessed the victims' experience of physical and verbal victimization, social scheming, and attacks on property. All of these experiences resulted in lower self-esteem, but social scheming, such as excluding the victim from taking part in games, was shown to be more likely to lead to post-traumatic stress, and verbal taunts were shown to lead to lower self-worth. The study also suggests that verbal bullying and social scheming can lead victims to a sense of helplessness, and a sense that they lack control over their own feelings and actions (Mynard et al., 2000).

Dr. Judith Herman of Harvard University, in her landmark work *Trauma and Recovery: The Aftermath of Violence* (1997), suggests that a new diagnosis, *"Complex Post-Traumatic Stress Disorder,"* is needed to describe the symptoms of long-term trauma (p. 120). While she presents this diagnosis in relation to situations where one is generally held in a state of "captivity," for example, a concentration camp or kidnapping, she also notes that in these situations the victim is "unable to flee and under the control of the perpetrator" (p. 74). This is consistent with Dr. Joseph's description of bullying victims feeling that "power and control lie with the bully" (Mynard et al., 2000).

Bullying victims with clinically significant levels of post-traumatic stress may experience the following symptoms of long-term trauma identified by Dr. Herman:

Figure 2.2 Symptoms of Long-Term Trauma

- Alterations in emotional regulation, which may include symptoms such as persistent sadness, suicidal thoughts, explosive anger, or inhibited anger;

- Alterations in consciousness, such as forgetting traumatic events, reliving traumatic events, or having episodes in which one feels detached from one's mental processes or body;

- Alterations in self-perception, which may include a sense of helplessness, shame, guilt, stigma, and a sense of being completely different from other human beings;

- Alterations in the perception of the perpetrator, such as attributing total power to the perpetrator or becoming preoccupied with the relationship to the perpetrator, including a preoccupation with revenge;

- Alterations in relations with others, including isolation, distrust, or a repeated search for a rescuer; and

- Alterations in one's system of meanings, which may include a loss of sustaining faith or a sense of hopelessness and despair.

SOURCE: Herman (1997).

Blaming the Victim

Research shows that both students and teachers tend to place the blame for being bullied on the student who is being bullied. In their study *Victimization Among Teenage Girls,* Owens, Slee, and Shute (2001) categorized students' and teachers' perceptions of victims in two ways: (1) "that it was the victim's own fault," and (2) "that the victims were vulnerable or easy targets." The girls saw bullying as a form of reprisal for annoying or indiscreet behavior. The teachers in this study "were more likely to blame the victims' lack of social skills . . . or having a home background that did not model constructive conflict resolution." Both students and teachers identified some girls as being particularly vulnerable to relational bullying. They described these girls as "having few or no friends, being new, being unassertive, and perhaps being a little different or 'geeky'" (p. 223). It is also significant that chronic victims frequently blame themselves for being a victim (Sullivan, 2000).

Students who seem to provoke bullying are known as *provocative victims.* According to some researchers, provocative victims make up only 10% to 20% of all victims (Olweus, 2001). Provocative victims often have attention deficits and irritating behaviors that can turn a whole class against them. They are contrasted with passive victims, who do nothing that can be considered provocative, and bully/victims, who both provoke aggression in others and instigate aggression toward their own victims (Sullivan, 2000).

Both individual bullies and groups of students tend to justify and minimize their bullying behavior by claiming provocation, regardless of how passive a victim may actually be. Olweus reminds us that while provocative victims may require intervention with the behavior problems that are exacerbating the bullying, this does not legitimize harassment by their peers. In fact, too much attention is often paid to trying to change the behavior of the victim rather than addressing the whole dynamic (Olweus, cited in Juvonen & Graham, 2001, pp. 12–13).

Signs and Symptoms That May Indicate a Child Is Being Bullied

Common signs and symptoms of bullying can help the teacher identify students who are possibly being victimized. Figure 2.3 lists things to look for in a potential bullying victim.

Figure 2.3 Signs and Symptoms That May Indicate a Child Is Being Bullied

- Personal belongings, including books, papers, homework, money, or other items are taken, damaged, or scattered around
- Bruises and physical wounds, including scratches, cuts, and torn clothing, appear on the victim without a natural explanation given by the victim
- Exclusion or isolation from peer groups during recess/break or lunch time
- Lack of good friends in class
- Being chosen last or among last for "team" activities
- Attempts to be proximate to adults (teachers, aides, other adults) when recess/breaks or other unstructured activities take place
- Appearance of being depressed, unhappy, distressed, withdrawn, anxious, or insecure
- Gradual or sudden drop in school performance.

SOURCE: Olweus (1993).

SIX POWERFUL PRACTICES FOR DETECTING BULLYING AND HARASSMENT IN SCHOOLS

The following are practices that can and should be implemented by every adult in the school setting to reveal and identify bullying behavior among students:

1. Be observant and document what is seen. Monitor the schoolyard, classrooms, vehicles, and other places where students interact. If you observe taunting, name calling, mimicking, rude gestures, cruel or racist remarks, hitting, kicking, shoving, biting, scratching, hair-pulling, pinching, spitting, threats, intimidation, exclusion, extortion, insulting notes or graffiti, or unwanted sexualized behavior, you may be observing bullying and/or illegal harassment. All such behavior should be documented, reported, and investigated. Patterns of behavior are more easily caught if written reports are consistently turned in to a central complaint manager. (See Chapter 8 for a complete discussion.)

2. Encourage children to report incidents that they experience or observe. By listening carefully to what is being said and by taking all complaints seriously, you will encourage students to report bullying that they experience or observe. If you are the investigator, you must listen for the involvement of silent partners or "ringleaders." These children are bright, popular students who get others to do their "dirty work," knowing that adults in the community will not suspect them of misconduct.

3. Be on the lookout for "Bully/Victims." These bullies are themselves victims of abuse who have learned aggression from others and are, in turn, aggressive toward weaker children. When a bully is identified, further investigation of the child's circumstances may reveal patterns of violence toward the child. The child may need counseling or other preventive intervention.

4. Listen to and report rumors of bullying, harassment, or abuse that you overhear among students. Among girls, covert bullying behavior includes spreading malicious gossip, shunning, isolating and ostracizing a particular girl, and manipulating friendships. (For example, "Lisa's not your best friend anymore. She likes Sandy better than you.") Administrators should investigate rumors. Often they provide a bread crumb trail to student misconduct.

5. Watch for signs that a child is being victimized. Watch for isolated, lonely children. Investigate why a particular child likes to stay in the classroom during recess. Why does another child stay near adults on the playground? Watch for torn clothing, injuries, and missing belongings. (See the list of signs and symptoms in Figure 2.3.)

6. Provide close supervision to vulnerable students. Children with special needs are two to three times more likely to be bullied and more likely to bully than others of their age (Rigby, 2001). Other commonly targeted groups include racial minority students; the minority gender in nontraditional education settings (e.g., girls in metal shop or auto mechanics class); and gay, lesbian, or transgender students. Children who have been sexually abused or experienced other childhood trauma may be particularly at risk for victimization as well. In addition, children with certain emotional and behavioral difficulties, such as attention deficit hyperactivity disorders (ADHD) or oppositional defiant disorders, may be at risk for bullying others.

SAFE, RESPONSIVE ADULTS ARE THE KEY

There are many programs and intervention strategies designed to "bully-proof" students. Those with the best practices and research behind them are worth implementing. These programs are necessary, but *they will not protect you in a court of law.* It is a major pitfall to think that training children to interact differently is a replacement for monitoring the environment, intervening, and investigating.

Students—both victims and bystanders—want adults to *intervene* in bullying and harassment behavior. However, most children do not feel safe telling an adult that the behavior is occurring. The code of silence is strong: *Do not tell or things could get worse for you. Adults won't do anything anyway. Teachers just tell me to be tough and fight my own battles. Nobody likes a tattletale.* Teaching students the difference between telling and tattling, then giving strong positive reinforcement by taking effective action, increases the likelihood that students will report.

Training students how and when to report what they observe and experience is an important part of a legally fit approach to bullying, but you should not *expect* them to report. Relying on children to protect themselves and each other is illogical and irresponsible. The adults in the school system must encourage students to report while keeping an eye out for the warning signs that bullying is going on. It is more likely than not that the students will not report situations to the adults, so the adults must take the initiative in combating bullying. Every employee in the school, from the front office staff to the school crossing guards, must get involved.

Being a Safe Adult

For students, a safe adult is someone who will take them seriously and take prompt action when told about peer harassment. *Safe adults clearly distinguish between the role of "friend" or "confidante" and that of a guardian.* They know that their first priority is the safety of the child and any other victims who may be experiencing abuse by the bully or bullies involved.

Safe adults know that to protect students they must report what they hear. They also know how to put children at ease with the process, assuring them that while they cannot promise confidentiality, they can and will keep the matter as private as possible. *Safe adults act quickly.* They demonstrate that bullying and harassment will not be tolerated. *Safe adults protect victims and witnesses from retaliation.* If you want to create an environment in which more children report peer abuse, you have to demonstrate that it is safe and worthwhile to tell. *Safe adults respond effectively and stop the bullying behavior.*

Being a Responsive Adult

Often we hear from kids that reporting harassment is simply not worthwhile. Why? Because the response they got was either ineffective or left them more isolated than ever. Chapters 6, 7, and 8 will describe the elements of effective action. However, one of the most critical aspects of being a responsive adult is to *monitor the situation.* You have to follow up.

Did the problem really stop? How will you know that the situation is fully resolved? What will be your measure for success? Is the victim receiving sufficient assistance in the aftermath of the incident(s)? Is there more to do? These are essential questions if your response is to be both legally fit and educationally sound.

Getting Everyone Involved

Bullying behavior itself is often hidden from the view of adults. Children who bully others often wait for opportunities to act unobserved. One of the best ways to find out what is going on is to look for signs in possible victims.

You can enlist the assistance of the entire school community in this endeavor. Lunchroom monitors, playground supervisors, maintenance staff, front office administrative personnel, bus drivers, and other classified staff often see or overhear things that classroom teachers are not privy to. In addition, children sometimes see these adults as less threatening or easier to talk to than teachers and administrators and will confide in them.

Parents should also be advised of your anti-bullying efforts and trained in how to identify warning signs that their child is bullying or being bullied by peers. Of course, it is easier to get parents to protect their children than it is to convince them that their own child might be the source of the trouble, but it is not impossible. A parent of a middle school boy had this to say about her own efforts to impact her son's behavior: *Doug had begun to hang out with a group of students known to be bullies at his school. Tall for his age, Doug found it easy to intimidate others.* His parents cooperated with the school and successfully intervened with Doug, who is now hanging out with a *"nicer"* crowd of students.

Another parent spoke of her success in stopping a group of children from bullying her nine-year-old son at the bus stop. Twice he walked home from the bus covered in spit. She enlisted the help of the ringleader's parents. The abuse ended.

THE NATURE AND SCOPE OF ANTI-BULLYING INTERVENTIONS

Anti-bullying initiatives based on socioemotional interventions are very recent; their development and implementation spans only a little more than two decades. In their introductory chapter to *Bullying in Schools: How Successful Can Interventions Be?*, editors Smith, Pepler, and Rigby (2004) caution,

> It is difficult at this stage to identify the crucial elements in the anti-bul-
> lying programmes or to say which programmes are the most effective.
> Most of the programmes to counter bullying have resulted in a degree
> of success, at least on some outcome measures. This is encouraging. But
> the task of describing what is the "best practice" for schools to follow
> on the basis of evaluative studies of interventions remains. (p. 2)

Smith and his associates provide an overview of the types of anti-bullying interventions being developed by researchers and adopted by schools worldwide. One of the difficulties in comparing programs is that they are so varied in their approaches.

Common features of these programs include strategies for:

- developing staff and student awareness of the problem;
- taking a "whole school approach," defined as coordinated action at the school, class, and individual student levels; and
- implementing an anti-bullying policy. (Smith et al., 2004)

There is general agreement that all of these common features are necessary, but additional program features vary widely. Some programs emphasize preventive procedures while others lean toward intervention.

Program features may include:

- ways to develop a positive classroom environment,
- curriculum work and training in countering social prejudice and undesirable attitudes,
- assertiveness training for victims,
- anger management programs for bullies,
- training of bystanders to report behavior and stand up for victimized students,
- teacher and staff training and monitoring of the environment,
- peer mediation; and
- conflict resolution. (Smith et al., 2004)

Smith and his associates tell us that the widest variance among intervention programs lies in how students who engage in bullying behavior are dealt with. Suggested strategies are shown in Figure 2.4.

 Figure 2.4 Strategies for Dealing With Bullying Behavior

1. Rules and consequences: Rules are established and specific consequences are set for breaking them.

2. Bully courts: Students set sanctions for bullies who break the rules.*

3. Community conferences: Victims confront their tormentors and "express their grievances" in front of the family and supporters of the bully; the operating principle here is to invoke shame, but in the presence of a caring community who can support the bully in reforming.*

4. Non-punitive, problem-solving approaches such as peer mediation are implemented.*

5. The No-Blame approach: Developed by Robinson and Maines (1997), in this approach the "person conducting the intervention" meets with the victim and gets the facts; a meeting is then held with the bully or bullies, the victim, and other student supporters. The adult explains what has happened and its impact and "seeks a proposal on how the situation can be improved" from the students who decide the outcome; the adult then monitors the situation. *

6. Pikas' Shared Concern Method: A series of meetings is conducted with the victim, with each student perpetrator, and finally with all students involved with the intention of establishing workable relationships and ending the bullying behavior.*

SOURCE: Smith et al. (2004)

NOTES: All of the asterisked (*) items in the figure above involve some form of peer mediation or conflict resolution strategy that requires the victim to confront the perpetrator(s).

BUT IS IT LEGALLY FIT?

The mindset that there is a "conflict" involved reveals a misunderstanding about the fundamental nature of bullying and harassment. Bullying is not a conflict but a domination of another, an abuse of power.

The U.S. Department of Health and Human Services ([USDHHS], 2004) puts it this way:

> Bullying is a form of victimization. It is no more a "conflict" than are child abuse or domestic violence. Mediating a bullying incident may send inappropriate messages to the students who are involved. . . . The appropriate message to the child who is bullied should be, "No one deserves to be bullied and we are going to do everything we can to stop it." The message for children who bully should be, "Your behavior is inappropriate and must be stopped." Mediation may further victimize a child who has been bullied. It may be very upsetting for a child who has been bullied to face his or her tormenter in mediation.

There is no evidence to indicate that conflict resolution or peer mediation is effective in stopping bullying (USDHHS, 2004). Furthermore, conflict resolution and peer mediation are not legally fit responses to bullying behavior. In cases of actionable harassment, the Office for Civil Rights ([OCR], 2001) has stated that a victim has the right to not confront the perpetrator. Encouraging such action may heighten the risk of liability.

Other intervention strategies mentioned in Figure 2.4 have their pros and cons, and no one best practice has yet to surface, if it ever will. There appears to be no magic formula for changing kids—either the bullies or the bullied.

LEGAL AVENUES FOR EFFECTING CHANGE

A completely different avenue for effecting systemic change is the law. Many difficult societal issues had to be legislated and litigated first before human behavior began to shift. The law gives guidance on expectations for student conduct as well as educators' duty to provide a safe learning environment. Pay attention to managing and monitoring what is happening and apply legally fit, educationally sound strategies for enforcing justice and fairness at school—including your school district policies and procedures.

Subsequent chapters in this book present a step-by-step guide to fulfilling your duties to train students and employees, monitor the environment, investigate rumors and complaints, and take remedial action to stop the behavior and avoid further harm. Most important, the McGrath SUCCEED System that follows is designed to create a school culture in which children trust adults to act in their best interests and communicate when something is amiss.

If adults in the school system take their responsibilities seriously and train themselves in legally fit and educationally sound actions, and then take those actions promptly and consistently, they will establish an environment in which students trust adults to protect them. This environment will encourage students to come forward when there is a problem. The ultimate goal of this book is to significantly reduce bullying in schools for the protection of all involved.

SUMMARY

This chapter discussed the impact of bullying on the victim. The physical and emotional effects, signs and symptoms, and the long-term impact of bullying (including chronic trauma and post-traumatic stress) were reviewed. A safe, responsive adult in the school community was defined and six powerful practices for identifying victims in need of assistance were presented. The common features of intervention programs whose aim is to reduce bullying in schools were identified, along with the pitfalls of using conflict resolution and peer mediation strategies with bullying. Finally, the benefits of approaching bullying from a legal perspective were looked at.

Two current trends in the bullying research are discussed in the next chapter: social scheming—particularly among girls—and "technobullying." The chapter also addresses aspects of the school culture that keep bullying in place and what can be done about them.

3

Social Scheming and Technobullying

You will never, all your life, forget the rank order of popularity in your sixth grade class, or the rules of the middle-school food chain: You will prey upon anyone who appears remotely more vulnerable than you are.

—Linda Perlstein, *Not Much Just Chillin':*
The Hidden Lives of Middle Schoolers

Stephanie (not her real name) is a bright, articulate seventh grader. She attends a Southern California junior high school with approximately 530 seventh- and eighth-grade students, gets good grades, and participates in extracurricular activities. She says,

Bullying to me is not just somebody ganging up on someone or trying to just hurt them, it's sometimes their way of getting things out, and they don't realize they're doing it. And sometimes it's peer pressure. Because in junior high it's huge, and sometimes they think it's cool. . . . It means taking advantage of somebody that's less fortunate in different ways. It might be physical but sometimes it's just somebody who needs a friend but they can't get one because nobody wants to be seen with them. We all have our own little groups. The cool people have their group. They don't go around bullying everybody. It's just they enjoy making fun of people, and they don't think it's bullying. They just go around having fun with their friends. Then if they pass somebody they're like "look at her hair" or they text message mean comments to her.

(Interview with the author, April 1, 2005)

Stephanie demonstrates an awareness of the manipulative emotional and relational interactions often prevalent among students, particularly girls. These behaviors have been around perhaps from the beginning of time, yet they have only recently been recognized as forms of bullying. Stephanie also describes new technologies for perpetrating bullying that involve the Internet, cell phones, and pagers. Both areas are worthy of further exploration.

MEAN GIRLS

In *Odd Girl Out*, Rachel Simmons (2002) writes, "There is a hidden culture of girls' aggression in which bullying is epidemic, distinctive, and destructive. It is not marked by the direct physical and verbal behavior that is primarily the province of boys" (p. 3). By middle school, the backbiting, exclusion, rumors, and social scheming among girls is at its height.

Marion K. Underwood (2003), in *Social Aggression Among Girls*, notes that relational bullying is not the sole province of girls. Boys engage in it too. Nor do all girls bully others in this manner. However, this is the main way that adolescent girls bully other girls.

What Does Relational Bullying Look Like?

When I asked her about the bullying she had observed, Stephanie talked about Lisa (not her real name):

There's this girl that nobody likes because of her reputation last year, but of course I didn't go to that school last year, so I was her friend, and she's really nice. And they say, "Are you hanging out with Lisa? Is she your friend?" Literally, they say that. And I say, "Yes, she's really sweet." But now I know what everybody thinks of her, and I don't understand why because she's really cool. I'm half the time on her side because I consider myself her friend. But when they're saying Lisa does this stuff all the time and she's really imma-ture, I don't stand up for her because of peer pressure. . . . Sometimes I do, I'm like guys, just stop, she's cool. But sometimes I don't and I get really upset with myself because I could have.

Let's look again at the behaviors that constitute relational bullying. Exclusion, dirty looks, cold shoulders, being called a "ho" or a "slut" by people thought to be friends, being set up to look stupid, rumor spreading, public humiliation—it's all there. Students watch it happen to others and pray that they don't do the wrong thing to set their friends against them. They stay silent while others are being victimized, hoping that their silence will keep them safe.

Figure 3.1 Relational Bullying

- Using negative body language or facial expressions
- Gossiping
- Starting/spreading rumors

- Threatening to end a relationship
- Undermining other relationships
- Passively not including in group

- Playing mean tricks
- Insulting publicly
- Ruining a reputation
- Ignoring someone to punish or coerce

- Exclusion
- Ostracizing/total group rejection
- Arranging public humiliation

Range of Severity

What's the Harm?

In her discussion of social aggression among girls, Underwood (2003) states that the intended objectives of physical aggression (that the behavior harms and the victim feels hurt) also apply to instances of relational bullying. The difference is that the victim may not know the perpetrator's identity in relational bullying (p. 16).

Underwood (2003) describes the developmental stages of social aggression:

- **Preschool:** "If you won't do what I say, I won't be your friend." (p. 65)
- **Middle School:** Gossip—phone calls, online communication, note passing (p. 93)
- **Adolescence:** Rumor spreading, moral negotiations, and strategic interactions to inflict social harm (p. 134)

A full description of these stages is beyond the scope of this book, but Underwood's (2003) comprehensive exploration of current research is highly recommended. She cautions her readers: "That such behavior undermines our deepest-held assumptions about what it means to be female might tempt us to pathologize all forms of girls' aggression rather than to seek to understand why girls might engage in them" (p. 183).

Preliminary evidence in this new area of research shows that there are "developmental and psychosocial consequences" to social aggression in girls. There are impacts on both the perpetrators and the victims. Studies show that both groups report internalizing difficulties and higher levels of loneliness and depression than students who were neither victims nor perpetrators. In addition, self-reported victimization is also correlated to poor self-concept (p. 186).

Social aggression hurts because it undermines girls' need for belonging and social acceptance. In their qualitative study of victimization among teenage girls, Owens and his associates (2001 pp. 222–223) address the effects on victims. Their findings were "consistent with those of other researchers who have reported the harm that indirect harassment inflicts upon girls," including Crick (1995), who found that girls experience more emotional distress as a results of indirect harassment than do boys, and Galen and Underwood (1997), who reported that "girls found indirect harassment to be *just as hurtful as physical aggression* (and to be more hurtful than boys found it to be)."

In their report *Relational Victimization in Childhood and Adolescence: I Hurt You Through the Grapevine* (2001), Crick, Nelson, Morales, Cullerton-Sen, Casas, and Hickman also address the issue of harm. They point out that "relational victimization can be experienced at varying levels" of frequency and intensity. Single incidents may have no lasting impact, but like other forms of bullying, the more frequent and severe the behavior, the greater the harm.

Crick and her associates indicate that the majority of studies of relational bullying have been conducted in middle schools, where the behavior is most prevalent. In a 1998 study, Crick and Bigbee found that relational victimization in middle schoolers was "significantly associated with peer rejection, submissiveness, loneliness, emotional distress, and lack of self-restraint" (Crick et al., 2001, p. 205). In 1998, Grotpeter, Geiger, Nukulkij, and Crick explored the impact of relational victimization on middle school friendships. As compared with non-victimized peers, "relationally victimized children reported significantly higher levels of negative qualities (e.g., physical aggression and conflict) and significantly lower levels of positive features (e.g., help and guidance, conflict resolution, intimacy, validation and caring, companionship and recreation) in their reciprocated friendships" (Crick et al., 2001, p. 207).

THE MARVELS OF MODERN TECHNOLOGY

As said before, relational bullying is nothing new. Children's author Laura Ingalls Wilder devoted many pages in her autobiographical *Little House* series to the treachery of her schoolmate Nellie Olsen as they pioneered the Midwest at the turn of the twentieth century. However, modern technology offers the twenty-first century teen altogether new and inventive ways to bully. Today's children participate in a variety of "technobullying" behaviors via Web logs, text messaging, cellular telephones, pagers, personal digital assistants (PDAs), and other electronic devices. A person no longer needs to be bigger than the other guy to bully in this way, just to be wired.

This type of bullying and harassment is widespread among students. A 2004 study of 1,566 students by i-Safe America, a non-profit Internet safety group, found that 58% of fourth through eighth graders reported having had "mean or hurtful things said to them online" and 53% admitted to having engaged in such behavior with others. Nearly 33% had been threatened. Forty-two percent said that they had been "bullied" online. Yet 58% of those who experienced hurtful behavior did not inform their parents of the incidents.

Three-Way Calling Attacks

In *Queen Bees and Wannabes: Helping Your Daughter Survive Cliques, Gossip, Boyfriends, and Other Realities of Adolescence*, Rosalind Wiseman (2002) introduces readers to what she terms "three-way calling attacks." This form of social scheming is particularly treacherous because the target never knows who may be listening in on the call. Here is what this behavior looks like: The objective is to get one girl on the phone (Girl A), then conference in another girl (Girl B). Girl B doesn't know that Girl A is on the line. The originator of the call then traps Girl B into saying something mean about Girl A. At this point, the mastermind has completely undermined her friend. This can, of course, be done with multiple callers on multiple phones. It can include boys ("Do you like Brad?"). The possible configurations are endless and downright chilling.

Instant Messaging

Instant messaging is the afterschool (and often in-school) social networking activity of choice for secondary school children. As soon as they get home, they log on to "talk" to their friends. Not all instant messaging is friendly, however. In a 2004 *New York Times* article on *cyberbullying*, Amy Harmon reported on an incident that started with a stolen pencil case that contained makeup. Eighth grader Amanda, the victim, reported the theft that had been perpetrated by girls in her class. An argument then ensued at school. According to Harmon, "it did not end there. As soon as Amanda got home, the instant messaging started popping up on her computer screen. She was a tattletale and a liar, they said. Shaken, she typed back, 'You stole my stuff!' She was a 'stuck-up bitch,' came the instant response in the box on the screen, followed by a series of increasingly ugly epithets."

Amanda then went to a basketball game for the evening. There she continued to receive the "electronic insults." Fifty text messages were forwarded from her computer to her cell phone during the game—the maximum the phone holds (Harmon, 2004).

In the case of 13-year-old Ryan Halligan, the consequences were deadly. According to his father, John Halligan, he discovered evidence after his son's death that his suicide was preceded by "a very disturbing IM [Instant Message] exchange" with "another boy who was harassing Ryan in a very disgusting sexual way. . . . Ryan never mentioned this boy's name. We learned later that Ryan hung out with him a few times in person but mostly online since he lives a few hours away. Had we met this child in person or had the chance to ask other parents about the boy, we would have never allowed [our son] to associate with this kid" (Halligan, 2004).

Experts speculate that on the Internet, children are farther removed from the effect of their words. They seem to say much nastier things to each other online than they would ever say in person. Kathleen Conn, author of *Bullying and Harassment, A Legal Guide for Educators*, says, "Because cyberbullies do not have to confront their victims directly, they may feel emboldened and uninhibited, making their messages more vicious than they would be in a personal confrontation" (Conn, 2004, p. 164).

Bullying by instant message can include insulting remarks, racial slurs, sexualized comments and threats of harm, gossip, and rumor spreading. Students post hurtful comments about other students on their instant message profiles. They also participate in online exclusion tactics by shutting specific students out of their "buddy lists" or private chats.

Blogging

Web logs—known simply as "blogs"—are another weapon for relational bullying. A 2005 study by the Pew Internet and American Life Project revealed that one in five kids aged 12 to 17 keeps a blog. That is four million American children. Twice that many children read blogs regularly (Lenhart & Madden, 2005).

Blogs are personal or shared Web sites where kids journal. Hotbeds of gossip, rumors, and harassment, the blogs provide a place for kids to gossip and complain about everything and everybody—often anonymously. Make someone mad today and you risk being added to an online list of the school's "10 Biggest Whores" tonight. Of course, there is nothing private about these Web pages. It is the social equivalent of writing something nasty on the bathroom wall or passing a note in class, only a blog is vastly more public, available to millions of Internet users worldwide.

The creation of Web sites dedicated specifically to social networking, such as MySpace, Xanga, LiveJournal, and others, has added to the mayhem. According to Nancy Willard, Director of the Center for Safe and Responsible Internet Use, "the thing is that young people appear to be totally oblivious to the fact that everything they post in these sites is public, permanent, accessible from throughout the world, and easily transmittable to anybody" (Paulson, 2006).

Bullying Online, an organization dedicated to cyberbullying prevention, posted the following on their Web site: "We recently closed down a series of message boards in the Hertfordshire/north London area where pupils were being identified by name, school and year and others were invited to post abuse about them" (Carnell, 2006).

The problems identified by Bullying Online on these message boards included

- "A death threat"
- "Numerous threats of violence"
- "Racist comments"
- "Numerous bogus messages posted in the names of people being targeted"
- "A girl who tried to kill herself due to abuse"
- "A boy who lost all his friends as a result of postings made in his name"
- "A teenager on antidepressants and afraid to go out due to threats"

No Privacy on the Internet

Forwarding private material can be even more devastating. Videos of student sexual encounters, revealing digital photos, and private e-mail messages revealing personal secrets are easily forwarded to classmates or posted to public Web sites. Once forwarded, they are impossible to stop and can be excruciatingly embarrassing for the subject of the e-mail. Children are learning the hard way that there is no guarantee of privacy online.

In a 2004 *New York Times* article, Amy Harmon notes, "Psychologists say the distance between bully and victim on the Internet is leading to an unprecedented—and often unintentional—degree of brutality, especially when combined with a typical adolescent's lack of impulse control and underdeveloped empathy skills." She goes on to describe a number of incidents in which private information sent by e-mail was widely disseminated to others, humiliating the original sender. For example, an eighth-grade girl sent a digital video of herself masturbating to a boy on whom she had a crush. It was soon posted on a file-sharing network where there was unlimited public access. The girl was clearly identifiable. A 15-year-old girl sent her boyfriend a nude picture of herself by e-mail; he sent it to his friends; it is still in circulation on the Web (Harmon, 2004).

Online Impersonation

Online impersonation is an especially devious way to "get" someone. According to the Bullying Online Web site, kids have been known to steal each other's screen names and send hurtful, insulting, or embarrassing messages to friends or crush objects. And how can the victims ever prove that they did not send the incriminating messages?

What Can Schools Do?

Kathleen Conn (2002) gives guidance in *The Internet and the Law: What Educators Need to Know*. She suggests having well-articulated discipline policies or codes of conduct, establishing acceptable use policies for the Internet on campus, and requiring students and teachers to report Web sites that mention the school in any way so that they can be monitored. While she recommends caution regarding out-of-school behavior and First Amendment rights, she advocates keeping parents in the loop. The latter may well have the best ability to stop the behavior when they hear of it or see it online (pp. 20–23).

Why Kids Don't Report

In the case of technobullying, children say that they are afraid of losing their computers, cell phones, PDA, or Internet privileges if they tell. Katie, now 14, received a death threat via instant message at the age of nine. In *Teaching Tolerance* magazine she writes,

> Afterward, I didn't tell anyone for a long time. I was convinced that I had done something wrong by clicking to accept that message. If I told, my parents would assume that the Internet wasn't safe and would take away not only my computer privileges but . . . my older siblings' privileges. It remained a secret, keeping me off the computer in fear. (Jackson, 2006, pp. 50–54)

Of course, among children there is also *The Code*.

THE CODE

Stand among a group of children after an incident of misbehavior and ask, "Who did that?" You are unlikely to get a response. Why? There is an unwritten but generally inviolable code of silence among children when it comes to reporting another child's transgressions.

A child's status in the group often depends on his ability to keep silent. He or she will collude in bullying, grateful to be on the sidelines rather than the target. Once this happens, the bystander may remain silent out of fear of being next, out of guilt at his own passivity, or out of a sense that he will lose peer acceptance by telling.

Most adults in the school setting unwittingly reinforce the code with statements like "Don't be a tattletale" or "Fight your own battles." They harbor a mistaken notion that children should learn to work things out and that a victim of bullying just needs to "toughen up."

In his article *Breaking the Code of Silence: How Students Can Help Keep Schools—and Each Other—Safe,* Samuel J. Spitalli (2003) writes,

> The code of silence evolves from habits formed during the first years of life. From an early age, children are taught how to get along with their siblings and friends, how to share, how to be fair and how to play together. They learn to negotiate with others, to compromise, to compete, to win and to lose. In time, unfortunately, they also learn to manipulate, to be vindictive, to hurt, to bully, to retaliate, to victimize, to defy and a multitude of other negative responses to life's challenges. Children learn these "skills" from their peers, their brothers and sisters, their parents, television and a whole new generation of computer-based entertainment.

> Somewhere along the line, they also learn to tattle. Because tattling is self-centered and typically is used only to get someone else in trouble, parents often discourage their children from telling on each other, encouraging them instead to get along, "play nice" and work out their own difficulties without adult intervention. Over time, this reluctance to tattle evolves into a code of silence—an unspoken yet clearly understood commitment to their peers that they will not disclose even the most disturbing and dangerous information about each other to adults. (p. 56)

Spitalli reminds us of the case of Andy Williams cited earlier. Williams told friends he was going to bring a gun to school, and no one reported it.

Changing the Adult Response

According to Spitalli (2003), "students also need to hear that the collective benefit of reporting or informing adults about unsafe activity is that they get to attend the kind of school they want to attend, a school where the climate is friendly, warm, respectful, and supportive" (p. 57).

This brings us back to the concept of the safe, responsive adult in the school setting. If we are to break the code of silence, the adults in school must demonstrate that student reports will be taken seriously and that there will be swift, appropriate, and effective consequences for bullying behavior. Adults must welcome and encourage reporting of these matters and enlist the support of parents in these efforts.

THE COMPLEX ROLE OF THE BYSTANDER

There are other phenomena that contribute to the culture of bullying in schools. The remainder of this chapter will examine aspects of school culture that help perpetuate the problem and provide some strategies for addressing them.

Having examined the role of the bystander in maintaining the code of silence about bullying, let's now examine the complex role of the third party or bystander in more depth. What makes the bystander role complex? Isn't a bystander just an onlooker who happens to be in the vicinity? Isn't the role of bystander that of a passive witness? Absolutely not. Bystanders are both affected by and participate in bullying incidents in a variety of ways. Responses range from active complicity or collusion in the bullying behavior, to tacit approval, to fear and traumatic injury from what bystanders are witnessing (Nishina & Juvonen, 2005b).

Then there is the legal lens. First, every bystander is a *witness* to the alleged incident(s) and may later be called to testify about what was observed. Second, bystanders may turn out to be *victims* with legitimate claims of illegal harassment if the environment is proved to be sufficiently hostile and intimidating so as to interfere with studying and learning. Finally, bystanders may be *perpetrators* themselves if their own behavior is found to constitute bullying. It is also important to note that school officials who witness bullying may be accused of negligent supervision or deliberate indifference if they stand by and do not intervene when witnessing bullying behavior. A bystander could, therefore, be an untargeted victim, a bully, a witness, or a supervisor. Bystanders may even play multiple concurrent roles, and students, school employees, and parents may all be bystanders.

Group Dynamics

The public nature of bullying is particularly humiliating for the victim. For the most part, bystanders neither report bullying nor attempt to stop it. In an observational study of playground bullying among first- through sixth-grade Canadian school children, Wendy Craig and Debra Pepler (1997) found that peers were involved in some way in 85% of bullying episodes. Among other things, this involvement consisted of active participation in the episode (30%) and observing the interaction (23%). Peers intervened in only 12% of the episodes observed. Furthermore, peers were coded as being respectful to the bully in 74% of the episodes but respectful to the victim in only 23% of the episodes. The range and prevalence of responses may stem from the bystander's fear of being victimized himself or from doubt about having any power to actually stop what is happening. Inaction may even stem from a bystander's opinion (as discussed in Chapter 2) that the victim somehow deserves what is happening.

This lack of "standing up" for a victim can cause fear and a general sense of malaise among a group. It reinforces a sense of powerlessness and can also increase fear among the group (Sullivan et al., 2004).

A group can adopt bullying as a problem-solving technique, particularly with provocative victims. When that happens, the entire class may become desensitized to the harm that this behavior is causing the victim (Olweus, 1993, p. 33). The general learning environment of the class is contaminated, and students do not have the will or the skill to deviate from the expected norm of behavior. In essence, they become powerless in the face of peer pressure and bullying. In an environment of fear, discomfort, and powerlessness, student learning is often inhibited.

The Role of the Defender

Bullying is usually, although not exclusively, a group activity. In *Bullying in Secondary Schools,* Sullivan and colleagues (2004) contend that bystanders are more important in stopping bullying than either the bully or the victim because bullies need an audience for their power plays and "bullying can only go on if the bystanders let it" (p. 19).

Among bystanders, the first three types—witness, victim, perpetrator—abdicate responsibility; however, the fourth group, defenders, can shift the dynamic. Bullying experts agree that increasing the number of defenders among a peer group and training them to actively show their disapproval of bullying behavior can stop bullying behavior (Beaudoin & Taylor, 2004; Coloroso, 2003; Davis, 2004; Sullivan, 2000; Sullivan et al., 2004).

Being a defender is not easy for most children and adolescents, and according to Sullivan and his coauthors, defenders are rare (Sullivan et al., 2004). Young people need models of compassion and social conscience. Yet these virtues are all too often actively discouraged by parents, mentors, and peers alike. By adolescence, the prevailing drift is toward alienation, resignation, and disengagement.

Shifting the Dynamic: Training Bystanders

Effective interventions with students must include the whole group, including bystanders. Salmivalli (2001) distinguishes three areas of development:

1. Awareness training,
2. Opportunities for self-reflection, and
3. Rehearsal of new behaviors.

Awareness training must include awareness of the group dynamics involved in bullying. Students need to understand their roles and how they may be unintentionally contributing to the bullying behavior that they witness.

ጢ— **Figure 3.2** Peer Bystanders *ጢ*—

Sullivan and his associates categorize peer bystanders into four types:

1. **Sidekicks** (who join in at the bully's bidding),

2. **Reinforcers** (who laugh and encourage the behavior),

3. **Outsiders** (who do not take sides but distance themselves and remain silent), and

4. **Defenders** (who comfort the victim and try to stop the bullying).

SOURCE: Sullivan (2004).

Shifting the dynamic so that there is a significant increase in the number and frequency of defenders (students who stand up for and defend victims of bullying) is essential. One way to accomplish this increase is to practice the roles with students. Have the "cool" or "popular" kids—the kids the others look to for leadership—be the defenders. Start a trend. Make defending "cool."

Resources such as videos, films, and works of fiction that depict bullying can stimulate self-awareness and offer opportunities for group and paired discussion. Incidents in the school setting can also be used as *teachable moments* in which students reflect on their behavior.

Perhaps most important is the opportunity to practice new behaviors. Drama and role-playing can be used to rehearse skills such as defending another child, reporting an incident, or telling another child to stop. It is important that such activities include players in all of the roles so that students get to deal with their fear and other emotions that could stop them from taking action when a real incident occurs.

"I'M AFRAID TO WALK IN THAT CORRIDOR"

Another key to prevention is identifying the "hot spots" where frequent bullying and harassment happen. These areas tend to be the less supervised parts of campus, congested hallways, or areas where groups congregate.

Make a map of your campus and take a walk. What do you see in the environment? Where is trouble brewing? Mark these spots on the map and create a plan for cooling off the hot spots. Your plan may include increased adult presence in these areas, the breaking up of large groups, managing the traffic flow, rearranging furnishings, or making an area off limits.

Students report that most bullying takes place on the way to and from school, including on the school bus, in classrooms, on playgrounds, and in locker rooms and rest rooms. Training the adults who supervise students to intervene in, report, and prevent bullying and harassment is critical to a legally fit, whole school, whole person approach.

IS YOUR DISCIPLINE CODE ADEQUATE?

In some districts, policies against bullying and harassment will provide for disciplinary sanctions. If your policy does not contain penalties, it should cross-reference other policies that spell out sanctions, such as the student discipline code.

Take a look at your student discipline code and any anti-bullying and harassment policies and procedures. Do they allow for flexibility in determining your response? Consult your legal counsel if you are unsure whether the policies are adequate for dealing with bullying and illegal harassment by students.

WHAT DOES RETALIATION LOOK LIKE?

Retaliation or reprisals can include threats, bodily harm, graffiti aimed at the complainant, further bullying and harassment, ridicule, pranks, taunting, and organized ostracism or exclusion. It can happen student to student, but all too often it also happens employee to student.

Watch out for peers or siblings of the alleged harasser "ganging up" on the complainant. This includes faculty or staff mistreating a student who has complained about a popular student, star athlete, or school employee. Community members, the media, or both may also make things difficult for a student who "makes waves."

HANDLING GRAFFITI

Not all inflammatory text messages appear online. Bullying and retaliation for reporting bullying may include taunts, threats, and intimidation via graffiti. Depending on the content, graffiti can violate state laws against vandalism, malicious destruction of property, threats and intimidation, and hate-motivated offenses. The graffiti itself is tangible, legal evidence of the crime. An approach should be planned in advance to deal with the collection of the evidence and prompt removal of the offending graffiti.

Take the following actions to deal with graffiti:

1. All school custodians should be trained to report graffiti that is sexually explicit or discriminatory toward a protected classification of students (based on race, ethnicity, gender, etc.).

2. Law enforcement agencies recommend that evidence of graffiti be preserved for investigation when the graffiti is persistent; is located in places of high visibility; identifies particular targets; identifies the perpetrator; contains incitements to violence, threats, or intimidation; and/or targets particular groups.

3. Cover the graffiti so that it does not continue to create a hostile or offensive environment.

4. Request that law enforcement photograph the graffiti as soon as possible. If the content is not sufficiently provocative to warrant law enforcement's attention, photograph it yourself.

5. A camera should be readily available to take photographs of the area where the graffiti is. Custodial or office personnel should be instructed in how to take the photographs in case a site administrator is not available.

6. Remove the graffiti completely after law enforcement inspection and after photographing it.

SUMMARY

Two new trends were explored in the study of bullying behavior. The first topic, social scheming or aggression among girls, has been around for generations, but understanding of the phenomenon as a social and developmental issue is still in its infancy. Knowing the behaviors involved and the impact on victims will increase educators' sensitivity to this type of bullying and facilitate appropriate action.

We also entered cyberspace and looked at the world of bullying opportunities that new technologies make available. Children, it appears, are no longer safe from bullies in the privacy of their rooms. School personnel can have an impact by monitoring online activity on campus as well as staying alert for signs that students are being victimized in this way.

The chapter concludes back on the school campus with an examination of a range of phenomena that contribute to the *status quo*, keeping the bullying culture in place, including the code of silence, bystander passivity, unmonitored campus hot spots, and fear of retaliation.

PART II

The Legal Context of Bullying

4

Bullying Through a Legal Lens

School directors want safe schools as well as schools with a climate that attracts students and fosters learning. They seek a balance between regulations and conditions that prepare students to live responsibly in a free society. They want common sense to prevail in choices that students make and in the actions of teachers and principals who must enforce the rules.

—Washington State School Directors'
Association, *Using Common Sense* (1999, p. 2)

Fourteen-year-old Michael Delaney was repeatedly harassed and beaten up by older teammates on the Andrew High School varsity basketball team—on bus rides to games, in the locker room at away games, and at basketball practice during basketball season. The "hazing" by upperclassmen included severe beatings with a leather belt. Threatened with reprisals if they told authorities, Michael and Reed, the other freshman on the team, kept silent about what they were experiencing. However, on the way to yet another game, they asked their coach if they could sit in the front of the bus because they were afraid of getting beat up. The coach told them to sit in the back. The assault that followed lasted 25 minutes. The incidents finally came to light when Michael passed out in class one day, and another student, worried that the beatings had caused an injury, called her parents for advice on what to do. Michael's parents sued the school district for negligent supervision. The jury awarded the family $100,000. (de Souza Guedes, 2002)

It is vital that any campaign for the eradication of bullying behavior, and the school district's responses to that end, be understood from a socio-emotional view, as previously discussed. It is just as critical that bullying be understood in a legal context. More and more students and their parents are suing school districts for their failure to take steps to prevent or intervene in persistent, pervasive, and/or severe acts of social and physical bullying. They are suing, and many of them are winning substantial settlements and judgments.

The monetary awards are occurring because many school officials, administrators, and employees are not fulfilling their duties. There are currently three main causes of action that are being brought in suits against school districts and a variety of incidents and injuries for which they are being held liable.

Main causes of action:
- Failure to take preventative action
- Deliberate indifference
- Negligent supervision

Types of injuries and incidents:
- Bullying
- Suicide
- Threats of violence
- Sexual harassment
- Anti-gay discrimination
- Physical assault
- Verbal harassment
- Civil rights violations

For a more in-depth examination of a sampling of current cases, refer to Resource B at the end of this book. You will find a number of representative cases organized by type of lawsuit and state.

Subsequent chapters of this book will provide detailed instructions on how to address bullying in a legally fit and educationally sound way—a way that both protects students from harm and you and your district from liability. However, first it is necessary to consider that in many school districts, current practices meant to prevent and intervene in bullying are not legally fit.

IN LOCO PARENTIS

School administrators and employees are obligated to provide a safe educational environment for the children they are supervising. This is not just common sense. It is the law. Fail to do this, and even governmental immunity (should your state have such a law) may not protect your school district. Act with deliberate indifference, and you may even be personally liable for the injury suffered.

You have a legal duty to take steps to prevent harm to students by training students and staff, by adequately supervising and monitoring the environment, by *thoroughly* investigating allegations and rumors, and by taking effective remedial action to prevent further abuse.

You did not go into education to become a lawyer. Fortunately, you do not need a law degree to follow the law in this area. What is needed is a legal primer that provides guidance.

THREE BODIES OF LAW

There are three bodies of law that govern bullying:

1. Civil law
2. Criminal law
3. Administrative law

What Is a Civil Action?

A civil action is a lawsuit entered into for the purpose of enforcing a civil or personal right. Although there are other scenarios, a civil action typically involves someone seeking monetary damages for the fact that they were hurt or, on occasion, an injunction against further harm by the alleged perpetrator.

In situations involving bullying, in certain states a civil action may be brought against the school or district for some failure in its duty to take reasonable measures to protect a student from harm, including:

- negligent acts where the harm was foreseeable,
- harassment or discrimination to which it was deliberately indifferent, or
- a violation of a student's rights.

What Is Criminal Law?

Criminal law is public law that deals with crimes and their prosecution. This area of law is usually governed by state or federal statute or ordinance.

Varying from state to state, a duty exists to take steps to protect students from assault, battery, rape, sexual abuse, hate crimes, theft, extortion, and other crimes that may be committed on or off campus while the student is under school supervision. This includes crimes committed by third parties on school grounds, on school transportation, or at school-sponsored activities.

Bullying behavior may also be criminal conduct. In such cases, you may be cooperating with law enforcement in an investigation of the matter. This does not relieve you of your responsibility to conduct a district-level investigation and to remedy the situation.

Crimes are very narrowly defined. There are specific parameters for criminal investigations: time limits, rules of evidence, definitions of age of consent, criminal intent, and so on. The district attorney or prosecutor will decide whether to try the case, or the case may be plea-bargained. There are a variety of things that may happen with the case that have nothing to do with the truth of the criminal charges.

Criminal prosecutors must prove their case "beyond a reasonable doubt," which is the highest standard of proof required under law. Reasonable doubt is a lack of sufficient certainty, based on the evidence, that an accused person is actually guilty of a particular crime. One might say that the prosecutor must present a case that leaves the judge or jury about 95% to 98% certain.

The standard of proof for civil and administrative proceedings is a "preponderance of the evidence." This means that if 51% or more of the evidence for one side supports the facts of their case, that side wins. Even if 49% of the evidence says it was not established, the case is won on the 51% that says it was.

What Is Administrative Law?

The third body of law that regulates the behavior of school employees and students is administrative law. This is the area of law dealing with governmental agencies. You are responsible for knowing and following administrative law.

Administrative law includes, but is not limited to, policies, procedures, and regulations of:

- your school district's governing board;
- federal regulatory agencies such as the Equal Employment Opportunity Commission and the Office for Civil Rights; and
- your state's education code, government code, and administrative regulations.

You must know and enforce your school district's policies and procedures. In fact, you are a governmental agent charged with responsibility for enforcement of those laws. If your local school district policy is more stringent about something than federal or state law, the school district's higher standard will prevail unless it violates someone's constitutional rights.

Familiarize yourself with your district's anti-bullying and harassment policies for both students and employees, emergency and crisis plans, accident and incident reporting forms and procedures, collective bargaining agreements and due process standards, and any other policies and procedures that apply to you and your students. Keep copies in a convenient location and refer to them often. You should be able to locate a policy, plan, or procedure quickly when it is needed.

Never assume that you know what a policy or regulation says. Review the policy before taking action on something related to that particular policy. There have been numerous cases in which a school administrator took action without reviewing the policy, only to discover later that she had skipped a step or missed a mandated timeline.

WHAT IS LIABILITY?

Liability is legal responsibility. It entails the obligation to do something or not do something. To say that a person or entity is "liable" for a wrongful act is to indicate that they are responsible for compensating another for that wrongful act. Liability is determined in a court of law, either by a judge or jury, and is the outcome of a civil, not criminal, action.

You may be personally named in a lawsuit, and there are circumstances in which you could be held personally liable. Regardless of whether you may be held personally liable for an act, you have an obligation to minimize the risk of harm to students and liability for your employer.

What Is Governmental Immunity?

The doctrine of governmental immunity came from English common law. It provides that no government body can be sued unless it gives permission. In many states, school districts are immune from lawsuits under this doctrine. Today, many states have waived their governmental immunity except in instances involving discretionary acts. To deny immunity, courts often look at the duty of care, whether reasonable care was taken, whether the injury was foreseeable, and whether the governmental entity had prior knowledge of the condition.

WHAT IS NEGLIGENCE?

A large area of individual and institutional liability is based on the law of negligence. Not only are people responsible for the intentional harm they cause, they are also responsible for any failure to act under certain circumstances. *Failure to act as a reasonable person is expected to act in similar circumstances, when a duty exists toward the person affected,* is considered negligence. Negligence, if it causes injury to another, can give rise to liability.

Negligence is always assessed in light of the circumstances and the standard of care that would reasonably be expected of a person in similar circumstances. This is known as the *reasonable person standard*.

Where Does Negligence Fit Under the Law?

Negligence can be viewed on a continuum of behavior. On one end of the continuum is deliberately causing injury to others, which may be a criminal offense and may result in punishment of the perpetrator.

On the other end of the continuum are injury accidents that occur when the circumstances that give rise to the accident or injury are totally unforeseeable; thus, no one can be held responsible for the injury.

In between these two ends of the continuum are negligent acts—acts that are not deliberate, but in which the injury is foreseeable. Although there is no criminal offense, the injured party may seek financial compensation in a civil suit if a duty is owed him or her by the involved parties.

Between negligence and the intentional or criminal act there lies yet another, more serious type of negligence, which is called gross negligence. Gross negligence is any action or omission in reckless disregard of the consequences to the safety or property of another.

What Is a Duty of Care?

In civil law, a duty of care is a legal obligation imposed on an individual requiring the exercise of a reasonable standard of care while performing any acts that could cause foreseeable harm to others. For an action in negligence, there must be an identified duty of care in law. We owe this duty of care to anyone for whom we have accepted responsibility (e.g., students in general, student athletes we coach, neighbor children in our homes, or employees we supervise). The duty of care requires individuals to consider the consequences of their acts and omissions and to ensure that those acts or omissions do not give rise to a foreseeable risk of injury to another person.

What Is the Standard of Care in Civil Actions for Negligence?

The standard of care is the degree of prudence and caution required of an individual who is under a duty of care. A breach of the standard is necessary for a successful action in negligence.

The requirements of the standard of care are closely dependent on circumstances. Whether the standard of care has been breached is determined by the trier of fact and is usually phrased in terms of how a reasonable person would have exercised caution under similar circumstances.

In certain industries and professions, the standard of care is determined by the standard that would be exercised by the reasonably prudent manufacturer of a product or the reasonably prudent professional in that line of work. A special standard of care also applies to children, who are held to the behavior that is reasonable for a child of similar age, experience, and intelligence.

Simply following a customary practice never constitutes a complete defense against negligence. For example, one might argue that coaches "turning a blind eye" to hazing rituals is still common practice within the profession. This argument will not protect you or your district if a coach fails to protect a student from foreseeable harm.

While in most cases what is reasonable is, in fact, the common practice, this is not always the case. A whole industry may be lagging in adopting reasonable safety precautions; therefore, the industry may not set its own tests for a standard of care.

In the end, the courts set the standard of care. The test is *what a reasonable person under the same or similar circumstances would have done.*

How do the courts determine whether an educator or administrator is negligent? There are four questions that are fundamental to the courts' determination of negligence (see Figure 4.1).

Figure 4.1 How Do the Courts Determine Whether an Educator or Administrator Is Negligent?

This is accomplished by asking four questions:

1. Did the educator have a legal duty to the injured person?
2. Did the educator fail to fulfill this duty?
3. Was there an injury to the person to whom the educator had a duty?
4. Did the educator's failure to fulfill the duty directly or proximately cause the injury?

If a case is brought on the basis of negligence, the answers to all four questions in Figure 4.1 must be "yes." This is why, to date, most bullying cases involving negligent supervision in which juries have found in favor of the plaintiff have involved physical bullying. Injury is easier to substantiate in these cases. However, more courts are finding that a failure to prevent verbal harassment that is sexual in nature constitutes a Title IX violation for sexual harassment, for example, failure to prevent a heterosexual male student being called a "fag" by classmates over the course of several years (see Resource B).

Not all lawsuits are brought on the basis of negligence. Lawsuits for bullying behavior that is also unlawful discrimination may be brought under a variety of civil rights laws. One such law is Title IX, the federal law prohibiting discrimination based on sex, which includes sexual harassment. Another is the Civil Rights Act of 1871 § 1983, which creates liability for anyone acting on behalf of a state who causes the deprivation of any rights, privileges, or immunities secured by the United States Constitution and federal laws, if the person acts in an official capacity with deliberate indifference.

Under What Conditions May an Individual Be Found Individually Liable?

While the conditions vary and some states bar liability under negligence standards altogether, a general rule is that any school official with a practice, custom, or policy of disregarding, dismissing, concealing, and/or discouraging student or employee complaints of misconduct, discrimination, hazing, or other harmful acts or omissions may be held personally liable for harm to the complaining student or employee. The liability may be found under negligence law, as described previously, or under the civil rights protections provided to certain protected classifications of people.

Individual liability for civil rights infractions is more often found under the Civil Rights Act of 1871 § 1983. As stated above, § 1983 creates liability for anyone acting on behalf of a state, who causes the deprivation of any rights, privileges, or immunities secured by the United States Constitution and federal laws, if the person acts in an official capacity with deliberate indifference.

ℳ   **Figure 4.2** Personal Liability   *ℳ*

Liability may be established under federal civil rights laws if the complainant proves:

1. The supervisor/school official received notice of a pattern of improper acts by a teacher, employee, volunteer, or student;

2. The supervisor/school official demonstrated deliberate indifference to or tacit authorization of the offensive acts;

3. The supervisor/school official failed to take sufficient remedial action; and

4. Such failure proximately caused injury to the employee or student.

What Qualifies as "Notice"?

Under the laws of negligence, a school has notice if it actually knew (actual notice) or, in the exercise of reasonable care, should have known (constructive notice) about the harassment. As long as an agent or responsible employee of the school received notice, the school has actual notice. Under Title IX, the notice requirement is different.

In the landmark *Gebser* case, the U.S. Supreme Court found that an official of the school district must receive actual notice to be liable for monetary damages for sexual harassment under Title IX. In this case, the Court was concerned with the possibility of a money damages award against a school for sexual harassment about which it had not received actual notice (*Gebser v. Lago Vista Independent School District*, 1998).

A key question in current federal litigation is who within the school system is considered a school official for purposes of receiving actual notice, particu-

ℳ   **Figure 4.3**   *ℳ*

Schools Receive Actual Notice If

- A student, parent, or other individual contacts appropriate personnel such as a principal, campus security, bus driver, teacher, an affirmative action officer, or dean.

- An agent or responsible employee of the school has witnessed the conduct.

- OCR receives a complaint and notifies the school.*

Schools Receive Constructive Notice If . . .

- The school could have found out about the bullying or harassment through a reasonably diligent inquiry.

- Known incidents should have triggered an investigation that would have led to the discovery of additional incidents.

- The pervasiveness of the bullying or harassment should have made it obvious to the school.

*NOTE: When the OCR receives a complaint of a civil rights violation, they will always notify the school of a potential violation and give that school an opportunity to correct the situation before pursuing fund termination or other enforcement mechanisms.

larly in the Title IX cases. For purposes of notice to the school district, school principals have been held to be school officials, but not teachers. Given the contentiousness of this issue, it is likely that the U.S. Supreme court may accept a case on this issue in the near future in order to give direction to the lower courts.

Even if the school district did not receive actual notice, the Office for Civil Rights (OCR) has made it clear that as an administrative agency, its duty is to enforce a higher standard of compliance with Title IX. Its standards include constructive notice or the "should have known" level of notice. OCR has the power and the right to enforce this standard in review of the adequacy of the actions taken by the school district during compliance audits (Office for Civil Rights, 2001).

How Does a School Receive Notice?

A school can receive notice in many different ways, depending on what it has specified in local policy.

What Are Deliberate Indifference and Reckless Disregard?

According to the Supreme Court, *deliberate indifference* means that an official's response or lack of response was "clearly unreasonable in the light of known circumstances" (*Davis v. Monroe County Board of Education*, 1999).

Reckless disregard is ignoring instances of known high-risk misconduct and endangering a person as a consequence.

WHAT IS DISCRIMINATION?

Discrimination is the area of law dealing with unfair or unequal treatment of a person or persons based upon their belonging to a protected class. These laws protect both students and employees.

Many states include additional classes under protected status, such as sexual orientation, marital status, and others.

What Is the Difference Between Bias, Prejudice, and Discrimination?

Bias is a tendency, inclination, or outlook: a subjective point of view. We all have biases.

Prejudice is a negative bias or disliking of people because they belong to a particular group one dislikes. The group is often an ethnic, racial, or other social category.

Discrimination differs from prejudice in that it includes action. When this action is unfair or unequal and is directed toward a member or members of a protected class, such action is illegal discrimination. Educators have a right to their biases and prejudices, but they may not act on them in a way that affects students or other employees.

Figure 4.4 Classes Protected Under Federal Law

- Age
- Disability
- Gender (including sexual harassment)
- National origin
- Race
- Religious affiliation

What About Students' First Amendment Rights?

First Amendment rights apply to the speech of students, employees, and third parties, though they do not exist at the same level as they do for adults outside the school setting.

> Free speech rights apply in all programs and activities of public schools:
>
> - class lectures and discussions;
> - public meetings and speakers on campus;
> - campus debates;
> - school plays;
> - cultural events;
> - athletic events; and
> - student newspapers, journals, and other publications.

The intent of civil rights laws is to protect students from discrimination, not to regulate speech. In order to establish a violation of an antidiscrimination law, the harassment must not be merely offensive but also sufficiently serious to deny or limit a student's ability to participate in or benefit from the education program. In the K–12 school system, free speech rights may be significantly circumscribed for purposes of the orderly running of the school.

The First Amendment and Retaliation: A Case in Point

The First Amendment also protects students from retaliation when they report bullying, harassment, or other misconduct. That includes retaliation by school employees as well as students. While courts have been somewhat lenient with schools that make some effort to remedy ongoing problems, they have generally shown little tolerance for those that respond by retaliating against students who report harassment.

In 2001, a federal jury awarded damages to a football player who was the victim of hazing almost a decade earlier (*Seamons v. Snow*, 2001). The court held that the football coach had violated his First Amendment rights by retaliating against the player for going to the police.

According to a 2002 article in *Trial* magazine (Brownstein, 2002),

> In 1993, Brian Seamons was a second-string quarterback for the Sky View High School Bobcats in Smithfield, Utah, when his fellow players decided to initiate him into the team. One day after practice, they bound him naked to a towel rack in the locker room, affixing his wrists, ankles, and neck with athletic tape. The boys then ushered in Seamons's date to an upcoming dance.
>
> Seamons's attorney, Robert Wallace of Salt Lake City, decided not to bring the suit against the players—in his eyes, they were just kids. And the school district, Wallace believed, did not have the kind of warning of the attack that would have given rise to a negligence claim. . . .
>
> When Seamons reported the episode to police, one of the players who participated told him at practice that he had betrayed the team and should apologize. Seamons later testified that the football coach said nothing during the exchange. The coach made Seamons sit out of a scheduled game and take the weekend off to "think" about the situation. The perpetrators of the assault, meanwhile, continued to play football as news of the incident spread through the school. Seamons was suspended from the team and ultimately cut. . . .
>
> At an evidentiary hearing, the coach was asked what he had hoped to accomplish by telling Seamons to take the weekend off to "think." His reply: He expected the student to "reconsider" his report to the authorities. (p. 62)

RESPONSIBILITY FOR THE BEHAVIOR OF THIRD PARTIES

While school officials are not responsible for third parties' behavior, they do have a duty to take steps to protect students and employees from harassment or abuse by them. For the school to be liable, it must be determined that the school's failure to take these steps was the proximate cause of the injury by that third party.

School officials are required, upon notice, to take prompt action to eliminate any hostile environment that is created by third parties, to prevent its recurrence, and to remedy its effects on the victim(s).

Your responsibility includes:

1. monitoring the environment,
2. training students in their rights regarding harassment by third parties,
3. investigating rumors and complaints, and
4. remedying behavior.

/ᑎ⎯   **Figure 4.5** Third Parties   /ᑎ⎯

Third parties include but are not limited to:

- Vendors
- Volunteers
- Consultants and independent contractors
- Public speakers
- Performers at dances, assemblies, and social events
- Repair persons and construction workers on campus
- Coaches, athletes, and fans from other schools or the community
- Referees, umpires, and other league officials
- Visiting parents/guardians, siblings, and community members
- Visitors to dormitories or other overnight accommodations
- Security personnel or temporary workers from outside agencies
- Customers at campus bookstores, cafes, theaters, libraries, etc.
- People in off-campus locations during school-sponsored field trips
- People in off-campus locations directly related to school work or activities such as leadership conferences, work-study jobs, internships, job shadowing, or mentoring programs

Who Is Considered a Third Party?

A third party is anyone who enters your employment premises, school grounds, or school property (including vehicles) and who is not a student, school employee, or board member, or anyone whom students and/or employees encounter off campus while participating in official school functions.

Public School Students in Employment Settings

Many school districts, as a regular part of their curriculum, place students with either government or private employers in an internship, community service, job shadowing, or employment capacity. School districts may not place students with an employer that allows illegal harassment or discrimination in the workplace.

Both the school and the employer have an obligation to investigate any student allegations of illegal harassment or misconduct. It is crucial that both the school district and the employer coordinate their responses to any allegations of misconduct or illegal harassment that are made by or about a student in such an employment setting.

ENACTMENT OF STATE LAWS

At this writing, 23 states have already enacted anti-bullying legislation and 15 more state legislatures have introduced such bills. In Resource B, there is a sample law from the state of Washington. This particular statute got an "A" grade from www.bullypolice.org, a Web site dedicated to tracking and evaluating the prevalence and efficacy of state anti-bullying legislation. It should be noted, however, that each state's legislation is unique in its scope and intent, so this law, while an example, is not representative.

While Congress has enacted a number of federal civil rights laws pertaining to protected classifications, until recently it seemed to be leaving anti-bullying legislation up to the individual states. Federal law may interfere with state sovereignty if there are constitutionally protected rights involved. That has not happened yet in the matter of bullying. If we move into bullying as a civil rights violation, it is likely to be unwieldy in terms of enforcement and adjudication.

At this writing there is a bill in Congress. Known as the Anti-Bullying Act of 2005, this bill would amend the *Safe and Drug-Free Schools and Communities Act* to specifically require districts and schools to prevent and appropriately respond to instances of bullying and harassment as part of an ongoing effort to keep students safe. The bill, HR 284 (109th Congress), was introduced by Rep. John Shimkus of Illinois and 39 cosponsors on January 6, 2005, and referred to the Subcommittee on Education Reform. It requires schools to have discipline policies against bullying and harassment, to establish complaint procedures for students and parents, and to notify parents annually of new anti-bullying policies and procedures (Jackson, 2006).

SUMMARY

In this chapter the basics of the law as it applies to liability for actionable bullying and harassment have been reviewed. Remember, families do take legal action, and your best intentions may not carry the day. Even if your current practices for managing and investigating complaints are consistent with those of neighboring school districts, you may be held liable if you do not meet the standard of care.

There are a variety of laws under which you and your district may be sued, including the civil rights statutes that protect specific classifications of people. If you are found to be deliberately indifferent to a situation that took place under your supervision, you may be held individually liable. Be vigilant also in monitoring third parties who come in contact with students, including those in work-study or other school-sponsored student employment settings. There is potential for liability there as well.

Finally, depending on the law under which a lawsuit is filed, you may not need actual notice of bullying behavior to be held accountable in a court of law. All you may need is constructive notice, which is to say that you "should have known" even if you were not approached directly about the incident.

The next chapter will continue Part II: The Legal Context of Bullying with a discussion of the criteria for determining when bullying or harassment behavior is illegal. The best practices for protecting yourself and your district from liability under all of these circumstances will be covered in Part III: Legally Sound and Principle-Based Action.

5

When Bullying Is Legally Actionable

The Davis case shook the cage. It was an awakening. Davis did set the bar high, but it also showed that five justices felt very strongly that liability should be imposed against schools for egregious violations. . . . I think we're in an evolution here. People aren't winning cases right and left, but the fact that they're being brought at all shows how much times have changed.

—Mary Jo McGrath, in Brownstein (2000, p. 14)

Heralding a trend in litigation based on student-to-student bullying and harassment, 2002 saw a rising tide of costly jury verdicts against U.S. school districts. Now, several years and many verdicts later, it is clear that the issue of lawsuits over student-to-student behavior is not going away any time soon. Parents of children who have been injured will have their day in court. School administrators must be prepared to minimize the risk of harm to students and liability to the school district with legal awareness and sound practices.

To assist educators in determining what makes student misconduct legally actionable under state and federal harassment and discrimination law, the McGrath Five-Point Criterion has been developed. However, before the criterion is presented, it will be helpful to clarify where bullying falls in terms of its "legal status."

Unless a state has adopted legislation regarding bullying (see discussion in Chapter 4), bullying in itself is not a legally recognized harm for which an action may be brought in a court of law. The only people who can definitively say, "Yes, that was illegal harassment" or "Yes, that was a violation of the state anti-bullying statute" are judges and juries. School administrators do not have that authority and will never be called upon to make that kind of legal ruling. School districts typically take action against bullying using their administrative law powers to enforce the student code of conduct and board policies. If necessary, they may involve law enforcement to pursue the matter under the criminal code.

A judge or jury may find that illegal harassment or bullying took place at the school site, yet find in the school district's favor regarding its liability for the conduct. Juries do not find against school districts *because* the behavior happened. They find against school districts that did not take appropriate action when they knew (or in some cases, should have known) that the behavior was occurring.

It is particularly important to recognize that taunts that have been around for a very long time may now be recognized as behavior that interferes with a student's educational opportunities and causes great harm. A highly illustrative case is out of Tonganoxie, Kansas. In December 2005, 18-year-old Dylan Theno received a $440,000 settlement from his former school district. Theno sued the school district in federal court under Title IX in May 2004, claiming that he was bullied because other students believed he was gay even though he testified that he is not. He says that the harassment started when he was in seventh grade, and continued until he quit school in eleventh grade. His lawsuit claimed that he had to quit because the bullying was so severe. (Note: Gay or straight, Theno's cause of action would have been the same.)

Although the age-old issue of bullying has traditionally been considered from a socioemotional perspective, in today's world it must also be looked at through a legal lens. This is not a bad thing. The judicial system has played an integral part in moving many social issues forward, such as integration and gender equity. Looking at behavior through a legal lens gives objectivity and clarity on how to proceed and effect change.

THE CRITERION: POINT BY POINT

Point 1: Is a Protected Classification Involved or Is There Intent to Harm?

If bullying behavior is directed at a member of a protected class of people, it must be addressed as potential illegal harassment and discrimination. An example of behavior related to a protected classification would be when a child is taunting another child about race, ethnicity, or disability. Similarly, if the behavior is sexual in nature—for example, if a student is groped or sexually explicit remarks are made, as in the Theno case above—the bullying behavior may fall into the category of illegal harassment and discrimination.

ん—   **Figure 5.1** The McGrath Five-Point Criterion   *ん—*

Illegal Harassment	Bullying
1. Is the behavior related to one of the following protected classifications? *(Intent is not an issue—impact is the issue)* sexual in nature gender age race religion national origin disability sexual orientation (in some locales)	1. Is there intent to harm?
2. Is it unwelcome or unwanted?	2. Is it unwelcome or unwanted?
3. Is it severe or persistent or pervasive?	3. Is it severe or persistent or pervasive?
4. Does the behavior substantially interfere with work or study?	4. Does the behavior substantially interfere with work or study?
5. Does the behavior meet the subjective/objective tests or standards related to its level of interference with work or study?	5. Does the behavior meet the subjective/objective tests or standards related to its level of interference with work or study?

The same behaviors may be classified in four categories:

1. under a protected classification (e.g., protection against discrimination based on sex) and justifying a civil rights action;
2. under the school administrative law and policies prohibiting bullying and justifying action under the student code of conduct and board policy;
3. under criminal law (e.g., hate crimes); and
4. under state statutes relating to anti-bullying provisions or even negligence.

The very same behavior may violate all four areas of law at the same time. It is a lot to think about.

Intent Is the Key Factor

The biggest difference under most anti-bullying statutes between bullying and illegal harassment and discrimination is the intent of the perpetrator to harm. The key question with bullying is *Did the perpetrator intend to cause harm to the victim?* With illegal harassment, the perpetrator's intent or lack of intent to harm the victim is irrelevant. The hallmark of illegal harassment is the emphasis on the impact of the behavior on the victim, rather than the perpetrator's intent.

Establishing intent can be tricky. Often intent has to be inferred from the actions of the alleged perpetrator. Rarely does a person say, "Yeah, I meant to bully that weasel and given the chance, I'd do it again!" There are places to look to get a window into the mind of the alleged perpetrator where intent resides. First, ask the student why he or she did what he or she did. *When you were doing that, what were you trying to do? What did you mean to cause?* Second, any documentation you have of the student's history or prior allegations may point to the student's state of mind.

Once you have established into which of these two arenas the behavior falls—illegal harassment or bullying—the other four points of the Five-Point Criterion are identical in their legal requirements between the two categories.

Point 2: Is the Behavior Unwelcome or Unwanted?

Two boys are exchanging insults about their respective mothers' sexuality, socking each other on the shoulder and sharing a bag of french fries. Is that bullying or illegal harassment? The defining question is *Is the conduct welcome by the recipient?* In the example here of the two french fry–eating boys, to all appearances they are having a mutually agreeable, good time together.

What is welcome differs with gender and with culture. For example, we have seen cases of African American children who call each other the "n word," and among them it is not unwelcome. Yet this word would be completely unwelcome from a student or teacher of another race or even from another student who is of the same race but outside their group.

Consent does not mean that the behavior is welcome. With bullying you have an imbalance of power. The target may be consenting, yet that consent may be a defensive reaction. This is especially common with sexualized behavior. A person may not feel like he or she can say "no," so he or she goes along. But going along does not mean the behavior was welcome. Furthermore, there are people who cannot legally consent to sex, including minors, people with certain disabilities, and those who are intoxicated.

Point 3: Is the Behavior Severe or Persistent or Pervasive?

To be bullying or illegal harassment, behavior only has to fit one of these three criteria: Is it severe or persistent or pervasive? It may, in fact, be all three.

Severe behavior can be established with a single action. Actions that would typically be considered severe include physical assault resulting in injury or severe bodily harm, the threat of severe bodily harm, or the threat of severe bodily harm to one's family. The more severe the conduct, the less you need a pattern of behavior to establish bullying or illegal harassment.

Persistent behavior, as the term implies, happens repeatedly. As a drip of water on the top of a hill eventually erodes the hill, a small action done persistently has a compounded impact and can cause harm cumulatively. (See the discussion of trauma and post-traumatic stress in Chapter 2.) Intent to harm can be inferred from a pattern of persistent behavior in which a child has been warned by the target, "I consider this harmful," and then repeats the behavior.

Pervasive means the unwelcome behavior is everywhere one goes within the school environment. Like Theresa in the case study in Chapter 1, there is no respite for the victim. There are many schools in which the climate and culture allow pervasive harassment or bullying to take place. There is a tolerance for vicious behavior among students that has been cultivated and prevails.

Point 4: Does the Behavior Substantially Interfere With the Student's Education?

The legal standard for illegal harassment and discrimination claims requires that it be proved that the behavior *unreasonably interferes* with the student's ability to get an education. In a civil lawsuit for the recovery of damages, the intent to harm or even gross negligence won't carry the day without actual harm to the student being proved.

Point 5: Does the Behavior Meet Both Subjective and Objective Tests Related to Its Level of Interference With Student Education?

Unreasonable interference with education is assessed through a two-pronged test: subjective and objective. Subjectively, did the alleged victim experience unreasonable interference? Objectively, would a reasonable person similarly situated to the alleged victim be unreasonably interfered with, given the totality of these circumstances?

For example, Sally comes to you saying, "The way Tommy looks at me makes me feel uncomfortable. He's sexually harassing me, and it's hard for me to pay attention in class." Sally is experiencing what she considers to be interference with her schoolwork. That is the subjective test.

You make some informal inquiries and find out that Tommy has cerebral palsy. He has trouble controlling his head and neck and often appears to be blankly staring to his right or left. There is no evidence that any behavior on Tommy's part is sexual in nature, nor does any intent to harm exist. No other students have a problem with Tommy and they enthusiastically support and include him in class activities. This is the objective test. It is clear that Susan is not reacting as a reasonable girl of her age and background would react under the totality of these circumstances.

Again, even though this is not a legal matter, there is still action to take. Those actions may include educating Susan about cerebral palsy and helping her to adjust to the inclusion of students with disabilities. This is not a case of illegal harassment or bullying, but one that calls for education.

Quid Pro Quo Sexual Harassment: An Exception to the Five-Point Criterion

For *quid pro quo* sexual harassment cases, only points 1 and 2—the behavior is sexual in nature, and the conduct is unwelcome—need be answered affirmatively for liability to attach. An example of *quid pro quo* sexual harassment (and sexual abuse) is trading sex for favorable treatment in class or grades. Usually *quid pro quo* sexual harassment occurs adult to student.

In Review

The Five-Point Criterion determines whether certain bullying behaviors are legally actionable harassment or discrimination. (See Figure 5.1 on pg. 57 to refresh the components in your mind.) The Five-Point Criterion may also be used for determining whether bullying behavior may be legally actionable in a negligence suit or actionable under the state's anti-bullying legislation. The criterion for illegal harassment and the criterion for bullying are identical except for the first point. The first point for illegal harassment or discrimination is that the conduct must be against a protected classification of people. For bullying that is not also illegal harassment or discrimination, the first point is that there is intent on the perpetrator's part to cause harm.

FOLLOW YOUR POLICY

Any time you have a state or federal law and a policy in place, you have the potential for a lawsuit right behind it. You *cannot* prevent lawsuits. You *can* shield yourself from liability. You must have the sophistication to follow your policy and implement it to a "T." Ultimately, the law will not second-guess your discretion as long as you follow your own criteria. It will not supplant your decision making if somebody questions the process you use or the decision you make, as long as that process is legally fit and educationally sound.

Bullying Policy Highlights

Every school district should have an anti-bullying and harassment policy in place and disseminate it regularly to students. In fact, most state anti-bullying laws enacted to date mandate such a policy. What are the elements of a sound anti-bullying policy? The following chart outlines key points to include. You will also find a sample policy in Resource B.

A Cautionary Note: The Importance of Being Strategic

Aggressive intervention in all forms of bullying behavior is essential, whether or not the behavior is legally actionable. That being said, it is important to note that if the school district crafts a very high standard of anti-bullying in its board policy, it will be held to that standard in all legal actions that may come along. Anything written into a school policy has the weight of law. Consider whether it is wise to put all the highest-level practices for administrators and staff to follow into board policy or regulation. Perhaps some of the best practices are better left for discussion at staff meetings rather than being elevated to the rule of law.

YOUR DUTY TO PROVIDE A SAFE ENVIRONMENT: THE COURTS ARE SPEAKING

You probably entered the field of education as a certificated or classified employee with a commitment to making a difference. At some point, you may

Figure 5.2 Points to Include in an Anti-Bullying Policy

General Policy Statement

- Intent of the governing board to maintain a learning and working environment that is free from bullying based on a person's race, color, sex, national origin, disability, sexual orientation, or economic status.
- Intent to promote positive interpersonal relationships between all members of the school community.
- It is a violation of this policy for any student or staff member to bully another while attending school or school-sponsored events.
- It is a violation of this policy for any school employee to tolerate bullying during school or at school-sponsored events.
- The School District will promptly and thoroughly investigate reports of bullying.

Definition of Bullying

- Use a definition that is consistent with local or state laws if applicable.
- Bullying is distinguishable from roughhousing or friendly teasing in that bullying is intentionally hurtful and motivated by the desire to harm/hurt the victim.

Examples of Bullying

- Physical acts
- Nonphysical acts

Duty to Act

- Students who experience bullying are encouraged to report it.
- Students know who to report to (designated complaint managers at your school site).
- Any employee of the District who observes bullying or receives reports of it is required to act immediately and forward an Incident Report to the Principal for prompt investigation.

Sanctions for Bullying

- For students, these sanctions must be appropriate to the seriousness of the incident(s) and may include suspension and/or expulsion or other discipline in accordance with accepted common sense application of the district discipline policies.
- For staff, sanction(s) must be appropriate to the seriousness of the incident(s) and may include termination or other common sense discipline in accordance with contract provisions or other policies of the District.

Retaliation Prohibited

- Retaliation includes, but is not limited to, any form of intimidation, reprisal, or harassment used against a person who reports incident(s) of bullying in good faith.

False Reporting

- There will be no repercussions toward people who make reports in good faith where insufficient proof of misconduct is found.
- Deliberate fabrications will not be tolerated and anyone who fabricates a report will be disciplined accordingly.

have stepped into a larger accountability—that of an administrator or a department manager. You may even be a superintendent or other district-level administrator. Whatever your position, as an educator you are concerned for the safety and well-being of each and every student. This is a given. So why go into your duty to provide a safe environment here? Isn't it inherent in your commitment to your students' welfare? Absolutely.

However, while your foremost concern will always be the protection of students, as an administrator you are also responsible for protecting the school and yourself from the liability that may attach when bullying and harassment claims are not handled properly. For this reason, we will review exactly what the courts mean when they refer to your duty to provide a safe educational environment for students.

The courts have found the following bases for the duty of educational institutions to safeguard students from bullying, harassment, and abuse.

- School personnel have a duty to protect students from known or reasonably foreseeable harm occurring during or in connection with school activities.
- School personnel are responsible for properly monitoring and disciplining subordinates—students, teachers, and staff—over whom they exercise supervisory authority.

Established Guidelines for Protecting Students

Schools have administrative policies and procedures that are designed to protect the rights of both students and employees. These policies may extend beyond local, state, or federal law. As an administrator, you are obligated to follow up on all complaints that allege that employees, students, or both have violated administrative policies and procedures. You are also obligated to follow these policies and procedures when implementing an investigation and determining appropriate action.

In addition, the U.S. Department of Education Office for Civil Rights and the Equal Opportunity Employment Commission have issued extensive guidance regarding sexual harassment and abuse of both students and employees. (URLs for downloading copies of these guidance documents are available in the Bibliography and Resource E.)

Four Responsibilities Under the Duty to Provide a Safe Learning Environment

Educators must provide a safe learning environment for all students. Figure 5.3 defines your responsibilities for meeting that duty.

COVERING ALL THE BASES

It is impossible to cover all bases on which liability may attach; however, you can minimize the risk of harm to students and the risk of liability for the district by following the guidelines in Figure 5.4.

/h.— **Figure 5.3** Duty to Provide a Safe Learning Environment /h.—

1. **A Responsibility to Prevent and Train:** Providing appropriate training and instruction to all school employees and students with respect to the issues that surround bullying and illegal harassment. This includes dissemination of clear, understandable policies to all.

2. **A Responsibility to Investigate:** Establishing and implementing appropriate complaint and investigation procedures for employees and students to ensure that every rumor, incident, or complaint receives an immediate, appropriate, adequate, and comprehensive response.

3. **A Responsibility to Remedy:** Providing appropriate and adequate remedial steps and follow-through to ensure reasonable steps are taken to prevent further bullying or illegal harassment and to prevent retaliation.

4. **A Responsibility to Monitor:** Enabling a bullying and harassment-free school environment through continual monitoring and correcting of inappropriate behaviors.

/h.— **Figure 5.4** Covering All the Bases /h.—

- Have an explicit written policy against bullying and illegal harassment which clearly outlines a responsive, prompt complaint procedure.

- Follow the policy.

- Provide regular training and education to all supervisory and non-supervisory employees and students regarding this policy.

- Express disapproval of bullying and illegal harassment and explain the sanctions for such conduct.

- Maintain a procedure for complaint intake that encourages victims to come forward and does not require that they complain to the alleged perpetrator.

- Ensure privacy, provide effective remedies, and protect witnesses and victims against retaliation.

- Promptly and thoroughly investigate all reports or complaints of possible illegal harassment or bullying.

- Take immediate corrective action when needed.

- Implement appropriate consequences if allegations are substantiated.

- Promptly report suspected child abuse, sexual assault, or other criminal violations.

SUMMARY

In this chapter, the focus of the discussion shifted from examining the facts regarding bullying and its impact on the school community to examining the legal context and its effect on you and how you do your job. The Five-Point Criterion was introduced for determining whether behavior is actionable bullying or harassment that could be pursued through legal action. The elements of a comprehensive anti-bullying policy were provided. Finally, there was clarification of what is meant by an educator's legal duty to provide a safe learning environment for students.

Readers are likely to find themselves called into action by the previous discussion. It may be time to convene a team and re-examine school district policy. You may also begin to practice applying the Five-Point Criterion to the behavior that you observe at school. Picking up this new lens to view what is happening around you will sharpen your ability to detect abuses and enhance your ability to intervene early.

In the next four chapters, Part III: Legally Sound and Principle-Based Action, the McGrath SUCCEED System for identifying and responding to student misconduct will be presented, including the best practices for operating with legal integrity regarding bullying and harassment matters.

PART III

Legally Sound and Principle-Based Action

6

Daily Practices to Conquer Bullying

The natural world is now understood as an interdependent, relational, and living web of connections—inherently whole, abundant, creative, and self-organizing.
—Stephanie Pace Marshall, *The Power to Transform*, (p. xii)

The entire family, consisting of mother, older sister, older brother, and the twins, arrived at our inner-city school after coming across the border illegally from Mexico. The children had never attended any school or been involved in any social setting similar to the formal setting of a classroom. Javier was the twin who spent the majority of time with me in my office. Javier was a bright child; however, with no support for education or his homework, he soon began to fall behind his peers and by third grade was trailing significantly. After a year together, I left our inner-city school to open the newest school in our district and I lost track of the twins for approximately nine months.

Imagine my surprise, when on the first day of the following school year I heard familiar voices calling my name from down the hall. It was Javier and his sister. "Mrs. T! Mrs. T! We found you!" I was moved and touched to see these two children who had already won my heart, and who were so in need of support. They were now in fifth grade, and I knew this year would be critical.

I soon realized that Javier had moved on to more sinister things. He was bullying some of the Special Education students, using extortion and fear as his tools. I tried so many different tactics with him and nothing worked:

detention, inschool suspension, referral to the counselor, referral to outside support agencies, leadership roles with me, peer coaching—you name it, we tried it . . . to little or no avail.

Suddenly, a new idea occurred to me: "Okay, I have learned how to communicate with employees in a new way using the McGrath SUC-CEED System, and it really works. Why not try it with Javier?" The very next day, Javier was brought to my office after having hit another child. I sat him down and explained that I was going to try to talk to him in a different way than I usually did and that I needed him to really listen. That was one of the pluses we had going for us; no matter how tired Javier became of me or I of him, we truly cared for and respected one another.

I began with the FACTS: He had hit another child during lunch recess. Witnesses had seen the whole thing, and Javier did not dispute it. Because I was new at this with children, I found myself moving cautiously through the process. I stopped and waited to begin IMPACT. Then I told him that he had hurt the other child who was in the nurse's office being attended to. I stated that I truly cared for him, but that I was very, very disappointed in him. Next came CON-TEXT. How could I explain this to him in a way that he would understand? I stated that this was not the first time he had behaved in this way, and reviewed his history with him. I said that I was very disturbed by this pattern and felt as if all of our time together and all of our previous talks had been worth nothing, and that he was not trying to change his behavior as he continued to be a bully.

Because of our deep relationship, at this time I felt my own eyes fill with tears and told him that I needed to take a couple of minutes to decide what to do, and that I would just step out into the hall. When I stood up, I heard Javier begin to sniffle and he said, "Don't go, Mrs. T." I looked at him. It was the first time that I had ever seen him cry in front of anyone. I leaned down and explained that his behavior was becoming problematic for all of us and that I didn't know if I could trust him to change, as he had made me promises in the past. I then sat down and simply waited for him to respond.

ACTION: This street-smart young man with piercings and shaved eyebrows, denoting gang affiliation, began to sob and said that he would do whatever he needed to do, as I was one of only two people he cared for and trusted in the "whole wide world" (the other being his fifth grade homeroom teacher). I put my arm around his shoulder and we began to speak about the actions I would take in the future and what actions I would expect from him.

This was the beginning of a partnership and Javier has been growing from it in unexpected ways. So have I. The SUCCEED System, which was already my approach to employee growth and development, is now my daily approach to student issues.

Mrs. T. in the above story is Jennifer Terrazas, an educator with over 28 years' experience. She spent eight of those years as a building principal and is now a consulting principal for Las Cruces Public Schools in New Mexico, guiding other principals in their jobs. She is also a mother of three. Like every school administrator I have ever met (and in 30 years that's over 100,000 of them across the nation), Jennifer's story reveals a deep compassion for and commitment to her students that is both fulfilling and heartbreaking. She does her job well and with her whole heart. She wants kids to succeed, and she is willing to deal head on with whatever gets in the way.

AND THE COMPLAINTS KEEP COMING . . .

An administrator's daily life is fraught with complaints and concerns coming from all sides. That's the job, dealing with what is not working. In fact, all of the things that are working—individual students and teachers producing break-through results, families being impacted in positive ways, employees who go beyond expectations—can get little of a principal's time during the day, let alone the attention of the community. How can it when Tommy is in your office for the fifth time this month; Mrs. O'Shea wants her daughter transferred out of fifth-period study hall, immediately; and you just found out that an anonymous Internet blogger has been posting death threats against a teacher?

Given that 95% of an administrator's professional life is dedicated to com-plaint resolution, this is the area where strong communication and leadership skills are most needed. What if your approach to these complaints and concerns was transformative rather than just about fixing the problem?

In this chapter, the communication and complaint resolution aspects of daily school life will be addressed through use of the McGrath SUCCEED System. The system provides practical tools to use with bullying complaints. However, you will easily see the applicability of the same tools to all situations that require analytical thinking, clear communication, and principle-based action. Taking on this system will require intellectual effort and practice. With time and practice, however, a practitioner can expect to progress through the levels of mastery, from basic to advanced.

These are transformational tools. They intervene in the direction in which something is going and access new and unexpected results. *Imagine if today were the last time Tommy got an office referral!* The tools allow for constructive thinking and communication and have the potential to make an immediate and even lasting difference.

POWER TOOLS THAT BUILD A POSITIVE SCHOOL CULTURE

The McGrath SUCCEED System is designed to grow a healthy culture and facilitate the creation of a school environment of safety, caring, and excellence in education. The daily application of the principle-based tools of the McGrath SUCCEED System is directed at transforming the context, the very school environment, within which bullying thrives, and it leads to actions that effectively resolve the content issues at their most basic level. The McGrath SUCCEED tools support listening to and communicating with all of the constituents involved in bullying situations—students, parents, teachers, staff, community, and others—to enlist the entire school community in con-quering bullying. When applied promptly and thoroughly, this approach begins to create a school culture in which students see that their complaints will be heard, responded to, and resolved. Victims and bystanders are empowered to come forth, and those who bully begin to see that they are not going to get away with it.

The components of the daily practices will be addressed in this chapter. In the next chapter, the concurrent principles that power those practices will be added to the mix.

A LEGALLY SOUND RESPONSE

Like a hammer always has a claw, the McGrath SUCCEED tools always have the law. Built right into the SUCCEED System is everything you need to account for in following the law, including just cause and due process standards. Before the first tool is introduced, we will get our bearings within the procedural landscape.

BULLYING: THREE LEVELS OF RESPONSE

Procedurally, there are three levels of response to incidents of bullying or harassment:

Level I: The classroom teachers and staff are trained and empowered to intervene, take measures, and record incidents.

Level II: The behavior is brought to the attention of the administration, and an assessment is conducted to determine the appropriate next steps. Discussions are held with the involved parties.

Level III: A designated and trained administrator conducts a full investigation, using the McGrath Template III.

Level I Response: Training the Front Line

A Level I response to bullying and harassment incidents is the responsibility of teachers and front line staff (playground monitors, teachers' aides, para-professionals, counselors, coaches, etc.), whether on campus or at school-related functions. These educators are responsible for providing a safe learning environment—an environment free from bullying, harassment, and intimidation.

The Level I response should be part of a total school initiative to address these vital safety issues. Refer to Chapter 2 for a review of the various types of programs that are available for this purpose. All teachers and staff should be trained annually to recognize peer-to-peer bullying and harassment. I have had success with advising school districts to engage in a Training of Trainers model, where school counselors and administrators are instructed in how to train all staff on bullying and harassment issues and the appropriate responses to each. (See Suggested Anti-Bullying Training Plan in Resource C.) Figure 6.1 lists what to include in employee training.

ʌ⌐   **Figure 6.1** Teacher and Staff Training—Level I Knowledge   *ʌ⌐*

---

1. What constitutes bullying and what the school district's anti-bullying and harassment policies contain.

2. The difference between a bullying incident and a conflict (so that inappropriate referrals are not made).

3. The behaviors that constitute various forms of illegal harassment based on race/national origin, gender, sex, sexual orientation, or disability.

4. Their responsibility to supervise students and what the district may be liable for should they fail in this.

5. The signs and symptoms that a child is a target of bullying behavior.

6. Classroom or playground interventions and disciplinary actions that they can implement.

7. How to respond in a legally sound manner should a student report bullying or harassment to them (e.g., do not dismiss as tattling, do not promise confidentiality, be compassionate and nonjudgmental, do not blame the victim).

8. That the school district administration is serious about these issues and considers it their job to intervene in ALL instances of bullying and harassment that may occur.

9. Knowing the student code of conduct, and procedures and consequences for violations.

10. How and when to document and report incidents.

11. What types of matters to refer to site administrators.

Remember, the current paradigm in schools is one of stopping misconduct and behavior that disrupts order or safety—educators are looking for bullying behaviors, not victimization. It is important to train people to think about bullying from the point of view of the victim and to bring *patterns of victimization* to the attention of administrators. The *Theno* case mentioned in Chapter 5 is a prime example of what not to do. Many students taunted Dylan Theno at school over a period of five years, and school officials did not take effective action. School personnel must be on the alert for students who are being bullied and *act effectively on that awareness.*

Level I Response: Documentation

Specific methods of documentation at Level 1 should interface with the student classroom and playground discipline process unique to the school district. A general rule is where documentation is concerned, the more specific the better. You want to be able to show that you recognized the behavior and took appropriate action. Incidents that look isolated may, in fact, be part of a bigger pattern of victimization. Documentation will provide a paper trail for determining whether a pattern is occurring or is an isolated event.

Ideally, all behavior notes, student referrals, incident reports, and written complaints should be entered into a computerized schoolwide data system at regular intervals by office staff at the school site. Entries can be coded into the system according to student identification numbers. These data can then be extracted in a number of ways by the administration: identified by individual student perpetrators and victims, by infraction, by grade level, by location (classroom, lunchroom, etc.), or by time period. To avoid FERPA violations, determine with your legal counsel who may receive copies of this report.

Level II Response

A matter moves to Level II when:

- a *pattern* of bullying or harassment shows up in the tracking system,
- there is a *referral* by a teacher or staff member,
- a *formal complaint* is filed, or
- an *injury* has occurred.

Level III Response

A matter moves to Level III when there is a reason to suspect:

- sexual harassment;
- racial harassment;
- discrimination based on another protected classification;
- illegal or criminal activity;
- a pattern of taunting and harassment over time by the same perpetrator(s) and/or toward the same victim(s); or
- severe, persistent, or pervasive behavior.

Level II or Level III responses are called for when the matter is referred to the attention of the administration. This is where the McGrath SUCCEED System tools come into play. This chapter lays out the McGrath SUCCEED tools and practices involved in a Level II response. Chapter 8 contains a legally sound "To Do" list. It also provides the tools that will guide the administrator in the thorough processing of a referral or complaint and in determining whether a Level II or III response is appropriate. Chapter 9 sets out the McGrath Template III, an analytical tool for conducting an investigation and assessment of a Level III matter and determining the appropriate action steps.

THE McGRATH SUCCEED SYSTEM

Through use of the McGrath SUCCEED System, you can effectively lead, commend, encourage, improve, and discipline as needed the people involved in bullying incidents. The system organizes fundamental legal and ethical principles into a powerful methodology for resolving and transforming complex human situations. It is a layered approach to behavioral and performance issues that accounts not only for the content of the situation, the "who did what to whom," but also for the context of the situation. The context most often deals with the various relationships surrounding the events: relationships involving students, school, family, community, and even oneself.

Daily practice of the McGrath SUCCEED System brings out leadership qualities in the user, including:

- acting with honesty, compassion, and accountability;
- fostering trust, respect, understanding, and a commitment to growth;
- honoring the whole human being;
- addressing the varying needs of that whole human being; and
- providing a basic format to integrate all these qualities into daily life.

The McGrath SUCCEED System is designed to transform thinking, listening, and speaking and result in effective, principle-based action.

The McGrath SUCCEED System impacts the following four areas:

Thinking: To see things clearly, and assess and reflect on them honestly, without preconceived notions interfering with objectivity.

Listening: The ability to clear your mind so you can hear what is being said, whether or not you agree with it. Enhanced listening includes the ability to understand the *entire* situation in a holistic manner.

Figure 6.2 McGrath SUCCEED System Impacts

THINKING   LISTENING   SPEAKING   ACTION

Speaking: Transformative communication is more than words coming out of your mouth. It is a way to put masterful, holistic thinking and listening into action. When speaking is objective and fair, it can be more easily received and makes a difference.

Action: Right action is derived from understanding the whole of a situation and having a strong commitment to the growth and development of the people affected. Action that is based on transformed thinking, listening, and speaking evolves the people and their environment.

THE McGRATH FICA STANDARD: THE BASIC TOOL

When a Level II bullying or harassment matter comes to the administrator's attention, it is best to intervene as early as possible and correct behavior quickly. To accomplish this, the first tool in the McGrath SUCCEED System toolbox is used: the McGrath FICA Standard. Along with steps to resolve the complaint at hand, embodied in the McGrath FICA Standard are practices that build healthy relationships—creating a culture and climate in which bullying and harassment cannot thrive. Let's learn the practices.

The McGrath FICA Standard is a format that frames the school leader's thinking, listening, speaking, and action inside four fundamental questions:

- What happened?
- What apparent harm did it cause?
- What is known about anything preceding the event that is contributing to the situation?
- What immediate action should be taken, if any?

Implementation of the McGrath FICA Standard both requires and inspires a paradigm shift from confrontation to cooperation and from accusation to inquiry.

The McGrath FICA Standard is designed for use in daily thinking and communicating. Given that it is the most frequently used SUCCEED tool, we will cover the McGrath FICA Standard in depth. In this chapter, the McGrath FICA Standard *practices* will be explored. In Chapter 7, we will add the FICA *principles* to the mix and then watch the power quotient jump.

How to Evaluate Facts and Make Decisions

Consider that most of us do not have an impartial and just approach to assessing situations and making decisions. Instead, we are a product of whatever prior training or past experience has taught us. We are swayed by many factors that may have nothing to do with the situation at hand, including our emotional responses and biases. One of the hallmarks of the McGrath FICA Standard is the objectivity its use brings to the parties involved.

We are now going to walk through the McGrath FICA Standard together and train you to use this formula to organize, analyze, and evaluate every aspect of a bullying or harassment situation. Specifically, you will use the four-part McGrath FICA Standard to organize and evaluate the statements and evidence that you gather and to determine your action steps. What it will take for you to integrate and implement this training is a willingness to give up your old habits—even those that have been effective or expedient. What you will get in exchange are new practices that are legally sound and principle based and substantially more powerful.

Figure 6.3 McGrath FICA Standard

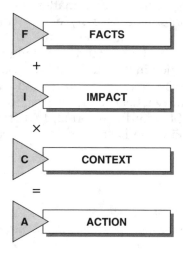

The FACTS: What Happened?

You have just received notice that a bullying incident occurred on campus. In dealing with the facts section of the FICA tool, you start by collecting information. To gather the information about the facts, you ask people who either participated in the event or observed it, **What happened here?** You want to be sure that people are describing specific, observable behavior that is based on the five senses. What did the complainant or witnesses see, hear, touch, taste, or smell?

"What happened" is usually within the five senses:

- What did you see?
- What did you hear?
- What did you smell?
- What did you taste?
- What did you touch?

In your conversations, you will assist people to think and speak in specifics rather than from opinion or interpretation. You want to train yourself to distinguish *what happened* from everything else that might enter into the picture, particularly any opinion about what happened. (See Figure 6.4 on page 76.) To illustrate the McGrath FICA Standard, we will use the story of Allison, which was relayed to me by a high school principal who uses the tool with his students. He began: *Allison, a freshman, walked into my office looking very scared and close to tears . . .*

Allison:	I found this note sticking out of my locker, Mr. Pogue. Cathy is really mad and is threatening to cut me out of our group of friends. I don't know why and I don't know what else she might do!
A typewritten note reads	You are in for it now, Miss Perfect. Everyone is so sick of you, nobody wants to be your friend. You better stay away from me. If you don't, someday you'll regret it. Your ex-friend, Cathy
Principal:	Thank you, Allison, for bringing this to my attention. When did you receive this note?
Allison:	I found it after second period when I went to my locker between classes.
Principal:	It was smart of you to come and see me right away. Have you and Cathy had any problems before?
Allison:	Not really. I haven't seen her, or some of the other girls I used to hang around with, that much since I joined the yearbook committee. I've been working during free period and after school on next month's publishing deadline.
Principal:	What are the names of the other girls you hang around with?
Allison:	Mostly, Cathy, Becky, and sometimes Sara.
Principal:	Thank you, Allison. Rest assured that I will start investigating this note immediately. I think you will be fine attending classes the next few hours. I will contact you before last period to bring you up to date on the facts I've gathered.
Allison:	Thanks Mr. Pogue.

Notice in this example that the principal did not express any opinion about what was happening; he just asked questions to elicit factual information: *When did you get this note? Have you and Cathy had any problems before? What are the names of the other girls?* He has remained emotionally connected with the student but factually impartial, and gathered what he needs to take the next step. Also, the principal has enhanced his credibility with the student by being objective rather than reactive to the situation, and by letting her know what his next steps are going to be.

Figure 6.4 Opinion

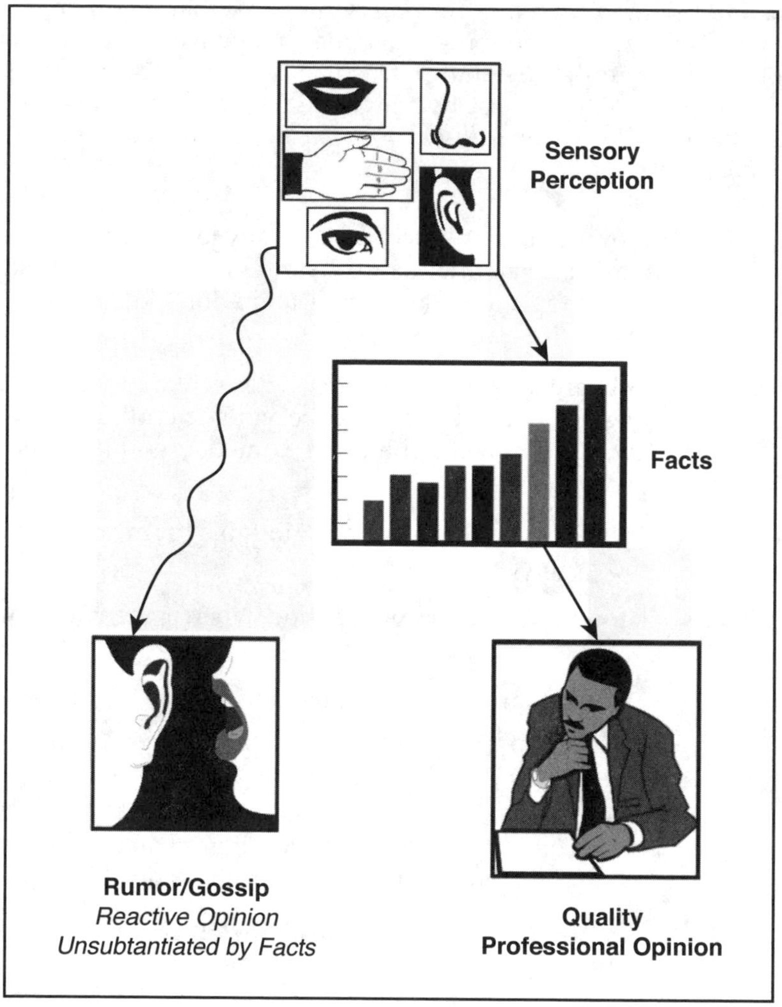

Sensory Perception

Facts

Rumor/Gossip
Reactive Opinion
Unsubtantiated by Facts

Quality
Professional Opinion

IMPACT: The Harm of What Happened

I M P A C T

Once you have a good bank of information that is factual, it is time to explore the impact questions:

- Who was hurt or may be hurt by this behavior?
- How were they hurt?
- Who else was impacted? How?

Impact refers to the consequences or repercussions of a person's actions. What actions? The actions revealed in the factual inquiry. The impact analysis does not refer to the foundational factual events themselves. Rather, it is the *outcome* of those occurrences.

Impact statements from a complainant could include:

- "I was afraid to go to that side of the building."
- "I won't use that hall anymore."
- "I arrived early to avoid her."
- "My grades dropped."
- "I wouldn't eat lunch in the cafeteria anymore because they eat there."
- "I can't sleep."
- "I am afraid he'll hurt me."

There is a cause-effect relationship between the facts and impact. The facts and their impacts should be directly correlated with one another. There is a logical flow from one to the other. For example, if I am your friend and I don't invite you to lunch (Facts), you may feel slighted (Impact). The impact is appropriately correlated to the facts—it is within the normal, predictable range of reactions. However, if I don't invite you to lunch, and you are so hurt that you intend to sell your house and move out of town, that is an impact that is not correlated with the facts as we currently understand them. Most people would doubt that the lack of a lunch invitation is actually the cause of your moving. There are other examples of the cause-effect relationship between fact and impact in Figure 6.5.

Think of the ripple effect on the surface when a pebble is thrown into a still pond of water. When bullying or harassment occurs on campus, it does not merely impact the two (or more) parties directly involved. Impacts will ripple far and wide throughout the school community and even beyond. Bullying affects bystanders who observe the incident, disrupts the classroom environment, takes the time and resources of the teachers who intervene and the school administrators who investigate, upsets the families of the students involved, and may even tarnish the reputation of the school within the surrounding community.

Figure 6.5 Facts Directly Relate to Impact

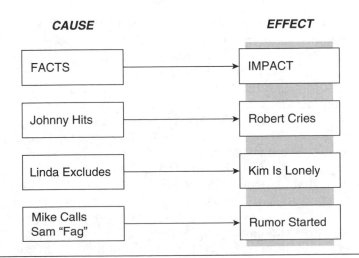

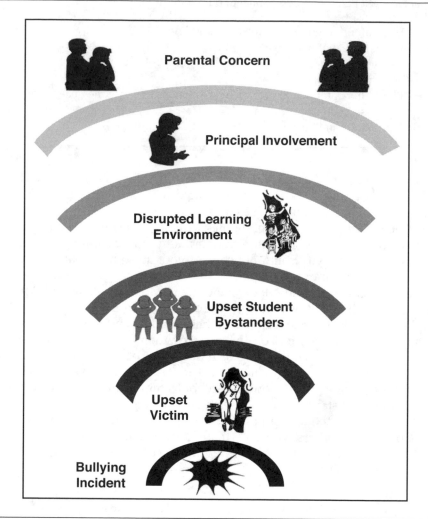

Figure 6.6 Impact Chain Reaction

Impact tells us why the situation is important—the greater the impact, the greater the significance of the situation. If something happens but the impact is minimal, it will be viewed quite differently from an event that has a catastrophic effect on the students and the school.

In using the McGrath FICA Standard tool, it is critical that you distinguish clearly between facts and impact. Understanding the impact of one's actions provides more opportunity for self-reflection when the impact is not collapsed with any factual data about what happened. Think back to the conversation between Principal Terrazas and Javier at the beginning of the chapter. In discussing the impact with Javier, she mirrored back to him the consequences of his actions (the way that his actions affected the world around him) and provided him with an opportunity to be responsible for those effects. In this part of the conversation, the practitioner is striving for self-regulation by the student and building an increased understanding of how actions taken affect other people. There is a deeper discussion of these phenomena in the next chapter.

When Facts and Impact Do Not Correlate

It is important to resolve any lack of correlation between the facts and the impact. If the facts and impact do not make sense taken together, then there is something about the situation that you do not understand yet. If someone is greatly upset about what appears to be a minor incident, the person may not be disclosing all of the facts. You have to be listening for a mismatch. The mismatch is likely pointing to something that is missing in the facts section—either because you didn't mention it or because you don't know about it yet.

For example, Judy Smith says, "Well, he said to me, 'How was your weekend?' and I was so distraught that I left school and didn't come back for a week." There is a lack of correlation between Judy's reaction and what she says happened. The lack of a logical balance between the two components tells you that there is something else going on here. It could be that she is oversensitive or it could be that Judy's allegations are a fabrication. It could also be that there is something else that happened that she is not comfortable telling you yet. All we know for sure is that the facts and the stated impact don't correlate with one another. Check it out further before you draw any conclusions.

Let's take a look at how Mr. Pogue proceeded with the *Allison* incident.

I called my Assistant Principal, Miss Jones, to meet with me and filled her in on the facts. Miss Jones called Cathy to her office and conducted an interview. Cathy said that she was sad and hurt that Allison was not spending as much time with her, but she denied that she was the one who sent the threatening note. Miss Jones asked Cathy if she had talked with Allison about her feelings. Cathy said that Allison was not interested in talking to her anymore and she started to cry. "Sara is the only one who understands what I am going through," said Cathy, "but I really miss Allison being my friend."

Miss Jones then spoke with Sara. Sara was indignant about being asked about the note to Allison. "Allison has been too busy with her yearbook friends to give me or Cathy the time of day. We are just fine without her," she said. "Cathy probably wrote that note just to scare Allison and get her out of her life." Miss Jones told Sara that Cathy was upset about the note and denied writing it. "Allison is not my friend anymore so I really don't care who wrote that note," replied Sara.

Miss Jones and I met to go over the interviews. The impact was clear— Cathy and Allison were both sad and upset, Sara seemed indignant. The facts were starting to take shape, but we needed to resolve the disparate statements regarding who wrote the note. We decided that an interview with their other friend, Becky, might shed some more light.

CONTEXT: The Other Factors Surrounding the Situation

C
O
N
T
E
X
T

Context refers to the circumstances that form the setting or environment within which the situation arose. The context must be taken into account for events to be fully understood and assessed appropriately and fairly. Context is the most elusive of the McGrath FICA components because it is not understood through a linear progression of thought. In the field of applied cognitive psychology, experts define context as *situational awareness of pre-existing factors*. I like to call it the "messiness" factor—those things that are in the mix that make the situation human and complex. The context amplifies or reduces the serious-ness of a situation. It does not excuse or justify behavior; it is simply factored in when making your determination about what to do next. This will become clear as we go along.

Context includes:

- **Discernment** of a pattern of behavior—Did similar behavior happen before (as described in the preceding Facts section) such that a pattern is detectable?
- **The setting:** What else was happening at the time of, or just prior to, the incident that influenced the events?
- **Cultural factors** that may be reflected in and influencing the participants' actions.
- **Prior intervention** or help given to a participant on a similar issue.

What may be revealed through your fact gathering is information regard-ing other matters that do not pertain directly to the immediate situation, but that are influencing the situation, for example, an alleged perpetrator who has Tourette's Syndrome and cannot avoid saying certain types of things or a person who is experiencing family problems at home and is acting out emo-tionally. These types of circumstances may be influencing the situation under investigation. Even though these circumstances are not primary facts about the bullying incident, they are factors that must be considered in making an appropriate decision about what next right action should be taken.

See how Mr. Pogue gathers facts for his contextual analysis:

While Miss Jones conducted her interviews, I looked to see if I had record of any prior incidents in my student communication log that involved Allison, Cathy, Becky, or Sara. Allison had no prior incidents. Cathy had been cited for inappropriate dress and served detention for skipping two classes, but had never been involved in any bullying behavior of record. There was nothing on Becky. Sara had one incident last month when she became upset during a history exam. She agreed to see the school counselor, and there had been no subsequent incidents. During our conversation, Sara told me that her parents were divorcing.

I also checked to see what anti-bullying and harassment training the students had received. In addition to sessions during their health classes, the girls had all attended an assembly at which the specific rules and con-sequences regarding making written threats had been discussed.

The context step functions as a "multiplier." This can best be illustrated by an exercise in which you take the same set of circumstances and alter the con-text; in other words, you make up several contexts for the same set of founda-tional facts and watch the appropriate action step change each time. Sometimes the context will show up as a factor that adds gravity to the situation. Think of it as a "positive" or increasing multiplier. At other times, the context will actually diminish the severity of the situation. Think of this as a "negative" or de-escalating multiplier. When you change the value of the multiplier, you come up with completely different action steps.

Let's try a game (in Figure 6.7a below):

/_   **Figure 6.7a** Context Game   /_

Guess what is going to happen next . . .

> The scene begins in the high school
> cafeteria. Senior Joe comes up to
> Freshman Jan from behind,
> wraps his arms around her waist,
> and pulls her close.

Solution on Next Page

Context: The Supreme Court Speaks

In reaction to a proposed emphasis on context, people often remark, "I don't care about the context. She did it. She wasn't supposed to do it. That's it." For educators, examining context can sometimes be a radical departure from earlier training. Considering only specific, observable facts is fine for measuring certain educational outcomes, but it is insufficient for compliance with the law.

In the landmark *Oncale v. Sundowner* case (USSC 1998) the U.S. Supreme Court found that same-sex harassment was illegal discrimination under Title VII (and by extrapolation, Title IX as well). In writing the unanimous opinion for the Court, Justice Scalia addressed the area of context in harassment cases as follows:

> The real social impact of workplace [or school-related] behavior often depends on a constellation of surrounding circumstances, expectations, and relationships which are not fully captured by a simple recitation of the words used or the physical acts performed. Common sense, and an appropriate sensitivity to social context, will enable courts and juries to distinguish between simple teasing and rough-housing among members of the same sex, and conduct which a reasonable person in the complaining person's position would find severely hostile or abusive.

Miss Jones Interviews Becky

Becky told Miss Jones that she did not know anything about the note. However, she shared that during lunch last week Allison and Sara had argued. Sara was upset because she wanted Allison to make her a copy of the yearbook picture of her boyfriend's winning soccer goal. Allison said that she would get in trouble for making copies and refused.

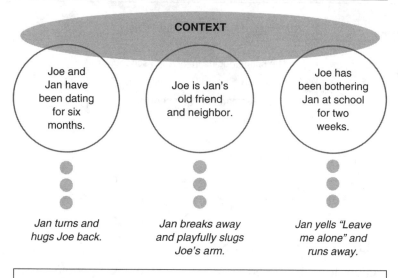

Figure 6.7b Context Game—Solutions

Scene: Senior Joe comes up to Freshman Jan from behind, wraps his arms around her waist, and pulls her close.

CONTEXT

Joe and Jan have been dating for six months.

Joe is Jan's old friend and neighbor.

Joe has been bothering Jan at school for two weeks.

Jan turns and hugs Joe back.

Jan breaks away and playfully slugs Joe's arm.

Jan yells "Leave me alone" and runs away.

As the context changes, so does the appropriate action.

When Miss Jones and I met again, the facts were starting to point to Sara. Miss Jones had cleverly checked the girls' class schedules and found that Sara was the only one who had Computer class first period that day and therefore had an opportunity to type the threatening note.

I called Sara into my office. I presented her with all the facts we had discovered so far. Without making any accusation, I asked Sara to try and tell me how she really felt about Allison. "Allison always gets what she wants. Everything is easy for her. Cathy is really sad that Allison doesn't hang with us as much anymore," Sara replied.

"How does that make you feel?"

"I don't care what Allison does; I just want to hang out with Cathy."

"Why is Cathy so important to you?"

"She is the first person who is really interested in what I have to say. My parents are always fighting; they are only interested in who is right and how much alimony my dad should pay. Cathy is different. I make her laugh, and she shares her clothes with me. We help each other with our homework."

"Do you feel threatened by Allison and Cathy's friendship?"

Sara's lip started to quiver and tears came to her eyes.

"Do you know who wrote the note?"

"I wasn't really going to do anything to her," said Sara with tears fully flowing.

"Did you type that note hoping Allison and Cathy would not remain friends?"

Between sniffs, Sara squeaked, "Yes."

After gathering details about how Sara had written and delivered the letter to Allison's locker, we discussed the impact on Allison, who received the veiled threats, and the impact on Cathy, who was innocent. I asked Sara about the impact her actions had on herself and she replied, "I may end up losing Cathy as my friend anyway." Upon further inquiry, I learned that Sara's mother had switched to the late shift, which leaves Sara alone most evenings. This provided additional contextual information within which to further understand Sara's actions.

I asked Sara what she thought would be the best solution to resolve this incident. "I guess I have to try and explain myself to Allison and Cathy and hope they forgive me."

ACTION: Taking the Logical Next Step

A
C
T
I
O
N

The action you ultimately recommend will be a product of your analysis of the preceding three components of the McGrath FICA logic formula—the facts, impact, and context. This analysis is rigorously organized into a logical progression, as follows: (Facts + Impact) × Context = Action.

Facts + Impact: The facts plus the impact are added together to give you the seriousness or "weight" of the incident.

Context: The weight of the incident (facts + impact) is then multiplied by the context. Determine what other circumstances were occurring at the

Figure 6.8 McGrath FICA Standard Formula

$$(F + I) \times C = A$$

time of the incident or preceding the incident, then look at the facts and impact against those circumstances. Sometimes bullying behavior appears more egregious in the light of the circumstances (e.g., the existence of a repeated pattern of misbehavior); sometimes the circumstances make it appear less egregious (e.g., the offending student has never been involved in conduct like this before, and outside circumstances, such as the parents' divorcing, are currently affecting his or her judgment). The context then informs your determination of a fair and appropriate response. That is what "understanding something in context" is about.

Here is an example of how the context shapes your recommendation, either diminishing or intensifying the severity of the situation: The alleged perpetrator is a newly arrived male foreign exchange student who patted a female student on the rear three times. This is a traditional greeting connoting honor and respect in his country. You will factor these cultural differences in when determining the appropriate remedial action—probably some cultural sensitivity training and an explanation that no disrespect was intended. Then you will monitor the situation. If the behavior is still happening two weeks from now despite efforts to remediate, the context changes dramatically because now it includes the lack of effort to correct, and the action you take will be proportionally more severe.

Spiraling Forward

Just one more piece is called for in order to totally understand the nature of the McGrath SUCCEED System's FICA Standard tool. As you may have discerned from the preceding discussion above, in any given situation the McGrath FICA analysis will repeat itself a number of times, such as with Allison, then in discussion with Cathy, Sara, and Becky, and then back to Sara. FICA is not a checklist; it is a repeating, dynamic, forward-moving, logical pattern.

Said again, the McGrath FICA is a recurring pattern in a forward-moving spiral fashion. In using the McGrath FICA pattern when you are thinking something through, ask yourself, What are the key facts here? How do these facts impact the situation? What is already occurring in the environment that is the context within which the facts and impact happen? Then analyze those three components together and determine the appropriate next step. The action you take will lead to new facts, have new impacts, and thus shape and inform the context in which it is all occurring.

Figure 6.9 McGrath FICA Spiral

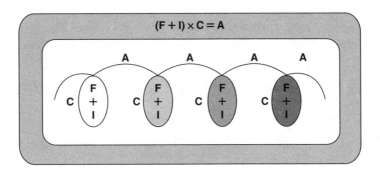

Back to Mr. Pogue

At this point I looked at the "whole picture." This is Sara's first offense of this nature, and our conversation established that while writing and posting the letter was an act of social scheming on Sara's part, it was also a result of insecurity and emotional upheaval in her life. Sara was going through a difficult time with her parents' divorce and her mother's change in work hours.

Sara showed a willingness to make amends. Cathy and Allison did not express any negative feelings about Sara during their interviews, so reconciliation seemed possible. That would be up to the girls. I would get back to both Allison and Cathy with my findings. Mediation would only be provided if they requested it, and it is typically not recommended in bullying cases.

All students in the high school were given the Code of Student Conduct at the beginning of the year and had attended an assembly at which the rules and consequences of bullying and harassment were discussed, including the consequences for making written threats. A first offense entailed 10 hours of community service.

I informed Sara that I would be contacting her mother about this incident and that it would be included in her discipline records. She would also be referred for further counseling. I asked Sara what other actions she could take to rectify writing the letter. Sara said, "I am going to apologize to Cathy and Allison and take the consequences. I also know that I will have to do community service for writing a threat, and I think it would be good for me. Is there a teacher in school who needs a volunteer helper during my free period?"

At times like this, I love my job.

Review Figure 6.10, the McGrath FICA Memo for this incident.

Figure 6.10 McGrath FICA Memo

Date: March 9, 2006

To: (Personal note for records)

Re: Sara Johansson

F Posing as Cathy, Sara typed a threatening note to Allison and placed it in Allison's locker. Sara denied writing the note until the second interview. Sara's action violated the Student Code of Conduct prohibiting written threats.

I Sara and I discussed Allison's distress upon receiving the veiled threats, and Cathy's hurt at being set up for something she did not do. Sara recognized that her actions may jeopardize her friendship with Cathy.

C This is Sara's first offense of this nature, and our conversation proved that while writing and posting the letter was an act of social scheming on Sara's part, it was also a result of insecurity and emotional upheaval in her life due to recent family issues. Sara shows a willingness to make amends.

A According to the Student Code of Conduct, a first offense for "writing a threatening note" entails a consequence of 10 community service hours. Sara will be placed in an in-school volunteer position for Community Service during her free period. A Community Service Tracking card will be issued to Sara, and the teacher to whom she is assigned will supervise and sign off on her 10 hours of service. Sara plans to apologize to Cathy and Allison. I will follow up with all three girls involved by conducting an informal chat with each during the week of March 20th–24th.

NOTES:

1. Be aware of FERPA restrictions on disclosure of student information.
2. The "F-I-C-A" in the left margin would not appear on the actual memo.

McGRATH FICA IN REVIEW

This is the McGrath FICA Standard: Facts, Impact, Context, and Action. These four practices are woven together in a logic formula, the purpose of which is to determine the next appropriate step. The McGrath FICA formula is designed to provide a consistent, logical approach that guides analytical thinking. Proper use of the FICA supports administrators in avoiding "the shoot from the hip" approach. The tool guides administrators in being thoughtful and completely informed about what actually happened, how much it hurt somebody, and how the current situation should be viewed in light of the known circumstances. With an understanding of these three components, wise action can be taken based on the logical analysis embodied within the McGrath FICA Standard: facts + impact × context = action.

When practiced consistently, the McGrath FICA Standard will become your daily building block for thinking, speaking, listening, and writing. You will find yourself problem solving on the spot. It will become your standard—the flag you are flying and your model for excellence.

Using the McGrath SUCCEED System is simple and logical, but its application is not necessarily easy. It requires a leader to be thoughtful and informed about an entire situation. This thoughtfulness may require a change in the way a leader has done business, moving away from what is expedient to what is principled. It is easy enough to learn a format for rote use. However, it is not as easy to allow a format to guide thoughtful consideration regarding all aspects of a situation, including our own behavior.

IMPLEMENTING THE
FICA CHAT INFRASTRUCTURE

A conversation in which you organize your thoughts and present them using the McGrath FICA Standard is referred to as a "FICA Chat." In many cases, you will have one FICA Chat with a student and the subject will never come up again; however, in other cases, you will find yourself intervening with the same student regarding the same issue on multiple occasions. In those cases, multiple FICA Chats will take place and they may include the parents, IEP team, school counselor, or other interested parties.

Let's take, for example, a case in which you are dealing with a minor incident of name calling. You use the McGrath FICA Standard to gather facts and analyze the situation, thinking through each section: Facts, Impact, Context, and Action. The evidence clearly proves misbehavior on the part of a particular student. Next, you have a FICA Chat with the student who perpetrated the name calling. In the action section, you state a warning that the behavior must not be repeated.

Three weeks later, the perpetrator is back in your office again. What is next?

You would apply the FICA to a maximum of two FICA Chats with the student. Each time you have a FICA Chat with a student, note that Chat in your calendar so that you have a record of who was involved, the topic, and any warnings given. Some administrators keep a separate calendar or dated log, referred to as a "Chat Book," for keeping track of all FICA Chats with students and parents. (Note: This is not your private journal. It is discoverable in a lawsuit, so be professional in your tone and consistent in your logging.) The goal of this Chat infrastructure is to address issues immediately and to get them turned around quickly. If after two successive chats the behavior escalates, you move to writing a FICA Memo or FICA Letter. When to discipline the student

_ℳ_   **Figure 6.11** Communicating With the McGrath FICA Standard   _ℳ_

Facts:

- Focused, clear, and precise descriptions.

- Specific, observable, relevant behavior.

- No emotional responses.

- No opinions.

- No minutiae.

Impact:

- Specific, observable impacts, along with your professional opinion, not your personal speculation, on how someone might be impacted.

- What happened as a result of this situation occurring?

- Watch out for attributing false cause to something. How do you know that there's a connection?

- Professional opinion and judgment do belong here.

Context

- What's the big picture that this incident fits within—the environment around the situation?

- For example, is there a family situation or other condition we should know about because it's affecting performance?

- Is there a pattern?

- Context is determinative—it gives meaning to the whole. Keep changing the context and you will keep getting a different appropriate action step.

Action/Growth:

- At this point you have choices depending on the outcome of working the McGrath FICA. It is a formula for growth, not a formula with a predetermined outcome.

- Because you have already included Facts, Impact, and Context with honesty, clarity, and specificity, you don't need to explain your rationale for the actions again.

  It is vital that the McGrath FICA be kept in its exact order. It is a logic formula, each section standing on the one that precedes it.

depends on the seriousness of the behavior involved. With less serious behavior you may not formally discipline the student unless you are sure the student understands what is problematic and yet continues to engage in the conduct. In the case of a serious offense, where there is injury to either another person or property, you will probably move immediately to discipline.

FICA Chat With Student. Begin by asking, "What is happening?" The conversation follows the FICA structure. A notation is made in the Chat Book. **(Note: If there is a serious health or safety issue involved, you jump steps and go directly to FICA Chat + FICA Memo so that your documentation is thorough and sound.)**

FICA Chat With Student + FICA Parent Phone Call. On the second occurrence, have another FICA Chat with the student and place a phone call to the parent. You are developing partnership. Make another notation in your calendar or organizer. Also schedule any future monitoring or follow-up required, for example, note on which date you plan to interview the classroom teacher or victim to see whether there have been any new occurrences.

By speaking with the parent on the second occurrence, you are not waiting too long to bring them into the loop. The first FICA Parent Phone Call develops partnership with the parent. A second call, if needed, "enlists" the parent for further intervention. Then, if a third call is necessary, they are not surprised by it. If you wait and call only to spring a disciplinary action on them, the parents may be rightfully upset and question the fairness of your decision.

Steve Lyng, a high school principal in Indiana, puts it this way:

> I want to build an alliance with the parent and that is why I include a FICA Parent Phone Call. It's a simple conversation: Here is what is happening. This is what your child is doing (FACTS) and here is the effect it is having on others and the school (IMPACT). Is there anything we should know about what is happening at home or school that could assist us in addressing this issue (CONTEXT)? We will be keeping an eye on him. You are so supportive of the school 's efforts to encourage and develop your son. I would greatly appreciate your help in ensuring that this type of thing doesn't happen again (ACTION).

Figure 6.12 illustrates what the FICA Chat infrastructure looks like over time.

FICA Chat + Memo or Letter. After a maximum of two FICA Chats, go to writing. The exception to this is a serious incident, which would go directly to a formal written record. At this point, you still have a FICA Chat with the student, but you follow it up with writing. After the conversation, recount the interchange in a FICA Memo or, if a more formal or weighty document seems appropriate, write a FICA Letter. Mention the subject and dates of the two prior FICA Chats. Attach any discipline contract that you develop in response to this issue. Make sure that a copy of the memo goes to the student and the parent(s). The memo should include a date, who it is to and from, an area for response, and a notation that the FICA Standard Memo is being copied to the student's site file.

Figure 6.12 McGrath FICA Chat Infrastructure

FICA Chat

Incident Facts, Impact, Context, Action

Chat With Student + FICA Parent Phone Call

Develops partnership with parents and enlists the parents for further intervention

FICA Chat + Memo or Letter

After the conversation, recount the interchange in a FICA Memo or, if a more formal or weighty document seems appropriate, write a FICA Letter. Attach any discipline contract that you develop in response to this issue.

By following the steps outlined here, the practitioner demonstrates a commitment to growing the student while creating a paper trail that documents all attempts at remediation. Having followed and documented such a clear course of action, any decision to go to discipline or recommend expulsion should be defensible in a parent meeting or disciplinary hearing.

SUMMARY

"The training that I have received in the McGrath SUCCEED System has changed the way I think about almost everything" (Steve Lyng, Principal, Northridge High School, Middlebury Community Schools, Indiana).

We have now introduced the four practices of the McGrath FICA Standard and illustrated their application with a Level II bullying incident. The McGrath SUCCEED System offers practices that put fundamental ethical principles into action. Each interaction flows from an application of the McGrath SUCCEED System's ultimate purpose, which is to develop people and the culture and climate in which they are operating.

In the next chapter, the ethical principles that power the four McGrath FICA practices will be discussed. Also discussed will be the all-important relationship between administrator and students and how to deepen and expand it. It is within the context of that relationship that the issue of bullying can be transformed for the individual student as well as within the culture of the school.

7

Powered by Principles

Lead with your heart while using your head.

—Mary Jo McGrath

As an alternative high school principal, I have the joy and heartache of help-ing at-risk students see their real potential, their deep-down dreams of living life successfully, and what that will mean for each of them. My students have wandered from the path of a life that leads to authentic fulfillment. I have lived enough of those messy moments with them to know that fulfillment and meaning do not come from a bottle, a winning lottery ticket, or a shallow rela-tionship, but from deep life-giving affirmations that come at crucial moments of indecision, moments when life can go either way, up or down.

At-risk students hear many voices in their lives—voices that berate and blame, voices fraught with frustration, voices that discipline with "don'ts" but rarely speak the "do's." They seldom hear words that encourage a stronger self-image or an attitude that "I can overcome no matter what obstacles are in my way." I see students daily who have been disciplined and corrected to change behavior but have never been communicated with in a way that helps them change the attitude of their hearts.

I leave my office and go mingle with my students in the hallways. I see typical American high school students: boys with beltless baggy pants, untied shoelaces dropping and dragging from designer tennis shoes, tattoos, and piercings—the badges of individuality but looking surprisingly like those marking their buddies as well; girls dressed in provocative, eye-appealing out-fits, chatting and giggling with their friends.

They are, in every way, products of the current media hype that tells them real success is "having things" and that living life is "just for the moment." And sadly, they believe it. I stop and, for a moment or two, have a chat with two or three of them. We talk about the facts of their lives—what is going on in school, at home, and with their friends during leisure time. The chat then moves on to what impact those facts are having on them: Did they have fun at the mall? Is it hard to study for exams and care for a newborn at the same time? Then we drop into the context—the often-difficult situations that they face in their home, school, and community lives and how they are growing and developing in response. Finally, to the action—what are they going to do about their daily decisions that will produce a fruitful future?

Just a chat—nothing long and drawn out, no great advice on life, no "gems" of wisdom. Just a chat—a snapshot in time that gives a picture of reality and encourages a sense of high self-efficacy (the belief that hard work brings about good things), rather than low self-efficacy (the belief that good things come about by luck or good karma).

As part of my daily routine, I have these little chats with my students. My school is small and I know the chats add up. We have rules and regulations— very strict rules. Our rules and regulations are very necessary for order, but they do not produce attitude changes. Those come—more and more frequently—as a result of the numerous chats I am having every day. Our chats produce growth in my students; they are our heart connection.

—Steve Young, Principal, Jefferson
Alternative High School, Idaho

W hen Mr. Young speaks about his daily practices with the McGrath FICA Standard in its informal phase, what we call "Chats," his mastery is evident—mastery not just of the "doing" aspects but of the "being" as well. So far, one tool in the SUCCEED System, the McGrath FICA Standard, has been introduced. This tool is the processing center of the system. It encompasses not only practical action—ask this question, look at other factors—but when united with its principles, the tool also provides access to a way of being that is ethical, connected, and honoring of people. When we bring in the principles from which the SUCCEED practices are derived, the practitioner's understanding of the SUCCEED approach alters and expands. Why? Because the McGrath SUCCEED System is a system of "being."

That's right, I said "being," defined as the nature or essence of a person. Why, you may ask, is a lawyer talking about being? Isn't this a book about bullying and legal strategies to address the problem individually and systemically? The answer is that any attempt to alter an organization's culture must access, address, and then shift who the people within the organization are being. It must ask questions that elicit new paradigms, choices, and ways of relating to each other and to the organization, or it is doomed to failure. More accurately, it will float on the surface as an additional thing to do, perhaps even as busy work, and never make a difference to anyone or anything of importance. It is the heart of the individual that contains the possibilities of the future, and that is only available through discovering what kind of human being he or she is. The McGrath SUCCEED System provides the tools for that self-discovery that, in turn, becomes transformative communication.

Beyond the individuals who practice and benefit from it, SUCCEED is an instrument of organizational culture change. SUCCEED embodies a duality of purpose and intent. Here the "must do'" of the law intersects with the possibility of the transformation of the individual and the culture. That combination is not really any kind of stretch because at the essence of the law are fairness and justice, fundamental human principles.

The McGrath SUCCEED System is about engaging people in choices, rather than talking down to them or punishing them into submission. The SUCCEED inquiry allows for unexpected and even seemingly impossible results to arise. In this chapter, both the underpinnings of the SUCCEED model and the far-reaching implications of its implementation as a catalyst for individual and organizational change will be explored.

THE "BE" AND THE "DO" OF CONQUERING BULLYING

What you can *do* for students pales in comparison to who you can *be* for them. So far this book has focused on what to do concerning bullying, and more guidance will be provided in that area. Equally important to your efforts is who you will be, and this will be addressed now.

Let's take another look at the McGrath FICA Standard (shown in Figure 7.1). On the left, we have the four practices: Facts, Impact, Context, and Action. On the right side of the diagram is an added dimension. These are the four fundamental principles of the McGrath SUCCEED System: Trust, Respect, Understanding, and Growth. The practices are the "what to do" part of the system; the principles give you "who to be." The principles infuse the system with heart and, hopefully, speak to the soul and spirit of the school leader.

Remember the Four Questions:

1. What happened?

2. What apparent harm did it cause?

3. What is known about anything preceding the event that is contributing to the situation?

4. What immediate action should be taken, if any?

Each question can be stated as a **Practice** with a corresponding **Principle:**

1.	Facts	Trust
2.	Impact	Respect
3.	Context	Understanding
4.	Action	Growth

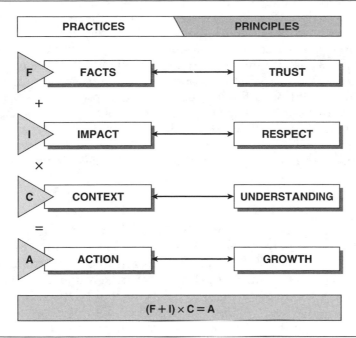

Figure 7.1 McGrath FICA Standard

WHY TRUST, RESPECT, UNDERSTANDING, AND GROWTH?

Facts With Trust

Being clear about the **Facts,** without judgment, in your analysis and in your communications, both conveys that you trust people (explained further in the next paragraph) and elicits from people their **Trust** of you. Communicating in a way that elicits trust is markedly distinct from the experience that we have all had where our accuser included "everything but the kitchen sink" in a berating communication. When this occurs we are often left in a swirl of emotion and resentment, feeling attacked and misunderstood, and not the least bit trusting of the attacker. Staying factual and aboveboard demonstrates your trustworthiness and earns you trust. You are simply stating what is occurring as reflected against previously conveyed standards of behavior, not passing judgment or impugning the student's character. The standards against which the behavior is measured in this section are the objective standards that have been relayed to all students through student codes of conduct and anti-bullying and harassment policies. You leave out adjectives that express judgment, for example, "mean," "rude," "obnoxious," or "disgusting"; they are neither objective nor fair. When you are being fair, aboveboard, clear, objective, and consistent in your approach to the facts, you are being trustworthy and concurrently bring forth Trust of you in others.

In addition, there is an underlying philosophical stance reflected in the principle of Trust that flows outward toward the student. This stance is in the order of, "I believe in you and trust that if you understand your behavior clearly, you will want to stop it. That is the kind of human being you are to me, and you cannot convince me otherwise." Hopefully, you can hear in this statement an immutable belief in the student—not because he or she has earned it, but because that is what *you* say is so. The student cannot prove you wrong because your stand is not based in evidence. You bring a stand into existence as an existential act. It is so because you say so, and for no other reason. The stand is yours to create from, based on nothing. A personal stand provides quite a port in a storm, and storms you'll see aplenty over the years to come. A stand is where your being may reside in the work you do with students. You remain steadfast and unflappable in your vision of who they really are. From this personal stand, your very being communicates, "I believe in you."

Impact With Respect

R E S P E C T

Keeping the **Impact** clear and distinct from what occurred factually creates a condition of **Respect** between the speaker and the listener. Why? To communicate the Impact dispassionately, and even compassionately, requires that you maintain the belief that most students do not want to harm others. (A wise exception to this belief will be discussed later in the chapter.) Even when they intend harm, they are not necessarily thinking ahead to the full impact of their behavior. Think about Sara in Chapter 6. Sara just wanted Allison's attention. She did not think about the harm she was doing. She was a teenager, with all the short-sightedness and self-centeredness that stage of life can reflect. When a student is presented with the full picture of the harm caused, the student can understand the rationale for any required behavior change. They also know that you Respect them when you do not "baby" them but, rather, hold them accountable for self-correcting and being responsible for the harm they have caused. Be sure that the cause and effect are in balance with one another as well, as discussed in Chapter 6. If your presentation of the Impact is balanced and is proportional to the harm done, you will garner Respect in return.

Context With Understanding

U N D E R S T A N D I N G

Putting things in **Context** generates **Understanding.** When you think about it, this makes perfect sense. How many times have you felt completely misunderstood by someone who did not recognize the preexisting factors that you were dealing with in a particular situation? It happens to most of us daily—that sense that no one really understands how it is for us. In childhood, especially adolescence, the need to be understood is predominant. It can preoccupy young minds 24 hours a day. Most young people feel that the majority of adults simply do not "get it."

It is important to be alert to the fact that the students' behavior is not occurring in isolation apart from the culture and climate of their homes, sibling relationships, circles of friends, pressures to make it and fit in, part-time jobs, health concerns, and academic demands. Being mindful of the "big picture" demonstrates compassion, awareness, and even recognition of the person as distinct from his or her behavior. A compassionate administrator who is genuinely interested in the Context will often uncover circumstances that completely alter the way a student's behavior can be understood in light of those circumstances and lead to unexpected and, ultimately, more effective pathways for remediation. This is Understanding at its most powerful.

Action With Growth

**G
R
O
W
T
H**

It is now time for **Action**. The underlying principle for the Action step is **Growth** (and if you are really in the game, **Mutual Growth**). Consider that while we might con ourselves into believing otherwise, the reality is that most resolution of student misbehavior and misconduct has little or nothing to do with Growth. Our principles for Action are more likely to include expediency, control, dominance, and even a degree of righteousness ("You have messed with me for the last time, buddy boy!"). Growth takes thought, planning, persistence, and diligence. It is also a hallmark of true leadership. When a commitment to Growth is driving the action selected, feedback, coaching, and self-correction can occur. Do not be surprised if the interaction contributes to your own Growth as well. In the process of using the McGrath SUCCEED System, you may learn things from your students that you never thought they could teach you. This principle will open you up to their wisdom and them to yours. When an administrator is a partner in a student's Growth, rather than someone who is out to punish, discipline, or dominate, a whole new future emerges for both.

FOUR LENSES: STRUCTURE, QUALITY, TONE, AND BALANCE

There are four lenses through which to examine your work product and develop your competency with the McGrath FICA Standard.

Structure Counts

Analyzing a McGrath FICA Standard communication for its structure is very straightforward. You are looking for all four parts—Facts, Impact, Context, and Action—in that exact order. Are they in the F-I-C-A sequence? Is anything muddled or out of place? For example, is an Impact being presented in the Facts section as part of "what happened?" The impact (or harm done) is not the cause of what happened; it is the effect of what happened. So yes, there may be facts that *describe* the harm, but they belong in a different section from the facts that *caused* the harm. The description of harm or impact is a description of consequences. Be sure that there are no Impacts in the Facts section. Refer to the annotated outline of the McGrath FICA Standard (Figure 6.11, page 87 in Chapter 6) as you analyze the structure.

Do not "cheat" on the F-I-C-A order of the communication; it is vital to the structural integrity and logical flow of the analysis. People often want to start with the context (the explanation for the occurrence) because it might help the "medicine go down" easier. Or, because the effects of what occurred are so distressing, the adult may go on a rant about the impact before describing "what happened." Be rigorous with the structure. You will see over time that the

(Text continues on page 98)

~~   **Figure 7.2a** McGrath FICA Standard—Comprehensive I   *~~*

PRACTICES

F   **FACTS: What happened, in specific detail?** ⟶

+

In your verbal or written communication, include a description of **specific observed behaviors without opinion.** This provides a mirror for the student to see a **reflection** of his/her own behavior, **rather than your judgment about that behavior.** If there is a pattern of behavior, prior occurrences should be mentioned after the current incident is described. **Beware of tinged words** that convey disapproval and rejection and obscure the point of the communication.

I   **IMPACT: What was the effect of what happened?** ⟶

×

The descriptions in the FACT and IMPACT sections should show a **cause-and-effect relationship between behavior and its outcomes.** Highlighting this relationship allows the learner(s) to **self-correct** by enabling them to understand the rationale for the requested behavior change. Further, the communicator needs to be sure the **FACTS and IMPACT are in balance,** neither one under- or over-stated.

C   **CONTEXT: Are there any preceding contributing factors?** ⟶

=

Factoring in **variables that may be influencing a student's behavior** makes this approach an open system, rather than a closed system. These variables may extend into **health, family, or personal issues** that are disrupting a student's ability to behave appropriately. Some personal matters may be addressed orally rather than in writing. The rule is **always talk first, write second.**

A   **ACTION: What are the next steps?** ⟶

Given that this is a logic-based formula for thinking and problem solving, the appropriate action step to be taken is determined by **working the formula: (FACTS + IMPACT) × CONTEXT = ACTION.** Because this is a dynamic system, each set of actions generates a new formula cycle: (FACTS + IMPACT) × CONTEXT = ACTION. Each action taken must correspond to the above formula.

Figure 7.2b McGrath FICA Standard—Comprehensive 2

PRINCIPLE

TRUST

When stating factual descriptions, be sure the **behaviors relayed are current** and not resurrected from past concerns not previously mentioned.The focus should be **specific,** rather than a shotgun approach. **Speak directly to the behavior only,** not to anyone's character. Lastly, be sure the standard against which the behavior is measured has been **previously conveyed** to avoid surprises.

RESPECT

Rely on the belief that **most students want to be kind people,** and trust that, once they understand how particular practices do not fulfill their intentions, students will alter their practices. In having this belief, you **treat students with dignity and respect**. At the same time, you **hold students accountable** for the consequences of behavior . . . instilling respect for the rights and well-being of others.

UNDERSTANDING

Students are **influenced by many different things** in their personal and academic lives. Without recognition of this dynamic, there could be a lack of compassion for the effect certain variables are having on a student's behavior, This principle allows for **behavior to be viewed from a "big picture"** perspective, and requires us to look at the **whole human being** and the system in which he/she is functioning, rather than a particular behavior in isolation.

GROWTH

Growth is the contextual principle within which **feedback, coaching,** and **self-correction** can occur. The intention is that correction or enhancement can be effectively accomplished immediately. The McGrath SUCCEED System allows everyone involved to more **naturally evolve in their competencies,** rather than be forced to utilize a "one size fits all" mismatched system.

∿   **Figure 7.3** Developing Competency With the McGrath FICA   *∿*

Review your FICA work product (verbal or written) through these four lenses:

STRUCTURE

Is each part in the right place, F-I-C-A? Is it logical?

QUALITY

Is the communication specific and objective?

TONE

Is the language used objective and impartial?

BALANCE

Does the action fit with the analysis?

structure will provide something you may not be able to see or experience now; the structure will literally train your mind to think in a new way.

Quality: Be Specific and Factual

Are you presenting the facts or are you presenting your opinion about the facts? This is a critical distinction. The quality of your communication is directly correlated with your ability to identify and eliminate opinion from the factual foundation. You may express your professional opinion, but it belongs in the Impact section where you recount the harm done.

Your opinion creates filters through which you perceive the world. (More on this later in the chapter.) Be responsible for how those opinions (filters) color what you perceive with your senses. For example, if your philosophy is that kids cannot be trusted, that filter may blind you to what is actually going on between the students. Get back to the five senses: What did you or someone else see, hear, touch, taste, and/or smell?

Emotional responses will also affect the quality of your communication. If you simply mirror back the facts for the student, the communication loses its emotionalism. For example, "Your filthy mouth makes me sick. You should be ashamed of yourself," versus "Mrs. Franklin heard you call Veronica a 'slut' three times during math class this morning." Your job is to hold up a mirror for the students to see themselves in, and your emotions and opinions, particularly in the Facts section, can cloud that mirror. We will return to this topic later in this chapter.

Tone: The Relationship Factor

Tone is the character or atmosphere of the communication. It is the relationship factor. An appropriate tone is essential for building relationships. Put your attention on what you "sound" like through your word choice, your vocal intonation, even your physical proximity. Ask yourself, Does the tone match what I intend to accomplish with this communication? Is the tone harsh? Is it neutral?

In writing, there are no facial expressions, body language, or tone of voice to rely on. Tone comes in through the choice of language. Does your word choice express negativity, frustration, or judgment? If so, then the tone of your communication is adversarial. Avoid this tone with students whom you wish to "grow." Choose supportive words over "fighting words." When it is time to discipline, and if you want to add a fear factor, then choose words consciously that are threatening and that evoke fear. Sometimes fear is an appropriate motivator—just not all the time.

Timing can also set the tone. Early intervention in a situation establishes a tone of partnership. Remember, you are the designer and architect of the communication, and through that, the culture and climate of your school.

Balance: Working the FICA Formula With Integrity

When looking through the lens of **Balance,** you are determining whether the action you are proposing fits with what you have learned through the use of the McGrath FICA Standard. Are you making your decisions using a thorough understanding and application of the formula **(Facts + Impact) × Context = Action**? You are always either using the formula or shooting from the hip. Refer to The McGrath FICA Standard: The Basic Tool in Chapter 6 for a refresher on the formula. Also, being in Balance entails rechecking yourself to be sure that you have used the principles to power the practices in all steps of the process. If you are just *doing* the McGrath FICA Standard and not *being* the principles of trust, respect, understanding, and growth, you have missed the mark.

IT'S ALL ABOUT RELATIONSHIP

The McGrath SUCCEED System is about changing culture one thought at a time, one communication at a time, one relationship at a time. On this path to transformation, you cannot merely think your way there; you have to *relate* your way there as well. How we relate flows from the way we:

- **think** about people and our world,
- **listen** to what others in the environment have to say,
- **speak** and express what is inside of us, and
- **act** in ways that make us a contributing part of the world.

The future is in each person's hands, moment by moment. We sometimes relate to the "system" within which we work, study, or live as something outside of ourselves. In these moments, we become like pawns on a chessboard and abrogate our leadership. Hopefully, over time you will begin to experience, through disciplined use, what the McGrath SUCCEED System is pointing to. You *are* the system. The "system" is not external and imposed. The system is driven by every interaction you have with your students and with other adults as well. Each relationship interaction "drives the behavior of the system" (Kaeufer, Scharmer, & Versteegen, 2003, p. 6) one thought, one act of listening, one conversation, and one action at a time. You can focus on what appears to prevent you from relating differently, or you can take ownership of your immense power to build the world in which you live, one relationship at a time. This is the choice that leadership makes possible.

Figure 7.4 SUCCEED Circle

THE McGRATH SUCCEED
LEVELS OF MASTERY

In *The Fifth Discipline: The Art & Practice of the Learning Organization*, author Peter Senge (1990) defines a "discipline" as a series of principles and practices that we study, master, and integrate into our lives. He states that a discipline can be approached at one of three levels:

- Practices: what you do
- Principles: guiding ideas and insights
- Essences: the state of being of those with high levels of mastery in the discipline (p. 373)

Each level provides a vital dimension. Each is necessary to the others if the culture of an individual and the culture of the organization are to grow. The McGrath SUCCEED System is a discipline with practices and principles.

The discipline of SUCCEED is designed to lead to the mastery of communication, relationship, and continuous growth.

Learning the McGrath SUCCEED System occurs at three levels: the Skill level, the Craft level, and the Art level.

The Skill level is attained using the McGrath FICA as described in Chapter 6, without any thought to the principles. This level will aid logical thinking, add quality and comprehensibility to any communications, and guide you in taking appropriate actions. Often, at this level, the System and its tools live in a drawer or notebook, to be pulled out by the user only in dire situations or when mandated.

The Craft level is achieved when the principles are added to the practices (e.g., FACTS + TRUST). These principles give users ethical guidance as they proceed through the actions dictated by the practices. At this level, the user has made the McGrath FICA Standard his or her own and uses it willingly and eagerly. Broader insights and understanding of one's students is achieved at this level, guidance is given based on those insights, and relationships are deepened and expanded.

The Art level is the state of mastery. At this level, you have so integrated the McGrath FICA Standard into your thinking that it is permeating your being as well. You are continuously learning about yourself, your students, and even the world. You are in a constant state of becoming a great communicator and relationship partner and loving the journey.

How one uses the McGrath SUCCEED System is a matter of individual choice. You cannot mandate becoming a master. The higher up in the levels one goes, the more fun the system is to use, and the more unexpected and transformational the insights attained and results achieved.

A TRANSFORMATIONAL APPROACH

The claim that the McGrath SUCCEED System is transformational at the level of an organization's culture is based on a two-step analysis. The McGrath SUCCEED System has its immediate focus on the individual: how that person thinks, listens, speaks, and acts. Culture can be simply defined as "the way we do things around here." Since an organization is made up of a collection of individuals, one could say that the actions of the individual *are* the culture of the organization. "Organizations learn only through individuals who learn. Individual learning does not guarantee organizational learning. But without it, no organizational learning occurs" (Senge, 1990, p. 139).

Kathleen Crume, Assistant Superintendent of the Academy School District 20, Colorado Springs, Colorado, brought a team of her leaders to be trained to teach the McGrath SUCCEED System in her organization. This was in 1995. Ms. Crume shared that this was one of the most meaningful changes they ever made in the school district. SUCCEED has become an integral part of the Academy School District culture. She commented that after the first five years of her own use of the system, it became an art. Ms. Crume found herself not only *thinking from* the McGrath FICA Standard but also *being* the Standard.

Ms. Crume reported that she now sees the world through the SUCCEED model, separating fact from opinion without effort, automatically looking for the correlated impact and whether there was harm or benefit from what occurred. She naturally considers the context within which the facts and impact are occurring and takes her next step based on these understandings. This approach is integrated into her thinking, listening, speaking, and the action she takes. She is even more excited today about what the System provides than she was over 10 years ago when she first learned to use it.

Academy School District 20 is ranked first among large (6,000+ attendance) school districts in student achievement in the state of Colorado (Academy School District 20, 2005).[1] Ms. Crume attributes this success in part to the disciplined use of the McGrath SUCCEED System throughout her district administration.

THE HEART OF THE MATTER

Who are you for your students? That may seem like a strange question, but consider that just as there are various levels of mastering a discipline, there are also various levels of relating to those who are under our care. You could be:

- a **Mechanic** fixing defects: You are disconnected from the process and providing the nuts and bolts of what is called for by the situation.
- an **Instructor** guiding behavior: The learner is expecting sage advice and guidance from you and you do not disappoint.
- a **Coach** assisting in thoughtful reflection: You guide the learner in stepping back, reflecting, and remembering what is important.
- a **Partner** in bringing forth new levels of aliveness: In working together, both you and the student become more fully who you are as human beings—creative, fulfilled, and fully self-expressed.*

*Adapted from, Senge, Scharmer, Jaworski, & Flowers (2005), *Presence: An Exploration of Profound Change in People, Organizations, and Society* and from Kaeufer, Scharmer, & Versteegen (2003), "Breathing Life Into a Dying System: Recreating Health Care From Within."

WHAT IT TAKES TO BE A PARTNER

In order to have positive adult interactions with students, we need to know more about the adult who is going to have those interactions.

Vital things to know are the adult's:

- philosophy of who the students are—"sneaky little creeps" or "creatures with limitless potential"? This could be called one's *worldview* regarding students;
- level of self-awareness, especially regarding what behaviors trigger emotional responses in oneself;

- ability to observe and break free from those paradigms or mental models that limit and constrain self-expression and that can interfere with the commitment to being fully present in each and every interaction; and
- capacity to take a stand day after day to continue self-examination for the purpose of being available to the students and others in one's life.

TURNING THE MIRROR INWARD

There are "deeply ingrained assumptions, generalizations, or even pictures and images that influence how we understand the world and how we take action" that Senge (1990) calls *mental models* (p. 8). We are often unaware of the impact of such assumptions on our behavior. A fundamental part of our task in pursuit of being a Partner is to catch ourselves in action, reflect on and learn from what we see about ourselves, and grow from that knowledge.

The McGrath SUCCEED System is designed to facilitate the work of self-reflection, but while a person is "on the court" in action, rather than as a passive observer. In other words, the game of the McGrath SUCCEED System is to:

- watch yourself not being objective, or
- watch yourself jumping to conclusions, or
- watch yourself "shooting from the hip."

In the act of watching yourself, you can learn the areas in which you are not thinking, listening, speaking, or acting in a way that is objective, fair, and impartial and grounded in the principles of trust, respect, understanding, and growth. The McGrath SUCCEED System prompts you to engage in self-reflection that empowers outward actions that are consistent with your purpose of being a Partner with students.

The McGrath SUCCEED System
as a Guide for Self-Reflection

It is nearly impossible to be a Partner with students (or anyone else for that matter) if you are reacting to something. It is also nearly impossible to turn the mirror inward and see what is happening internally when you are highly upset, emotional, angry, or volatile. However, you can determine whether or not you are being reactive (versus objective) by using the McGrath SUCCEED tools to look inward.

Start with the objectivity of the facts (quality) that are at issue (assuming you are even recounting the facts). Are the facts that you are communicating about a simple reflection of what occurred, or are they sprinkled liberally with your opinion and judgment? Simply assess your ability to just state the facts, and it will tell you how free you are to be objective. Then check on the Tone: Does your word choice reflect that you are consciously building a relationship or are you laying into someone with everything you've got, and not by choice, but by reaction?

You will find—in both the Fact analysis and the Tone analysis—the baggage of your past that you are bringing to the situation. From there, once you have perceived it (catching yourself in the act) the reactivity will loosen its hold on you. Being aware won't completely eradicate your reactivity, but the awareness will allow you to begin to transform the issues that gripped you.

Perceiving what is going on with one's self is the portal to being present. Being present allows for something other than the past to repeat itself. Being present allows for a self to arise that is separate from whatever reactivity has had you in its clutches. That self is then available to take actions that are consistent with a commitment to being a Partner. The McGrath SUCCEED System is about breaking down the barriers that we all have to being fully present, being related to others, and acting on our commitment to bring forth what is possible.

Use the McGrath SUCCEED "Mirror Inward Inquiry Questions" while using the McGrath FICA Standard practices and principles.

Mirror Inward Inquiry Questions:

- Are you being logical and objective, rather than reactive (STRUCTURE)?
- Is the information specific and nonjudgmental (QUALITY)?
- Are you bullying the bully, or are you building a relationship (TONE)?
- Does it all add up to the future you want (BALANCE)?

If the answer is "no" to any of the above questions, look inside and see what's up with you. One of the main reasons people are reluctant to engage in self-reflection is that they are afraid they may not like what they see.

The Internal "Imposter"

We tend to focus on what we do, rather than on whom we are "being," for students. It is often easier to do something, anything, than be with another person. And nothing gets in the way of being with another person faster than fear.

Professor Chris Argyris, formerly of the Harvard graduate schools of business and education, has made a career of catching people in the act of being human. He published an article in *The Harvard Business Review* titled "Teaching Smart People How to Learn." In the article, he classifies most professionals (also referred to as "Smart" people) as having "extremely 'brittle' personalities." He explains: "When suddenly faced with a situation they cannot immediately handle, they tend to fall apart." Professor Argyris attributes this brittleness to a fear of failure experienced by people (Argyris, 1991, p. 10).

In a 1994 follow-up article, "Good Communication That Blocks Learning," Argyris cites studies of more than 6,000 people, from which he concludes that *the defensive reasoning people use to place the blame for failure outside themselves is universal*, with no measurable difference by country, age, sex, ethnic identity, education, wealth, power, or experience (Argyris, 1994, p. 81). Argyris postulates that all of us design our behavior so as to (1) remain in unilateral control, (2) maximize "winning" and minimize "losing," (3) suppress negative feelings, and (4) be "as rational as possible" while doing all that (Argyris, 1991, p. 9; Argyris, 1994, p. 81). He concludes that the purpose of this strategy is to "avoid vulnerability, risk, embarrassment, and the appearance of incompetence" (Argyris, 1994, p. 80). The outcome of the strategy leaves very little room for being with other people intimately.

I believe that it is beneficial to go even deeper than a fear of failure. After reading Professor Argyris's work, I examined his theories using myself as a guinea pig. I saw that although I received good grades in my undergraduate studies and in law school, I was certain that those grades were serendipitous, a fluke that could disappear at any time. I began to consider that underneath every "Smart Person" is someone who is afraid of being found out as an "Imposter." I am not saying that the person *is* an imposter, but rather, the person *fears* that he or she is an *Imposter*—not really good enough to get the job done and about to be discovered as a sham or fraud.

I believe that people share a universal concern that sounds like, "I am faking it and today is the day 'they' are going to figure out that I do not know what I am doing." (Of course, this is coupled with a belief that the rest of the world *does* know what they are doing and that I will soon be shunned and abandoned for my deficiencies.) Safety and avoidance lie down the path of doing that which we already know how to do and foregoing any new ventures that could increase the risk of the internal *Imposter* being found out.

I tracked the *Imposter* into the life of Vaclav Havel, Czechoslovakia's president in 1990. In his acceptance speech after being awarded an honorary degree from Hebrew University in Jerusalem, he stated,

> This is far from the first honorary doctorate I have received, but I accept it with the same sensation I always do: deep shame. Because of my rather sporadic education, I suffer from feelings of unworthiness, and so I accept this degree as a strange gift, a continuing source of bewilderment. I can easily imagine a familiar-looking gentleman appearing at any moment, snatching the diploma from my hands, taking me by the scruff of my neck, and throwing me out of the hall because it's all been just a mistake compounded by my own audacity. (Havel, 1990)

Though Havel attributed his feeling of unworthiness to a sporadic education, people swimming in academic degrees often know that having those degrees does not necessarily make one feel competent or good enough to get the job done. The source of his sense of unworthiness appears to be a universal component of humanity that each of us does his or her best to keep hidden. What makes the sense of inadequacy, of being an *Imposter*, so dominating and overwhelming is the notion that it is unique to oneself alone; thus, the drive to hide the truth.

In hiding such "flaws," we distance ourselves from each other in fear, and in a reactionary fashion attribute blame to others so we will not be found out and left behind. It is often so much easier to just dominate a conversation, especially with someone you have total control over, like a student, than to engage in an interaction where you might not have it right.

Of course, the adult is not the only one with an internal Imposter running things. Consider the research discussed in Chapters 2 and 3: Students are driven to be "cool" and to fit in and are terrified that the opposite is the case.

They will turn on others, or stand by and let someone else be mercilessly bullied, rather than expose their own internal "geekiness."

The Personal Awareness Paradox

"Until a thing becomes what it is, it cannot change." Implied in that adage is that once we discover where we have been stopped or stuck, we can do something about it. Paradoxically, it is only when one embraces the *Imposter* within that one is granted any semblance of freedom from its grip. Senge (1990) addresses this paradox: "People with a high level of personal mastery are acutely aware of their ignorance, their incompetence, their growth areas. And they are deeply self-confident" (p. 142).

In 1995, Elizabeth Steinberger interviewed Margaret Wheatley on leadership change for *The School Administrator*. In the interview, Wheatley sums up what it will take for school leaders to let go of the defensive reasoning that blames others and shirks responsibility.

> On a personal level, it's a process of going from a clear sense of who I am, to letting in information that threatens me, to realizing the information is so important and so big that I can't stay the same and deal with it. It means going through a period of falling apart and letting go so that I can re-create myself to work better and fit better into the environment that has pressured me to change. (p. 20)

This "environment that pressures me to change" can be self-generated by the creation of a vision so big it cannot be fulfilled with us remaining as we are. We are called to change by our own commitment to what we say is worthy of our lives. We are empowered to move past the dominance of the *Imposter* and to put ourselves at risk for all that we can be.

The Questing Person

Are there only two aspects to a person—"Smart Person" and "Imposter"? No. We have all experienced another aspect of personhood. In my model, I call that aspect the "Questing Person." This person has a deep desire to make a difference, wants to reach out and impact the world in a positive way, and is eager to explore and risk. The questing aspect of being human is beautifully captured by George Bernard Shaw:

> This is true joy in life, the being used for a purpose recognized by yourself as a mighty one . . . the being a force of Nature instead of a feverish little clod of ailments and grievances complaining that the world will not devote itself to making you happy. (Shaw, 1903, p. 29)

> I am of the opinion that my life belongs to the whole community and as long as I live it is my privilege to do for it whatever I can. (Shaw, n.d.)

> I want to be thoroughly used up when I die, for the harder I work the more I live. I rejoice in life for its own sake. Life is no "brief candle" to me. It is a sort of splendid torch which I have got hold of for the

moment and I want to make it burn as brightly as possible before handing it on to future generations. (Shaw, n.d.)

People fluctuate in and out of their "Smart," "Imposter," and "Questing" aspects. We call all three together the *Whole Person*. These aspects never go away. Notice the chatter when your *Imposter* is talking. The model helps you know what is going on internally with yourself and others when you are interacting. This awareness will allow you to take responsibility for the inner dynamics of being human and have your commitment to being a Partner win out over any reactivity generated by your Imposter aspect.

The power of this model is that we are talking about fear and normalizing that emotion in all of us—particularly in our work and academic lives. The goal is not to erase fear, but rather, to bring a heightened awareness to the phenomenon of fear impacting people's thinking, listening, speaking, and actions.

Figure 7.5 Aspects of a Person

"SMART" PERSON

- Someone whose sense of self is highly invested in what he or she does
- Wants to be perceived by others as doing a good job
- Wants to be respected

"IMPOSTER"

- Afraid of being a fraud
- "Is today the day they'll find out I don't know what I'm doing"?
- Has a vocalizing instrument that some call the "constant critic"

"QUESTING" PERSON

- Has a deep desire to make a difference
- Wants to reach out and impact the world in a positive way
- Is eager to explore and risk

BEING A PARTNER: SHARED VISION

In a Fall 2005 policy brief to the community titled *Culture and Climate*, Superintendent Greg Firn of Milford Community Schools in Connecticut lays out his rationale for action, including comprehensive bullying and harassment training for the whole school community.

ℳ   **Figure 7.6** McGrath "Whole Persons" Model   *ℳ*

The case has been made for every person who has the ability to impact one of our students to inspire our children to achieve. Whether in the classroom, on a ball field, or at home, our children need to understand they must motivate themselves—and why. (Firn, 2005, p. 4)

After you have turned inward to embrace whom you are being, you are now in a place to start being a Partner in growing and developing your students in their own sense of self and assisting them in creating a vision for their future. Start by asking the student, *Who are you going to be as a person?*

- Are you going to be someone who hurts?
- Are you going to be someone who helps?
- Are you going to be someone who loves?
- This is always your choice—no matter what!

Train students to choose and to recognize that they are choosing. Any choice is fine. Just know that different choices give different futures. With every choice, you are shaping yourself (and life) for your entire life.

Remember Johnny from the Preface; he did not know how to be friends with Tim anymore. He said it was "hopeless." Then he came up with completing 10 acts of kindness. He invented and created his future. He did not come up with "no candy" as a punishment. He grew himself into the future he wanted—acts of kindness—and his mother became his partner in this shared vision.

The practice of shared vision involves the skills of unearthing shared "pictures of the future" that foster genuine commitment and enrollment rather than compliance. In mastering this discipline, leaders learn the counterproductiveness of trying to dictate a vision, no matter how heartfelt (Senge, 1990, p. 9).

Superintendent Firn concurs:

> The way a person behaves in our community greatly impacts teaching and learning in the . . . School System. Whether someone feels accountable for what he/she does—both in and out of school— impacts many other areas of one's life. How someone views the world and the people around them also impacts the climate found in our community. How people talk to each other and the degree to which they communicate is also vital to true community awareness across the board. These are all issues that must be discussed and brought to the forefront in order for real reform to occur. . . . The community expects a school system that offers safe, clean, and well-maintained facilities, filled with students and staff who proceed on a basis of trust and respect. (Firn, 2005, pp. 1, 5)

THE SOCIOPATH NEXT DOOR: A NOTABLE EXCEPTION

> *Minds differ still more than faces.*
>
> —Voltaire

Although most children are amenable to such growth, there are some who are not. They are the sociopaths among us. We are accustomed to think of sociopaths as violent criminals, but in *The Sociopath Next Door,* Harvard psychologist Martha Stout (2005) reveals that a shocking 4% of ordinary people— 1 in 25—have an often-undetected mental disorder, the chief symptom of which is that the person possesses no conscience. He or she has no ability whatsoever to feel shame, guilt, or remorse. These people can do literally anything at all and feel absolutely no guilt.

How do we recognize the remorseless? Most of the time, it is impossible. Except for the psychopathic monsters whom we sometimes see on television, whose actions are too horrific to explain away, conscienceless people are nearly always invisible to us (Stout, 2005). One of their chief characteristics is a kind of glow, or charisma, that makes sociopaths more charming or interesting than the other people around them. They are more spontaneous, more intense, more complex, or even sexier than everyone else, making them difficult to identify and leaving us easily seduced. Fundamentally, sociopaths are different because they cannot love. Sociopaths learn early on to show sham emotion, but underneath they are indifferent to others' suffering. They live to dominate and thrill to win.

For the most part, people whom we assess as evil tend to see nothing at all wrong with their way of being in the world. Sociopaths are infamous for their refusal to acknowledge responsibility for the decisions they make, or for the outcomes of their decisions.

> Instead, when confronted with a destructive outcome that is clearly their doing, they will simply say, "I never did that," and will, to all appearances, believe their own direct lie. This feature of sociopathy makes self-awareness impossible, and in the end, just as the sociopath has no genuine relationships with other people, he has only a very tenuous one with himself. (Stout, 2005, pp. 49–50)

The good news is that when a bullying incident takes place, you do not have to diagnose the child to determine appropriate action. If the child is conscienceless, the actions you take may make no difference, but you have discipline options to pursue in those cases. The McGrath FICA Standard is still your tool for analyzing these situations; it just might not lead to the desired level of growth or relationship with this type of student.

Most everyone is afraid of being found out about something or other, but most people are not sociopaths. Take care not to paint the Imposter, that niggling aspect of each of us, with the same brush as the *sociopath*. Where sociopaths are concerned, you are striking at the heart of bullying by distinguishing two different groups of people. There are the sociopaths who bully with no remorse, and then there is everyone else who goes along with it. Sociopaths are leaders; among children, they will get others to do their dirty work willingly. Kids are susceptible to following a leader who makes them feel superior to others—even if it entails putting those others down. It is essential for the school administrator to become a more attractive leader than the sociopathic student and to inspire the followers to return to who they are.

Fundamentally, the remaining 96% are good people. Sometimes their Smart Person takes over, trying to win and stay in control at all costs. Sometimes their Imposter runs the show, afraid that the crowd will think they are a "geek" and turn on them next. But young people are also Questing people. They want to make a difference and do what is right. Your job is to bring out the Questing Person in your students.

NO MATTER HOW MEAN THE STREETS

No matter how mean the streets, students have a choice. My own story is a victory over a terrifying and brutal past. The child of violent, abusive, alcoholic parents, I was homeless at age 17. By 18, I had a baby. One day, I had a conversation with Mr. Costner, a personal friend who was a high school principal. He told me, "You can be anything you want to be, but you can't be a runaround teen *and* a quality mother. Choose! Give your baby up for adoption or be her mother." That day I chose to be Adrianne's mother. I also started listening to the leaders around me rather than tuning in exclusively to my own internal dialogue. In partnership with these people, I began to invent choices for myself that were beyond survival. Eventually, that homeless teen became a lawyer. After nearly 30 years of practicing law, I am writing this book on legal strategies for educators. All these years later, I am still choosing my life and, in so doing, inventing my future. That was the gift that Mr. Costner, a principal, gave me.

When another recognizes you, that recognition draws the dimension of Being more fully into this world through both of you. That is the love that redeems the world.

—Eckhart Tolle, *A New Earth: Awakening to Your Life's Purpose* (2005)

YOU CAN SUCCEED

The McGrath SUCCEED System in its truest form is about facilitating love and life. There is a fantastic quote at the beginning of this book from newly elected President Michelle Bachelet of Chile. She went from torture victim to pediatric surgeon to president:

> Violence entered my life, destroying that which I loved. Because I was a victim of hatred, I dedicated my life to turn this hatred into understanding, into tolerance, and, why not say it, into love . . . You can love justice and be generous at the same time. ("Change and healing in Chile," 2006)

The McGrath SUCCEED System embodies that philosophy—loving justice while being generous at the same time. We are being generous when we stand for children's greatness and maintain our belief that if they do engage in bullying behavior or bystander complacency, this behavior runs counter to who they really are. SUCCEED in its truest form is meant to return people to who they are by removing them from the grip of the *Imposter*. In an environment of trust, respect, understanding, and growth, people have the capacity and the motivation to self-correct. If adults throughout the school consistently respond with the SUCCEED System tools, the culture will shift.

If we can reach the majority of children, and we reach them by using the McGrath FICA Standard and its principles in everything we do with them, something very powerful will start to happen. We have seen the power of the SUCCEED System in our work with administrators in U.S. schools for over 25 years. Now it is time to bring this power to the children they supervise and teach.

Rather than work on the organization at the highest level—having the organization adopt a different process or change itself completely—SUCCEED actually works from the lowest common denominator. It works on the individual's thinking.

In *Presence: An Exploration of Profound Change in People, Organizations, and Society,* Senge and colleagues (2005) maintain that the entirety of the whole is contained within the smallest unit. "A part, in turn, was a manifestation of the whole, rather than just a component of it" (p. 6). In *The Spiritual Dimension of Leadership,* Paul Houston and Stephen Sokolow extrapolate: "Instead of the whole being the sum of its parts, it exists within any of its parts. In fact, each and every point in the hologram can be used to create the whole picture" (Houston & Sokolow, 2006, p. 104).

The hologram is a useful metaphor for thinking about the potential of people in an organization.

> If you think about each person having the inherent qualities that you would like to see in your organization as a whole, that view can trigger an appreciation for every person's value, contribution, and impact on the totality. All you need to do is think of each person as a point in a hologram, which has the capacity to depict the organization as a whole. (Houston & Sokolow, 2006, p. 105)

If the entirety of the organization is in the smallest unit, then the whole exists in the individual's thinking. With the SUCCEED System, as we work on the individual's thinking, we are working on the whole organization.

Senge (1990) says that vision spreads because of a reinforcing process. SUCCEED is such a reinforcing process. So in every thought, every way we listen to another person, every way we speak, and in every action we take, we are consciously reinforcing the vision. And I am not providing SUCCEED on a "drop in when you need a moral lift" basis. I want people to operate from the profound realization that every thought they are thinking, when they are thinking consciously, is shaping not only their world as they say it will be, but also life itself.

Stephanie Pace Marshall (2006) phrases this beautifully in *The Power to Transform: Leadership That Brings Learning and Schooling to Life* when she says,

> Integral minds connect the fullness of our learning potentials. They integrate our multiple capacities for learning to know, do, be, and live together. They seek wholeness, notice patterns of relationships, and possess a connected sense of self and other. They are awake, holistic, full of wonder, and wise, and their vibrancy and wisdom come from their creative engagement with life. Integral minds navigate the landscapes of objective and relational knowing, scientific and indigenous knowing, and empirical and experiential knowing. They synthesize, fluidly weaving webs of connection between seemingly disparate concepts and perspectives. (p. 64)

LEAD WITH YOUR HEART

We cannot bully children into not bullying. We need to create an environment that calls for something different. And the children are watching. What will make a difference is all members of the school community modeling the kind of communication they want to see in the students. Trust, respect, understanding, and growth must be present both in the way that adults treat students and the way that adults treat each other.

The only thing that can stop us is fear. There is a simple, but not easy, way to be a driving force for a new possibility: Replace fear with trust, respect, understanding, and growth. Have simple, principled practices that are intended to reach each person's way of thinking and seeing the world, to reach the way we listen to other people, to reach the words we then speak, and to reach the actions we then take.

Just as one goes to the gym and does repetitions to build body muscle, one can use a pattern of trust, respect, understanding, and growth that builds "people-muscle." I was once quoted as saying, "The heart is not wimpy. It is one of the strongest muscles in the body." Lead with that tireless heart while using your head.

SUMMARY

This chapter introduced the four principles that are built into the McGrath FICA Standard and that give it its power to transform people and organizations. Four lenses were then described through which to examine your work product and develop your competency with the McGrath FICA Standard: structure, quality, tone, and balance. You can choose to make SUCCEED a skill, a craft, or an art form.

Then SUCCEED was discussed as a transformational approach to bullying. Inside this discussion, the focus was on who you are for your students and what it takes to be a partner. The McGrath FICA was distinguished as a tool for self-reflection, increasing personal awareness, and identifying reactivity. An overview was presented of current thinking regarding sociopaths, their prevalence among the population, and the lack of conscience that leaves them less amenable to intervention. Finally, how the SUCCEED System impacts the whole organization by working on the lowest common denominator—the thinking of the individual—was looked at.

In the final two chapters of Part III, legally sound processes and procedures for Level III investigation will be presented in detail. At this Level, a new tool in the McGrath SUCCEED System will be unveiled: the McGrath Template III. This tool includes everything an administrator must attend to when conducting a full-scale investigation of a bullying or harassment matter.

NOTE

1. Ninety-six percent of Academy School District 20 schools were rated High or Excellent on the state School Accountability Reports released December 6, 2005. Rankings are based on the Colorado Student Assessment Program tests that are administered in the spring of each school year. That is the highest percentage of High or Excellent schools in any district, when compared to districts of more than 6,000 students (Boulder, Cherry Creek, District 11, Jefferson County, Douglas County, Littleton, and Poudre).

8

A Legally Sound "To Do" List

Like all other arts, the science of deduction and analysis is one which can only be acquired by long and patient study, nor is life long enough to allow any mortal to attain the highest possible perfection in it. Before turning to those moral and mental aspects of the matter which present the greatest difficulties, let the inquirer begin by mastering more elementary problems.

—Sir Arthur Conan Doyle, *A Study in Scarlet, p. 15*

I t is time to learn a step-by-step approach to handling Level III bullying incidents and complaints, those that require a full investigation and involve:

- harassment or discrimination based on a protected classification;
- illegal or criminal activity;
- a pattern of taunting and harassment over time by the same perpetrator(s) and/or toward the same victim(s); and
- severe, persistent, or pervasive bullying behavior.

This comprehensive Level III approach minimizes the risk of harm to students, the risk of individual liability of school employees, and liability of the school district itself. It uses key pieces of the McGrath SUCCEED System to provide legally sound procedures and practices for complaint intake, management, and investigation.

In Chapters 6 and 7, the day-to-day communication and complaint resolution aspects of the McGrath SUCCEED System were presented. The tools of the system support listening to and communicating with all the constituents involved in bullying situations—students, parents, teachers, staff, community, and others—in order to enlist the entire school community in joining the team committed to eradicating school bullying.

The daily application of the McGrath SUCCEED System for interactions and communications with students, staff, and parents is also designed to transform the context within which bullying thrives, and to lead to actions that effectively resolve the issue at its most basic level. Most importantly, it is designed to grow a healthy culture and facilitate the creation of a school environment of safety, caring, and excellence in education.

THE CONTENT OF BULLYING THROUGH THE LEGAL LENS

When looking at the content of bullying through a legal lens, the four basic questions that were described in Chapter 6 are repeated at Level III, but in much greater depth. The four basic questions address:

1. What happened?

2. What apparent harm did it cause?

3. What is known about anything preceding the event that is contributing to the situation?

4. What immediate action should be taken, if any?

At the Level III investigation stage, the McGrath SUCCEED System adds sub-elements to the four key questions. These sub-elements, extensively described in the next chapter, **assure compliance with the due process and just cause rights of all involved and add a high level of legal security to the actions of the district.** The Level III investigation stage includes:

- identifying actionable bullying and distinguishing it from playful teasing, rough-housing, conflicts, disputes, and other types of interactions among students;
- implementing a uniform, system-wide approach for intake and management of complaints;
- applying legally fit and educationally sound procedures throughout the process;
- creating quality records of the actions taken; and
- Conducting and documenting a Level III investigation step-by-step.

At Level III, the administrative action required has moved well beyond warnings from administrators that some call the standard "knock it off" speech. The matter is now at a stage that can involve great harm to all involved if it is not handled with the utmost of care and expertise.

INITIAL INTAKE OF COMPLAINTS: PRELIMINARY STEPS

The Role of the Complaint Manager

A complaint manager is simply the person at the school site designated and publicized as the person to receive bullying and harassment complaints. In K–12 settings, the school principal often has this role (though sometimes he or she unfortunately does not know it). The complaint manager may receive complaints directly from students or may receive reports from teachers, counselors, and other third parties to whom the student has complained or who have personally observed the conduct. In either case, a prompt assessment must be made of each and every complaint received to determine the appropriate action to be taken.

A problem arises when the principal is publicized as the complaint manager but then hands the task off to an assistant principal who is responsible for the student alleged to have bullied someone. Often that assistant principal has not received the degree of training necessary to conduct a Level III investigation of a bullying or harassment incident. Sometimes he or she has received as little as one hour of training a year on the topic. The assistant principal then proceeds to use standard student discipline approaches in the situation, often using the aforementioned "If I catch you doing anything like this again, you're going to regret it" talk. The assistant principal most often keeps no record of the conversation with the student, or if a record is kept, many school districts have the problematic practice of destroying student discipline records at the end of each school year.

By failing to look up any student discipline records that may exist, either at the current school or where the student attended school before in the district, or by destroying student discipline records at the end of a school year, a pattern of behavior may well be overlooked. It is just such patterns that often form the basis of a lawsuit and a claim that the school district has been deliberately indifferent to the peril of the student. There may also be a claim that the school district negligently supervised students involved in the incident or the locale where the student was bullied. These types of claims are supported by the numerous incidents that may have taken place without the school providing additional intervention or adult supervision in that location.

Processing Incident Reports From Third Parties

When the complaint manager receives the Incident Report Form, check to see whether it is complete. If not, give the form back to the person and ask that it be completed fully. If the staff member is not fluent in English, provide assistance so that the Incident Report Form gets completed.

Once you are satisfied that the Incident Report is complete, the next step is to bring in the student who was the target of the bullying and get his or her statement on a Complaint Form. It is important that you take the complaint directly from the student, not just from a third party.

The complaint form should elicit the following information:

- When did the incident happen?
- Where did it happen?
- Who was involved?
- Describe what happened in as specific, objective, and concrete terms as possible.
- How many times did it happen?
- Who saw it happen?
- What are you requesting to happen?

(See Figure 8.1 on p. 118, sample Complaint Form.)

When a student or employee comes to you with a complaint, have him or her fill out a Complaint Form. Be sensitive, compassionate, and emotionally connected but factually impartial.

If the Complainant Cannot Read and/ or Write English Proficiently

Students, parents, and employees who are not proficient in English or have a disability that limits their ability to read or write need to be accommodated. Arrange for a secretary to take dictation or record what the person has to say and then have it transcribed. You should ask the questions exactly as they are written on the form and have the secretary write down what is said *word for word.*

When the Complaint Form is complete, have the person read it and sign it, or read it back and then have him or her sign it. Read it in short paragraphs and ask after each section, "Would you like to make any changes to that section?" Have the complainant initial each paragraph as you proceed.

You may also provide a translator who can read each question to the person in his or her first language, then give the person time to write the answers. Be sure that your documentation includes the name of any secretary or translator who participates in the complaint process.

Complaint Intake With Very Young Students

Use your judgment regarding whether complainants are too young to fill out their own Complaint Form. Children aged 10 and younger are probably too young. With these students, the complaint manager should ask the questions and fill out the form, then read it back to the student as described above and have the student sign the Complaint Form. Avoid using leading

Figure 8.1 Complaint of Alleged Bullying or Illegal Harassment

Complainant's Name: _____ Date: _____

Address: _____
               Street   City   Zip Code

Home Telephone Number: _____

Any other number where you can be reached during the day: _____

I wish to complain against: _____
                                        Name(s) of person(s)

Address or location* of person(s): _____

(*Location may include a specific class, school building, department, residence hall, etc.)

What alleged bullying or illegal harassment action was taken against you to cause you to file this complaint? (What happened? Where did it happen? Who was involved? Who witnessed the behavior?) _____

_____

_____

Date(s) of alleged bullying or illegal harassment: _____

What informal steps have you taken to stop the bullying or harassing behavior?

_____

_____

_____

Is there anyone who could provide more information regarding this complaint? Please list names, addresses, and telephone numbers of these people below.

Name   Address   Telephone

_____

_____

Remedy sought: _____

_____

_____

I certify that this information is correct to the best of my knowledge.

_____   _____
Signature of Complainant   Signature of Translator

Please use the back of this page if you need more room to write.

questions when talking with the student or employee. (Leading questions are typically those that can be answered "yes" or "no" and those that suggest what the answer should be.)

Informing the Parents

The most prudent practice is to inform the parents before interviewing a student. Parents often are angered when their child has been questioned without their knowledge, especially if it is by someone with whom they are unfamiliar—a central office employee or someone from another school site, for example. Unless the student comes straight to you with the complaint, it is possible to notify the parents even before the Complaint Form is completed. Minors have no right to privacy in this regard, not even if they have approached a school counselor.

Should You Audiotape the Child's Answers?

When later confronted in a meeting or discipline hearing, children (and adults as well) often say, "I didn't say that." Therefore, it is a good idea to audiotape the conversation. Ask the child's permission, and be sure to record his or her response authorizing the audiotape on the tape itself. It is doubly important to be cautious about your questioning techniques when an audio (or video) record is made of the session. At this stage, ask only the questions set out on the Complaint Form. In lawsuits, it is often claimed that the way in which the complaint was investigated was faulty. An audiotape provides more information to validate what was said but also more information with which to criticize the process used.

Completing the Conversation With the Complainant

Give the complainant an information packet. The packet should include:

- a one-page sheet detailing timelines and procedures used to process complaints taken from your policies, and
- a copy of the complaint procedures from your student bullying and harassment policies.

Don't Be Afraid of Documentation

Administrators often comment that they avoid putting complaints in writing to keep the process "informal." Putting the complaint in writing does not automatically mean that you must now resolve it "formally." The written nature of a complaint does not make it formal. Formal and informal procedures are a matter of individual school board policy. Understand the school district policy regarding the processing of complaints and follow it as it is written.

From a legal standpoint, it is highly problematic to have "oral" complaints for which you have never recorded the substance of the complaint and its

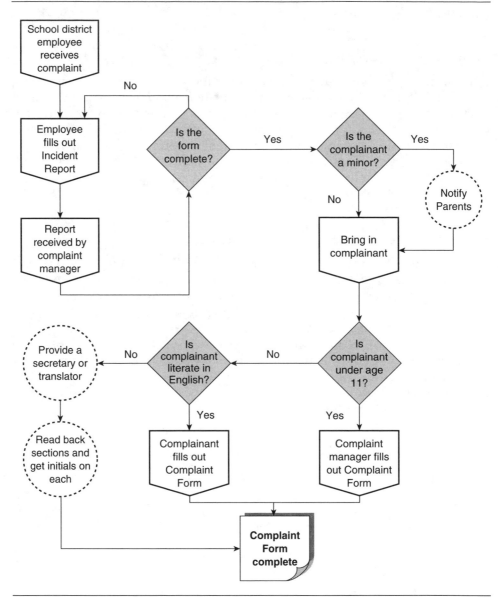

Figure 8.2 Initial Processing of Complaint

disposition in writing. If your policy does not allow for documenting all complaints, consider changing it.

Figure 8.2 is a decision tree outlining the initial processing of a complaint, for easy reference.

Deciding Who Investigates

Once the student has completed a Complaint Form and left the office, there is a critical juncture in proper management of the incident. It must be decided who should investigate the situation. One of the key concerns is whether a conflict of interest exists. A conflict exists when a person has a duty to more than one person or organization and therefore cannot do justice to the potentially conflicting interests of both parties.

Of most importance is an impartial, unbiased investigation. A conflict of interest would thwart that goal. Equally important is even the appearance of a conflict of interest. Is the accused a best friend of the daughter of the investigator? Does the investigator play golf with the complainant's father? Situations like these lend themselves to someone saying there is a conflict of interest.

If there is a conflict, or even the appearance of a conflict, hand the investigation off to someone else—another local site administrator or someone from another school site. If none of the above conditions is present, the complaint manager may proceed with the investigation.

Figure 8.3 is a flowchart for determining who investigates.

Figure 8.3 Determining Who Investigates

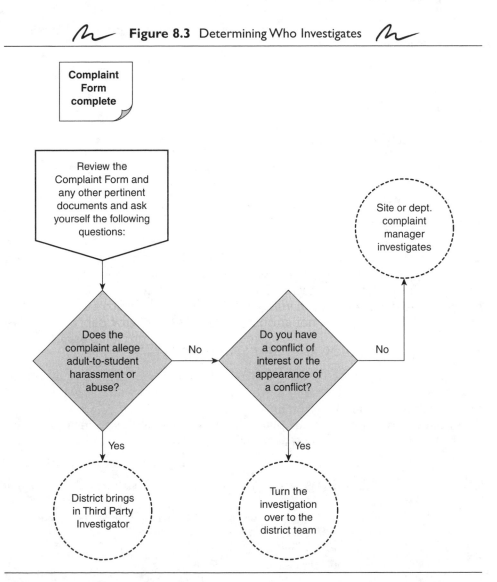

Handing Off a Complaint to an Investigator

In those rare instances in which you determine that it is necessary to hand off a complaint to another investigator, follow the guidelines in Figure 8.4.

/h—   **Figure 8.4** Handing Off a Complaint to an Investigator   */h—*

❑   Bring the investigator in quickly. Make contact within 24 hours.

❑   Document what you have done so far and keep copies of all notes and reports that you turn over to the investigator.

❑   Determine whether you will "stay in the loop." In most cases, the principal or assistant principal who received the complaint will be the logical liaison between the investigator and the complainant, the accused, and their parents.

❑   Document the name of the person who will serve in this "community contact" role, whether it is you or another responsible person.

❑   Schedule the date you expect to receive the first progress report from the investigator.

❑   Ensure that the investigation is moving forward.

❑   Always schedule the next progress report date and hold the investigator to that date or agree to an extension.

FIRST THINGS FIRST: EIGHT PRELIMINARY CONSIDERATIONS

The complaint manager has determined that it is appropriate to proceed personally with the investigation. There are eight preliminary considerations to address as the investigation gets underway. These considerations set the stage for a legally sound investigation (see Figure 8.5, p. 124).

1. Take Action on the Complaint Within 24 Hours

Prompt response is a cardinal rule of complaint management and investigation. Act immediately, even if it is to enter into your calendar when you will take your next action. Be ready to say, "Here is our schedule." Check the district policy to be sure that your plan is within the policy's specifications, and begin the investigation as soon as possible.

Look at the Complaint Form and ask yourself:

- Based on the information at hand, will this be a formal or informal resolution?
- What information is needed to make such a decision?
- Are the facts disputed or undisputed?
- Is it likely that others have been affected?

Unless you have already talked to the accused, you probably don't know whether the facts are disputed or not. Even if the facts are undisputed, investigate further to determine whether other parties are experiencing bullying or harassment by the accused or whether the environment is hostile or intimidating to others.

In creating the plan for conducting the investigation, be prepared to be flexible. People may not be available. Things will probably take longer than you think.

2. If Sexual Harassment Is Suspected, Use Two Investigators

Be sure that whoever investigates is trained to investigate, not just trained to do complaint intake. An investigation team of at least two investigators is preferable for sexual harassment matters. Why? Sometimes people have hidden biases of which they are unaware. Having a partner adds another perspective and keeps things balanced.

The other reason to have two investigators concerns gender. Having a mixed-gender team gives you flexibility and allows you to be gender sensitive. Ask the person being interviewed whether he or she is more comfortable with a male or a female. Do not assume that you know how he or she will respond. It varies. If you use a two-member investigation team, it is perfectly fine to divide the interviews between you. Both investigators do not need to take part in the same interview, except in very rare circumstances. Those rare circumstances would include any threat of violence toward the investigator. Also, if violence is feared, you may want to have a school security officer available nearby.

3. Create a Confidential File

There is a lot to this seemingly simple statement. As the investigation proceeds, you will be dealing with confidential material that may be of interest to people. This can range from nosy employees wanting to take a peek at the "juicy stuff" to someone snooping around for information to give to a plaintiff in a lawsuit. (This may sound a bit paranoid, but better safe than sorry.)

While investigating, keep the file in your possession. Do not assume that your administrative assistant is immune from taking a look, especially if it involves someone to whom he or she is related or a family friend. You should create a file that is not accessed by any person other than yourself, or your partner if there is a second investigator. The office filing cabinet is probably not a secure place to store the file. Many investigators keep the file locked in

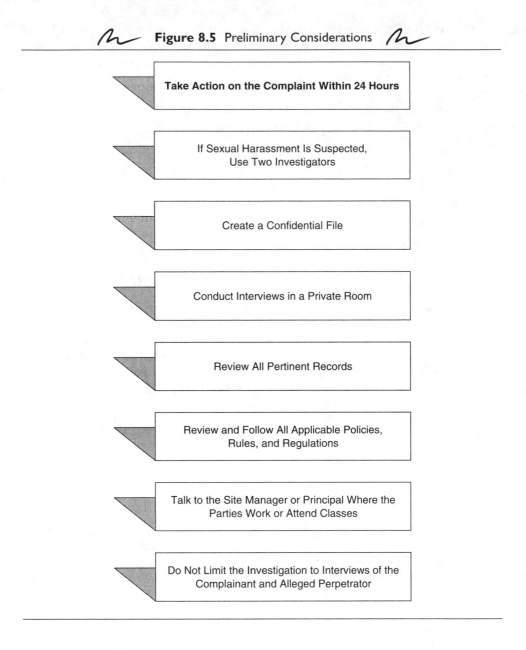

Figure 8.5 Preliminary Considerations

- Take Action on the Complaint Within 24 Hours
- If Sexual Harassment Is Suspected, Use Two Investigators
- Create a Confidential File
- Conduct Interviews in a Private Room
- Review All Pertinent Records
- Review and Follow All Applicable Policies, Rules, and Regulations
- Talk to the Site Manager or Principal Where the Parties Work or Attend Classes
- Do Not Limit the Investigation to Interviews of the Complainant and Alleged Perpetrator

the trunk of their car when they are away from their office or not reviewing the contents.

4. Conduct Interviews in a Private Room

It is very important to conduct all interviews in a private room. People seldom think through the nuances of privacy completely and they often end up making inadvisable choices.

Privacy means:

- all windows or glass partitions are covered or opaque;
- there is a separate entrance for the room and witnesses don't have to walk down a hallway or through a lobby, classroom, workspace, or conference room to get there;
- the location is out of the mainstream of traffic, where people can come and go without being seen;
- if people will be arriving by car, parking is unobtrusive; and
- the interview is as confidential and private as possible.

5. Review All Pertinent Records

When investigating alleged student misconduct:

- review the student's discipline and cumulative records for prior complaints, and
- determine whether the students have received bullying and harassment awareness or sexual harassment awareness training.

When investigating alleged employee misconduct towards students,

- review the employee's personnel file,
- review all relevant inservice attendance records, and
- determine whether there have been prior complaints.

The other two places to check are (1) your district's central repository for complaints and (2) records from the student's prior school site(s). If this step is neglected, indicators of a pattern of conduct that took place in prior years or in other settings may be missed.

6. Review and Follow All Applicable
Policies, Rules, and Regulations

Before taking action, review all applicable board policies and regulations, as well as the student Code of Conduct and discipline policy. Make sure that your copies are current and include the latest revisions.

Do not assume that you will remember the policy or regulation correctly. No matter how many cases you have investigated, you should always start by reading all policies again. Then follow them.

Relying on your memory can literally cost you in court. In an actual case, a human resources director called the school's legal counsel and said, "I need you to do an investigation of this matter." The attorney went out to the site immediately and began investigating. Neither one of them pulled out the policy that said, right at the top, "Informal resolution shall be attempted." This information was not presented to the complaining party, either.

The accused complained that she wasn't given an opportunity for informal resolution because the administration wanted to "get" her. She was sure that no one liked her, and this mistake fed right into her "conspiracy theory." All of this could have been avoided if the human resources director (or the attorney) had simply reviewed the policy before proceeding.

7. Talk to the Teachers With Whom the Parties Attend Classes

Have a conversation with the students' teachers, bus drivers, or other employees with whom the parties involved come in contact. Go to the location where the alleged bullying or harassment took place and be mindful of the following:

> - Do not go to the employee if that person is implicated in the bullying.
> - Do not go to the employee if you know that the person may have a conflict of interest.

Warn the teacher that this is an official investigation and the conversation must be kept confidential. Should he or she fail to maintain confidentiality and leak the information that an investigation is in progress, the employee may be held responsible and even be disciplined for any retaliatory conduct against the student or anyone else that ensues.

8. Do Not Limit the Investigation to Interviews of the Complainant and Alleged Perpetrator

Always look beyond what appears to be an isolated incident or situation. Look beyond the facts as presented by the complainant and alleged perpetrator, even if they are undisputed.

Figure 8.6 describes four situations in which it is critical that witnesses be interviewed.

Figure 8.6 Witness Must Be Interviewed When . . .

1. The facts are disputed and cannot be resolved simply by speaking with the two parties.

2. The complaint alleges a pattern of bullying that has gone on over an extensive amount of time and may even involve more than one school site.

3. Multiple victims or multiple perpetrators are involved.

4. Allegations have been made that may impact other people besides the complainant (e.g., child sexual abuse or hostile environment sexual harassment).

INFORMAL VERSUS FORMAL RESOLUTION

There is no universally applicable definition of "formal" or "informal" resolution of a complaint, nor are the terms "formal" and "informal" defined by law. Yet these terms are used frequently in regard to complaints and disputes in district policies.

You must carefully read your own district policies to determine how the school district is using these terms. The following is a general discussion of this ambiguous arena of formal/informal complaint management. Please keep your own district's interpretation of the terms in mind as you read.

A Working Definition of "Informal"

The American Heritage Dictionary defines informal as "not being in accord with prescribed regulations or forms; unofficial; being more appropriate for use in the spoken language than in the written language."

"Informal" as defined this way could be problematic for two reasons: Whichever mode of resolution you use, "formal" or "informal," it must always be "within prescribed regulations," and it is ill-advised to resolve complaints with "spoken language" only.

For purposes of this discussion, an "informal" situation is therefore defined as a situation that includes *all* of the following criteria:

- The complainant and the accused have agreed to "talk it out" and are satisfied with the result OR an administrator uses the incident as a "teachable moment" to educate the accused in appropriate behavior.
- The facts are undisputed.
- No discipline or sanctions are administered to the accused.
- The complainant is clear about his or her right to file a "formal" complaint and declines.
- The process does not move beyond the "inquiry" level into a full-blown investigation.

"Talking It Out"

In conflict situations, it is sometimes beneficial to resolve the matter with some form of mediation or "talking it out" between the victim and the perpetrator. A bullying situation is different. Bullying is considered abuse, not conflict. Mediation or face-to-face talks are not recommended (see U.S. Department of Health and Human Services, 2004). A victim of bullying has a right to *not* confront the perpetrator. The student who has been bullied already often feels powerless in relation to the perpetrator. *Again, bullying is an abusive act; it is not a conflict between two students of equal power.*

You should never push, coerce, manipulate, force, or entice the complainant into mediation. If you present it as an option, do so in an unbiased fashion and reiterate the complainant's right not to confront the harasser.

If the complainant insists on confronting the accused, have the complainant sign a statement acknowledging that he or she understands his or her rights and is voluntarily participating in the mediation process. This does not mean that the complainant is waiving the right to formal resolution. If at any time the complainant says, "I want to file a formal complaint" or "I want this handled through formal procedures," that takes priority. Formal procedures should be initiated immediately.

If mediation does take place, be certain that a trained school official facilitates the discussion. *Do not* use student mediators in bullying or harassment cases. Note that the *alleged perpetrator does not have a right to decline* to face his or her accuser. However, given the temperament of most perpetrators, they are unlikely to object to a confrontation, welcoming the opportunity for another go at the victim.

Anonymity

If a complainant asks to remain anonymous, let him or her know that this severely limits your ability to handle the complaint. Little questioning can be done without giving indications to others of who the alleged victim is in the incident. The ability to impose discipline is also greatly hampered, as well as the ability to remediate the behavior. The alleged perpetrator is simply going to ask, "Who said I did this and when?" If you cannot give him or her these details, then he or she is going to deny the accusation. If you do give the perpetrator the details about what happened but withhold the name, he or she will more than likely figure out the accuser's identity from those details. Attempt to persuade the complainant to allow the use of his or her name, with the reassurance that all reasonable efforts will be made to safeguard the complainant from retaliation.

Also assure the complainant that this information will only be given out on a "need to know" basis. Perhaps this encouragement will reassure the complainant enough that he or she will agree to be named. *However, if the person insists on anonymity, you still have an obligation to investigate to the best of your ability.*

Informal Does Not Mean Unwritten

Informal does not mean:

- casual
- unaccountable
- superficial
- unimportant
- off the record
- undocumented

If a written record of the complaint and how it was resolved is not kept, it will be difficult to establish the actions taken by the school should a dispute or litigation come about. There would be no tangible evidence that action was taken.

Unless expressly prohibited in district policy, document every complaint. If the district policy prohibits documenting "informal" complaints and their disposition, point out the problem to someone who is in a position to change the policy. Remember, written documentation is the best means of detecting patterns of harassment or abuse. Without it, the welfare of the students is at risk.

WHAT IS AN INQUIRY?

When a situation meets the previously established criteria for "informal" resolution, it is best to call the examination of the matter an Inquiry. An Inquiry (as opposed to a full-blown investigation) is limited in scope and fits the criteria for a Level II response, as detailed in Chapter 6. You have completed an Inquiry when, after interviewing both parties, you are clear that the facts are not in dispute. This would only be the case for very low-level matters in which no one's physical safety is jeopardized and repeated behavior is not alleged.

When witnesses and tangible evidence enter into the picture, the line of a Level III Investigation is crossed. An investigation is also required when a complainant requests a "formal" process. Investigation requires a trained investigator.

The U.S. Department of Education Office for Civil Rights (OCR) has this to say regarding the need to investigate "informal" complaints:

> In University of Maine at Machias, OCR Case No. 01–94–6001, OCR found the school's procedures to be inadequate because only formal complaints were investigated. While a school isn't required to have an established procedure for resolving informal complaints, they nevertheless must be addressed in some way. However, if there are indications that the same individual may be harassing others, then it may not be appropriate to resolve an informal complaint without taking steps to address the entire situation. (OCR, 2001, p. 38)

Cautionary note: The OCR stated in January 2006 that OCR cases are fact specific and do not constitute the official position or policy of the OCR on any particular matter (Monroe, 2006).

An Example of a Level II Matter

Susie, a high school sophomore, complains that during auto shop class, Billy, a 15-year-old student, yelled across the room, "Hey, Susie, would you pick up my *nut?*" with clear sexual connotations. She is requesting that you, the principal at Billy's school, "talk to Billy and tell him to knock it off."

Since you are Billy's principal, you don't need to speak with another administrator. There is no record of similar complaints in Billy's cumulative file or in the central repository. Billy's file does reveal that he received bullying and sexual harassment awareness training in health class last year.

You speak with Billy and he does not dispute what he said, so there is no need to interview witnesses. Billy claims that he meant no harm and did not intend his remark to be taken as sexual innuendo.

The Inquiry is now complete. Since this is a one-time incident, you use it as a "teachable moment" and review with Billy the definition and consequences of bullying and sexual harassment at school. You document the incident and the action you took, forward copies of the report to any appropriate parties (according to your district's policies), and let Susie know that the matter has been addressed. You also tell her that if there are any further comments or any other inappropriate behavior, she should let you know immediately.

Knowing that classes that have traditionally been unisex in the past are particularly vulnerable to hostile environment sexual harassment, you schedule a time on your calendar to "drop in" on the shop class to examine the environment further.

When Is Informal Resolution Clearly Inappropriate?

A more involved Level III response is required when the allegations involve:

- employee-to-student sexual harassment, misconduct, or abuse;
- multiple victims, multiple witnesses, and/or multiple harassers;
- threats to the safety of the complainant or others;
- bullying or harassment that has recurred after informal resolution attempts;
- a student who refused to identify the perpetrator of serious conduct; or
- suspected criminal behavior.

Figure 8.7 is a decision tree that outlines the steps for determining whether an Informal Inquiry or Formal Investigation is required.

Innocent Until Proven Guilty

Maintaining the presumption of "innocent until proven guilty" is one of the most difficult aspects of investigation. The first step is to acknowledge to yourself that as a human being you are simply not "wired" to maintain a presumption of innocence. In fact, if you are like most of the over six billion people on our planet, you have a propensity to jump to conclusions very quickly.

Test yourself: Get on a city bus or sit on a park bench. As you observe the people around you, listen to that "little voice in your head" commenting on people's lives, clothing choices, occupations, parenting styles, body piercing, attitudes, and so on. Notice how quickly you judge, evaluate, and even sentence people and how slow you are to question your conclusions.

This is not to say that something is wrong with you. You are fine, but you are human and have the usual human tendencies. Not only that, but most of us were brought up on television courtroom dramas that trained us to "catch the perp" and figure out "who done it" so we could "wrap up the case" in under 60 minutes (minus innumerable commercial breaks). Keep noticing

(Text continues on page 133)

Figure 8.7 Informal Inquiry Versus Formal Investigation

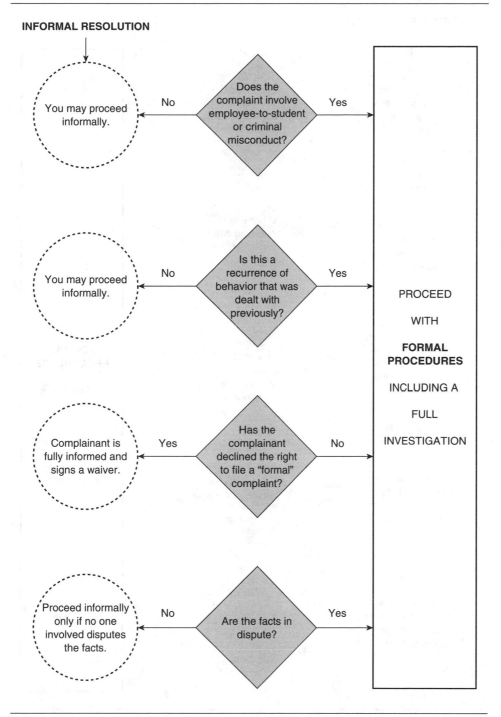

(Continued)

Figure 8.7 (Continued)

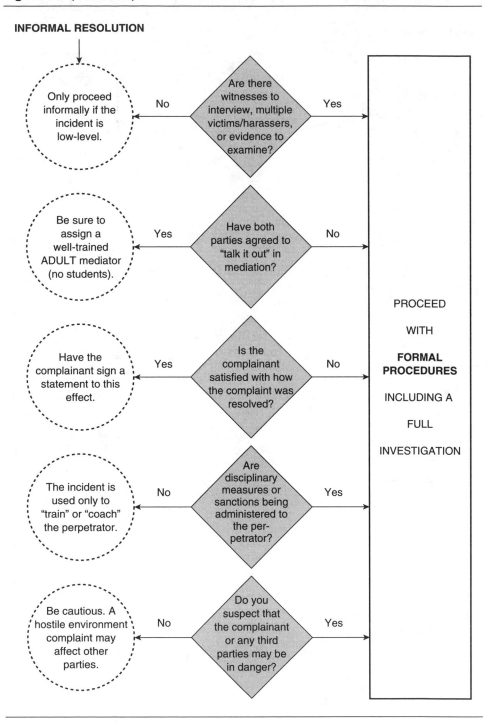

INFORMAL RESOLUTION

Only proceed informally if the incident is low-level.

No — Are there witnesses to interview, multiple victims/harassers, or evidence to examine? — Yes

Be sure to assign a well-trained ADULT mediator (no students).

Yes — Have both parties agreed to "talk it out" in mediation? — No

Have the complainant sign a statement to this effect.

Yes — Is the complainant satisfied with how the complaint was resolved? — No

The incident is used only to "train" or "coach" the perpetrator.

No — Are disciplinary measures or sanctions being administered to the perpetrator? — Yes

Be cautious. A hostile environment complaint may affect other parties.

No — Do you suspect that the complainant or any third parties may be in danger? — Yes

PROCEED WITH **FORMAL PROCEDURES** INCLUDING A FULL INVESTIGATION your prejudgments and let them go. Reality is often much more complex than initial impressions would lead us to believe.

But I Know the Kid Is Guilty

How do you "know" that someone is guilty? Consider that you and I have paradigms inside of which we operate. A paradigm is a decision you have made about some area of life that you assume is the truth, "the way that it is." Only you don't say to yourself, "I assume," you say, "I know." This is now the context or frame of reference from which you view that area of life.

Thomas Kuhn (1996) did his first groundbreaking research on the nature and impact of paradigms in the 1940s. Kuhn and his associates observed scientists as they tested various hypotheses. They found that these men and women would completely ignore physical events or data that did not support the hypotheses at hand. When asked about this, they said they simply had not seen the evidence that Kuhn and his team objectively observed.

Our paradigms blind us to what is in front of us. There is a tendency to ignore findings that might threaten our existing paradigm and trigger the development of a new and competing paradigm. Unless you are vigilant, you may just as easily miss evidence of innocence as of guilt. Ask yourself, Am I *fitting* the evidence and testimony to *my* conclusion? Listen to the evidence and testimony. What does it tell you?

In the long run, maintaining the presumption of innocence will support the most enduring resolution of the situation. Accused students who do not feel the burden of proving their innocence are less likely to resent the process and the outcome. If treated fairly and factually throughout the course of the investigation, accused students who are found to be guilty of misconduct are more likely to be receptive to a final determination that is not in their favor. Parents are also more likely to support the administration's actions as well.

/ʮ⁓   **Figure 8.8** The Ground Rules for Maintaining   /ʮ⁓
a Presumption of Innocence

- Be sensitive without expressing conclusions.

- Act consistently with due process rights.

- Balance your concern for the victim with the rights of the accused.

- Don't become an advocate for any party.

- Be sensitive to issues of gender, culture, language, and disability.

- Whenever possible, work with a partner or an investigation team.

- Keep your opinions private even when the details are personally distasteful.

- If there is a conflict of interest, or the appearance of a conflict, bring in someone else.

SUMMARY

This chapter discussed the necessary protocols, steps, and procedures for conducting a legally sound intake of a bullying or harassment matter, including preliminary steps, the role of the complaint manager, fundamentals of complaint intake, informing the parents, informal versus formal resolution, deciding who investigates, and maintaining the presumption of innocence.

There is a lot to master here, and readers may find the level of detail cumbersome. While it may take a little more time and attention to follow these steps, it is far better to tighten up procedures at the complaint intake level than to "sit in the hot seat" later while your investigation is being called into question by litigators. Get to work making a list of what needs to change. Be diligent now, or pay later.

9

Creating and Following a Game Plan

Level III Investigation

The secret of getting ahead is getting started.

—Agatha Christie

I n this chapter is a step-by-step guide to completing a legally sound Level III investigation. If a situation warrants a full investigation that needs to be beyond reproach, here is the approach that will make the investigation both legally fit and educationally sound. You might feel that this is far beyond what you want to do, but here's the rub. What follows contains the rules of the legal game. If you play by the rules, the likelihood of winning increases. What winning means here is that your investigation not only protects all the legal rights of the parties involved, but also, should you end up in litigation, your work is virtually unassailable. Knowing that, it is worth the effort to follow the instructions.

KNOW THE "PLAYERS"

There are often many people involved in a high-profile matter that warrants a Level III investigation, beyond the alleged victim, perpetrator, and witnesses. Analogizing to a football game, we call the participants "players."

Figure 9.1 is a diagram showing the cast of "players" in a Level III investigation.

Notice that every player has a counterpart on the "opposite" side of the diagram—not unlike a football game with its two opposing teams on the field. In K–12 situations, most of the students involved are minors. Family members, child protective services, law enforcement, and even IEP teams may play a role. Even if the young person is legally an adult, there is no need to follow a different procedure when dealing with a bullying incident in a school-related situation.

If any complaint of bullying or harassment is against an employee, the accused may choose to involve his or her union representative. If criminal conduct is suspected, law enforcement will also be involved. The school district's governing board and legal counsel also play a part in Level III investigations. (See discussion of Level III investigations in Chapter 8.)

Finally, while they may never know that an investigation took place, consider all students and all employees to be players because the entire school community is affected by the decisions made in the matter. Of course, when allegations become public, students and employees are more deeply impacted. The press and the surrounding community may also have a role.

The Complaint Manager's Role

As discussed in Chapter 8, each school in the organization should have a trained complaint manager for addressing student misconduct complaints. Usually the complaint manager is the principal, who in turn delegates the handling of the student matter to an assistant principal. Often schools will assign the students alphabetically to the assistant principals who handle complaints or impose discipline. This practice is acceptable, with one caveat. One person needs to be aware of all complaints so that patterns and trends can be noted. If there is not a central repository at the school site for all complaints, the risk is great that patterns of conduct could be missed or that unsafe locations in the building could remain unidentified.

The Response Team's Role

Review the complaint manager or designee roles and responsibilities in Figure 9.2 (p. 138).

It is preferable that a gender balance exist at the school site among the people assigned to investigations. That way, if a sensitive matter arises that the student is uncomfortable speaking about to one gender, the student can speak with an adult of the opposite gender. Because student misconduct investigations may result in discipline of students or even employees, the investigator should be a management-level employee with training in disciplinary matters and investigations.

Figure 9.1 Players Diagram

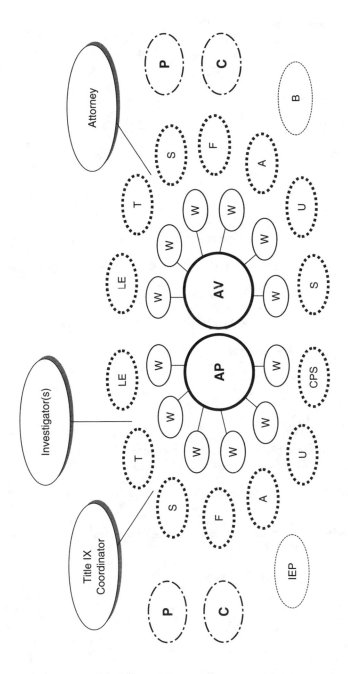

AP = Alleged Perpetrator
B = Board
F = Family Members
LE = Law Enforcement
T = Teachers

AV = Alleged Victim or Grievant
CPS = Child Protective Services
I = Investigator(s)
P = Press
U = Union

A = Administrators
C = Community
IEP = IEP Teams
S = Students
W = Witnesses

Figure 9.2 Response Team Roles—Summary

Complaint Manager

- Trained to address student misconduct techniques

- Needs to be aware of all complaints so that patterns and trends can be noted

Complaint Manager or Designated Investigator

- Initiates the investigation

- Interviews the complainant, alleged perpetrator, and corroborating witnesses

- Collects and records the facts and keeps track of any tangible evidence

- Evaluates the facts

- Prepares a detailed report of the factual findings and other data necessary for a determination

- Is sensitive to the issues and concerns that surround the reporting of bullying and harassment

- Is open-minded and non-judgmental when collecting the facts

- Is skilled in interviewing, often under delicate and emotionally charged circumstances

- Is capable of writing reports that are comprehensive, thorough, and articulate

- Is discreet and able to maintain confidentiality in all matters

Title IX Coordinator

- Conducts school visits to review policies, publications, grievance procedures, and hiring processes for compliance with Title IX

- Is accessible to students, educators, and staff and community members to answer questions about sexual harassment and to intake complaints

- Coordinates or provides for Title IX training (including sexual harassment) for students, staff, educators, and board members

- Stays current on the latest developments, laws, and regulations

The Title IX Coordinator may also

- Investigate complaints

- Compile documentation of complaints and report complaints as well as patterns to designated officials

- Regularly review the district's efforts to prevent harassment and suggest improvements

---

Traits of an Investigator

Review the investigator roles and responsibilities in Figure 9.2.

Level III investigators must have no personal connection with the people under investigation, in order to avoid a conflict of interest. It is vital to avoid any suspicion of bias or even the appearance of a conflict of interest. The investigators should have access to the district's legal counsel and to review reports, files, and confidential documents in student files and even employee files, if relevant. They should report directly to the principal, and, in turn, the principal should report to the superintendent, headmaster, or director on Level III bullying and illegal harassment complaints, regardless of his or her direct supervisor in other matters.

The Title IX Coordinator

Review the Title IX Coordinator's roles and responsibilities in Figure 9.2.

Federal law requires that school districts appoint a "responsible employee" to coordinate the school district's compliance under Title IX. The regulations require that the name, address, and telephone number of the Title IX coordinator be periodically announced in district publications. Title IX includes discrimination based on sex and student sexual harassment, but it has many other applications, all to safeguard against bullying that may amount to illegal harassment and discrimination based on a protected classification.

The Title IX coordinator should receive extensive training in the investigation of bullying, harassment, and abuse complaints. It is helpful for this person to serve as the central repository for student bullying and harassment complaints, in order to spot patterns of recurring conduct by individuals across a variety of locations, classes, or activities.

The Title IX coordinator should be aware of the latest developments, laws, and regulations that govern illegal harassment and discrimination, both federal and state, and may be helpful in answering questions that arise during an investigation of student-to-student allegations. The Title IX coordinator may also be assigned follow-up responsibilities. For example, when a hostile environment or bullying pattern has been proven, he or she may monitor the environment for indicators of improvement or recurrence.

The Role of Counsel

Legal counsel should remain separate from the investigation but be consulted at any stage of the investigation when questions, concerns, or problems arise that the investigator is having difficulty resolving. Legal counsel should not conduct the investigation. One of the main lines of defense in litigation is to attack the investigator. The opposition will challenge the methodology used, decisions made, perceived biases, and so on, of the investigator. It is not beneficial for the attorney representing the district to end up "on trial" while advocating on behalf of the school district and the actions it has taken.

Legal counsel must always be consulted before you discard any records of an investigation. The school district needs these records to provide a paper trail in the event that allegations are later made that a complaint was not adequately investigated or that the school district was deliberately indifferent to the plight of the student. Because state laws differ as to the amount of time a student has to file a lawsuit after attaining the age of majority, counsel should assist in determining whether and when it is appropriate to destroy records of an investigation.

Include All Players in the Game Plan

In planning your investigation, be sure to designate someone to be in communication with each of the identified players. When people feel uninformed, they often seek publicity in an attempt to get information or gain control of the situation. Clear, timely communication will help to minimize community backlash and ensure maximum privacy for all concerned. Using the McGrath FICA Model will assist with all of these communications.

> The following specific questions will help to keep track of who is responsible for communicating with each player:
>
> - Who is the liaison to the parents?
> - Who will deal with the press should the need arise?
> - Who is interfacing (communicating and cooperating) with law enforcement?
> - How will you take care of the community should the allegations become known?

The more serious the allegations, the more players will be involved. Plan ahead. As this chapter progresses, what can and cannot be shared during an investigation will be clarified.

THE FIVE PHASES OF AN INVESTIGATION

The five phases of a Level III Investigation are

Phase One:	Gather the Facts
Phase Two:	Check for Records of Concern
Phase Three:	Evaluate the Testimony and Evidence
Phase Four:	Write the Report
Phase Five:	Follow-Up Actions by School Officials

Phase One: Gather the Facts

There are four parts to the Fact Gathering Phase:

A. Review published documents, policies, laws, and regulations.
B. Review student files and/or cumulative records.
C. Gather testimony.
D. Gather tangible evidence.

A. Review Published Documents, Policies, Laws, and Regulations

The first step is to *always* review:

- policies;
- statutes;
- the Education Code; and
- any other documents delineating rules, regulations, policies, or procedures related to bullying, harassment, or student misconduct complaints in the school district.

Do not presume to know the policies "inside out." Every lawyer and investigator has a horror story about the time an extremely competent, trained, and experienced professional "got it wrong" by trusting his or her memory or not checking for legal updates or revisions. Pay attention to time limits and deadlines and plan your timeline accordingly. Make sure that you are honoring any applicable due process rights of the accused every step of the way.

B. Review Student Files and/or Cumulative Records

Next, review the student files and/or cumulative records of both the complainant and the alleged perpetrator(s).

This review will provide important information about:

- past occurrences,
- concerns,
- remediation measures previously taken, and
- any prior training received.

A thorough student background check includes reviewing attendance, disciplinary, and school counseling records. Also, check the records of any previous schools that the student may have attended within the district. For an employee, check attendance, inservice records, disciplinary records, and other employment records.

A common practice across the country is to destroy student discipline records at the end of a school year. This practice can present extreme difficulties in subsequent litigation. If a perpetrator has a history of violence and the pattern was undetected because prior discipline records were not reviewed or had been destroyed, it can reflect negatively on the school district.

When checking the background of an alleged perpetrator, look for other complaints that may have been filed at the current school or any prior school attended. Also check court records, to the extent possible, to determine whether the alleged perpetrator has a criminal record.

What About Freedom of Information?

The Freedom of Information Act is a federal statute and as such applies only to federal agencies. Each state has its own public access laws that should be consulted for access to state and local records. For example, some state laws provide that personnel records are not discoverable under Freedom of Information. There are states where all records are open. You have to read your particular state's statute in order to be specifically informed on this issue.

FERPA, The Family Educational Rights and Privacy Act of 1974, as amended (also referred to as the Buckley Amendment), is a federal law regarding the privacy of student records and the obligations of an educational institution, primarily in the areas of release of student records and the access provided to these records. Any educational institution that receives funds under any program administered by the U.S. Secretary of Education is bound by FERPA requirements. Institutions that fail to comply with FERPA may have federal funds withheld.

FERPA gives students the following rights: (1) the right to inspect and review education records, (2) the right to seek amendment of education records, (3) the right to consent to disclosure of education records, (4) the right to obtain a copy of the school's Student Records policy, and (5) the right to file a complaint with the FERPA Office in Washington, DC.

The other federal privacy law that may affect schools is the Health Insurance Portability and Accountability Act of 1996 (HIPAA). HIPAA is a set of rules to be followed by doctors, hospitals, and other health care providers, which took effect on April 14, 2003. HIPAA ensures that all medical records, medical billing, and patient accounts meet certain consistent standards with regard to documentation, handling, and privacy. In addition, HIPAA requires that all patients be able to access their own medical records to correct errors or omissions, to be informed of how personal information is shared, and to be notified of privacy procedures to be used.

The Kentucky School Boards Association and Kentucky Department of Education (KSBA) provide this guidance for school districts:

> Under a final rule issued by HHS [U.S. Department of Health and Human Services], health information contained within student educational records that are subject to the Family Educational Rights and Privacy Act ('FERPA') is exempt from the requirements of HIPAA. (See HIPAA, 24 CFR 164.501.) 'Educational record' includes individually identifiable health information of students under the age of 18 created by a nurse in a primary or secondary school receiving federal funds. In addition, medical records that are excepted from FERPA's definition of 'education records' under FERPA section 99.3[1] are also exempted

from coverage by HIPAA. The HHS reasoned that subjecting districts to both FERPA and HIPAA requirements as to these records would be confusing and unduly burdensome.[2] Of course, districts must continue to ensure that these records are received, maintained and transmitted in a manner consistent with FERPA. (KSBA, 2004)

For a current, comprehensive guide to FERPA, HIPAA, and other laws and regulations pertaining to student records, go to http://nces.ed.gov/pub search/pubsinfo.asp?pubid=2004330 and download the *Forum Guide to Protecting the Privacy of Student Information: State and Local Education Agencies*, published by the National Center for Education Statistics (2004).

C. Gather Testimony

During the course of the investigation, interviews will be conducted with the complainant, the accused, and any witnesses to the conduct. Start by planning the interviews.

- Who will be interviewed?
- When?
- Where?
- Who will conduct which interview?

Plan for the unplanned. People are often unavailable. Interviews usually take longer than you think. Fifteen minutes is barely enough time to establish rapport, so do not schedule any interviews shorter than 30 minutes. If your interview room does not have a back door, allow sufficient time between witnesses so that they can come and go without running into each other.

D. Gather Tangible Evidence

Gather tangible evidence quickly. Examples of tangible evidence are:

- Letters
- Torn clothing
- Graffiti
- Damaged property

Do not warn the students in advance of a locker search or a check for physical evidence. It is important to avoid the risk of someone tampering with or discarding evidence. If there is graffiti, it should be photographed and then removed quickly. Establish a protocol for taking photographs to be sure that the photographs capture all angles of the area containing graffiti. Store all evidence in a safe, secure location. Obviously, there are certain types of evidence that will remain in law enforcement custody if a criminal investigation is underway.

Phase Two: Check for Records of Concern

Check the central repository where complaint records are stored to see whether the complainant has filed any prior complaints. Also check with the Security Office to see whether there are any relevant incident reports there. Note how any prior complaints were resolved.

Check also for any prior complaints involving misconduct by the alleged perpetrator. If a record of the current complaint does not already exist, be sure to make a written record. Use an Incident Report Form, and send a copy to the complaint manager and to whoever is the central depository for records of bullying and harassment.

Phase Three: Evaluate the Testimony and Evidence

Using the McGrath Template III, you will be doing a 360-degree evaluation of all the evidence you have gathered. A detailed description of this tool is presented later. (See The McGrath Case and Report Organizer on p. 150.)

Phase Four: Write the Report

Use the McGrath Template III for organization of all Level III investigations and for drafting the final report. The backbone of the McGrath Template III is the McGrath FICA Standard that was discussed in depth in Chapter 6.

The McGrath Template III further elaborates on the logical thinking contained in the McGrath FICA Standard. The McGrath Template III contains all of the components required by law to satisfy due process and just cause standards. They are built into the instrument. The McGrath Template III is designed to guide the user throughout the investigation as information is gathered, and is designed to guide the writing of the Final Report regarding the matter under investigation.

The investigator may not be the district official authorized to make the final decision as to the remedial or disciplinary action to be taken. In most locales, the determination whether a student should be expelled is within the purview of the governing board, based on the recommendation of the school administration. The investigator may make recommendations in the final report, but it is important to be clear on who has the authority to impose the final consequences.

The following are the basics of report writing.

1. Draft a thorough, objective report

- Describe how and when the investigator first learned of the complaint.
- Provide exact details of the specific complaint. If the complainant filled out a complaint form or made a statement, attach that to the report.
- List all school district documents reviewed.
- Describe each interview, noting who was present, when and where the interview was held, the questions asked, and the answers given.
- Organize your entire report using the McGrath Template III in Figure 9.5 (pp. 157–159).

2. Indicate whether bullying, illegal harassment, or other misconduct has occurred and provide specific justification for your conclusion.

Some policies refer the conclusion of bullying or illegal harassment to the final decision maker. If the investigator does not make that decision, then the investigator is functioning as a fact finder. In that case, no final conclusion should be included in the report by the fact finder. The Final Conclusion section of the report should be completed by the final decision maker.

3. The final decision maker recommends corrective or disciplinary action if the investigation determines that the alleged conduct did occur and that it violates district policy.

- The penalty should match the conduct in severity.
- The discipline should be progressive, escalating from prior discipline imposed.
- The corrective action should not punish the complainant.
- The corrective action should be consistent with past discipline imposed by the school district in similar situations.

Phase Five: Follow-Up Actions by School Officials

Unless a private investigator is employed, the investigator's job is not over when the report is submitted.

The investigator must oversee the follow-up activity:

1. Submit the report to the decision-making official.

2. Follow up with the complainant and alleged perpetrator after the decision has been made.

3. Notify the victim of the corrective action taken and document his or her reaction (satisfaction or dissatisfaction) to the measures taken. (Be sure to follow FERPA, HIPAA, and other confidentiality regulations regarding what may be disclosed.)

4. If bullying, harassment, or misconduct has not been substantiated, counsel the individuals involved about the policy and complaint procedure.

5. Monitor the situation periodically to be reasonably certain that the misconduct is not recurring.

6. Continue educating all employees and students about bullying and harassment, developing effective complaint procedures, and approving and disseminating a strong anti-bullying policy.

If you are the decision-making official, when you receive the final report, you should:

- identify any deficiencies in the report,
- ask follow-up questions,
- conduct additional interviews if necessary,
- document all your actions, and
- make the final decision.

Figure 9.3 is a checklist to guide you through the Five Phases of your investigation. This is the game plan for ensuring a prompt, thorough, and legally sound investigation.

Corroborative Evidence

The key to a thorough investigation is to exhaust all reasonable opportunities to obtain corroborative evidence. As testimony is gathered, information on the impact of the behavior will surface from different people—the complainant as well as witnesses. It is particularly important in bullying and harassment cases to gather *corroborative evidence* regarding the impact of the bullying behavior on the complainant.

For example, Judy Smith says that she was too distraught to go to school and the attendance records show that she missed five days of school immediately following the alleged incidents. She told a friend, Tricia, that she was upset over the bullying behavior and did not want to go to school. Tricia goes on the list as a witness from whom you will gather testimony. Judy's doctor also testifies that Judy developed an ulcer during the time period of the alleged bullying. With Judy's parents' permission, he provides copies of x-rays and medical records.

Hearsay Evidence

Although it is not admissible in civil or criminal matters (except in rare circumstances that are beyond the scope of this book), hearsay may be admissible in administrative hearings. The opposite of hearsay evidence is called *direct testimony.* Direct testimony is information that someone heard, smelled, tasted, saw, or touched for himself or herself that has a direct bearing on the matter at hand. When there is direct testimony on a specific issue, then in administrative hearings, most tribunals allow hearsay information that corroborates the direct evidence to be introduced. Hearsay is loosely defined as information heard from other people.

The admission of hearsay into evidence is conditional on the hearsay information being the type of information that people regularly and routinely rely upon in the ordinary function of their duties. If it meets this standard, then it may be admitted in administrative proceedings as a backup for other direct testimony.

(Text continues on page 149)

Figure 9.3 Five Phases of an Investigation Checklist

	Date Completed

Phase One: Gather the Facts

Review published documents, policies, laws, and regulations: _____

Policies, statutes, the Education Code, and other documents delineating rules, regulations, policies, or procedures related to bullying, harassment, or student misconduct complaints in your district.

Review student files and/or cumulative records: _____

Past occurrences, concerns, remediation measures previously taken, and any training received previously.

Gather testimony. _____

Who will be interviewed? When? Where? Who will conduct which interview?

Gather tangible evidence: _____

Letters, torn clothing, graffiti.

Phase Two: Check for Records of Concern

Has complainant filed any prior complaints? _____

Check with the Security Office for any relevant incident reports. _____

Note how any prior complaints were resolved. _____

Prior complaints involving misconduct by the alleged perpetrator. _____

Complete Incident Report Form to record the current complaint. _____

Give a copy to the Complaint Manager and central repository of records of bullying and harassment. _____

Phase Three: Evaluate the Testimony and Evidence

McGrath Template III for a 360-degree evaluation of all the evidence you have gathered. _____

(Continued)

Figure 9.3 (Continued)

	Date Completed

Phase Four: Write the Report

Draft a thorough, objective report using the McGrath Template III.   _____

State a conclusion as to whether bullying, illegal harassment,
or other misconduct has occurred and provide specific justification.   _____

The final decision maker recommends corrective or
disciplinary action.   _____

The penalty should match the conduct. The corrective action
should not punish the complainant. The corrective action
should be consistent with past discipline imposed by the
school district in similar situations.   _____

Phase Five: Follow-Up Actions by School Officials

Submit the report to the decision-making official.   _____

Notify the victim of the corrective action taken and document
reaction. (Follow FERPA, HIPAA, and other confidentiality regulations.)   _____

If bullying, harassment, or misconduct has not been substantiated,
counsel the individuals involved about your policy and
complaint procedure.   _____

Monitor the situation periodically to be reasonably certain that the
misconduct is not recurring.   _____

Continue educating all employees and students about bullying and
harassment, developing effective complaint procedures, and
approving and disseminating a strong anti-bullying policy.

*If you are the decision-making official, when you receive the final
report, you should:*

Identify any deficiencies in the report.   _____

Ask follow-up questions.   _____

Conduct additional interviews if necessary.   _____

Document all your actions.   _____

Make the final decision.   _____

In administrative hearings, records and reports generally fall into the category of hearsay that is admissible, specifically under the business records exception to the hearsay rule of exclusion. In administrative matters, the hearing officer or the person who makes the final decision about a complaint determines whether the hearsay information is admissible.

CREATING A McGRATH CASE AND REPORT ORGANIZER TO GUIDE THE INVESTIGATION FROM START TO FINISH

Organize the Case File

Organize the case file using the McGrath Case and Report Organizer. The McGrath Case and Report Organizer uses the McGrath Template III as an outline and divider tabs for the Investigation Notebook. In the Investigation Notebook will be placed all of the policies, procedures, witness statements, and tangible evidence that are gathered in the course of the investigation. All the documentation and information needed to write the final McGrath Template III Investigation Report will be in the Investigation Notebook in the order in which it will be needed to write the Final Report. Take a look now at the McGrath Template III (Figure 9.5, pp. 157–159). Note: McGrath Training Systems has software available that supports the use of the McGrath Template III with bullying and harassment investigations.

To begin an investigation, get a three-ring binder. Label it with some "James Bond" code name so that it is not evident that this is the binder related to the case being worked on. Make dividers for each part of the McGrath Template III. Figure 9.4 contains a list of divider tabs for your McGrath Case and Report Organizer.

Everything you need to know to make a wise, informed decision is built right into the McGrath Case and Report Organizer and the McGrath Template III from which it is derived. If you organize your case files and reports in compliance with these tools, you will uphold due process rights, comply with just cause standards, meet deadlines, and everything will be in place to manage and decide the case in a legally fit and educationally sound manner.

As you go through the investigation, if a particular section of the Case and Report Organizer is not beginning to fill out, that tells you something about the case. Information necessary for a thorough and complete investigation is missing. For example, if you do not have any information about the training that students received regarding bullying and harassment, you may not be able to establish that the accused knew that what he or she was doing was in violation of policy and constitutes bullying. The goal is to let the McGrath Case and Report Organizer be the impartial, honest guide in conducting a quality, neutral investigation.

Figure 9.4 McGrath Case and Report Organizer Sections

Synopsis

TABS
- S1. Summary of Evidence
- S2. Conclusions
- S3. Recommendations

Facts

TABS
- F1. Timeliness
- F2. Authority
- F3. Facts

Impact

TABS
- I1. Impact of Conduct
- I2. Notoriety of Conduct
- I3. Motive for Conduct
- I4. Personal vs. Group Interests

Context

TABS
- C1. Student Training on the Issue
- C2. Extenuating/Aggravating Circumstances
- C3. Prior Help Given
- C4. Efforts to Correct
- C5. Likelihood of Recurrence

Action

TABS
- A1. Pinpoint Areas for Correction
- A2. Recommendations for Accomplishing Correction
- A3. Resources Available
- A4. Measure(s) of Improvement
- A5. Schedule of Follow-Up
- A6. Right to Respond

NOTE: McGrath Training Systems has software available to support the creation of the McGrath Case and Report Organizer and its dividers.

THE McGRATH CASE AND REPORT ORGANIZER

Synopsis

Make three divider tabs for this section to insert in your notebook. Label them as follows, with both the alpha and numeric indicators as well as the written description:

S1. Summary of Evidence

S2. Conclusions

S3. Recommendations

As with any good synopsis, it is not created until everything else is complete. You will use the other completed parts of your Case and Report Organizer to write the synopsis. Nothing gets filed behind these first three dividers except your final write-up.

Facts

Make three tabbed dividers for the Facts section:

F1. Timeliness

F2. Authority

F3. Facts

F1. Timeliness

Your *calendar* and all documents that give you a *timeline* or *deadline* go behind this divider.

- Look at your board policies, regulations, and guidelines, and make a copy of any page that has a timeline on it related to the subject matter of the investigation. Include any deadlines for taking matters to the governing board.
- Include deadlines for filing with regulatory agencies.
- Put a copy of each timeline instruction in your binder and highlight the important dates and time frames.
- Get a calendar and post all deadlines, due dates, and events on the calendar so that you can see them at a glance. Your calendar should include the date(s) of the alleged incident(s) and the date the complaint was received. Calendar every action that you take. I recommend that you mark all items that are due in the calendar five days ahead of the final due date, then put them in another color on the final day, as well. That way, you have an early warning system.

Note: McGrath Training Systems has software available to provide the scheduling function of the investigation and its part in the McGrath Template III.

F2. Authority

Here you put all of the documents that govern the manner in which the investigation is conducted. All of the relevant authority for the investigation being conducted is collected here:

- The entirety of the bullying and harassment policies
- Any specific education code sections or statutes relevant in your state
- Any specific provisions of board policy or the collective bargaining agreement that apply
- Any job descriptions, handbooks, student code of conduct, or class rules with which a student is to comply relevant to the conduct at issue

F3. Facts

The section should be organized as follows:

- A statement of the key issues to be decided in this case
- A list of potential witnesses
- Notes, transcriptions, and checklists from all interviews conducted

Impact

Make four tabbed dividers for the Impact section:

I1. Impact of Conduct

I2. Notoriety of Conduct

I3. Motive for Conduct

I4. Personal vs. Group Interests

I1. Impact of Conduct

The information in this section is not "What happened?" but "What was the effect or outcome of what happened?" In other words, how was someone, or the organization, or the community hurt by the behavior described in the Fact section?

In this section you will place:

- Quotes from the interviews that relate specifically to harm
- Other documentation that shows the effect on the alleged victim, such as
  - Tests which a student has failed
  - A report card that shows the student's grades have dropped
  - A note from a doctor that demonstrates that a student sought medical advice and/or treatment

I2. Notoriety of Conduct

The notoriety of conduct section contains information relevant to the educational community's reaction to the event. This is information that comes in from third party sources. It represents the reputation or public opinion about what happened.

This section includes:

- Publicity of any nature, including news articles
- Letters or e-mail from other people commenting on the situation

I3. Motive for Conduct

You are less likely to have any documentary evidence for this section. This is the material related to their "excuse," so to speak. You want to tease out what the alleged perpetrator said about why he was doing what he was doing. Be sure to write out the person's exact words here. Copy quotes verbatim. Do not paraphrase.

I4. Personal vs. Group Interests

In making your determination, you will weigh the interests of the group against the interests of the individual. Are there personal rights that are in conflict with the rights of the alleged victim or the rights of the school community to a bullying- and harassment-free environment?

Let's say the alleged perpetrator says, "You can't tell me that I can't tell someone they look sexy. It's my right of free speech. You can't limit me in that way." You put that comment in this section.

Say the principal tells a student who has been bullying others on the school bus, "You must sit in the front seat of the bus alone every day on the trip to and from school." All other students on the bus are free to choose any seat and to sit with their friends. Again, you have a collision of rights, so it goes here. You will analyze whether the rights of a member of the group to be free from bullying and illegal harassment and discrimination outweigh the individual's right to do as he or she pleases.

Context

Make five tabbed dividers for the Context section:

C1. Student Training on the Issue

C2. Extenuating/Aggravating Circumstances

C3. Prior Help Given

C4. Efforts to Correct

C5. Likelihood of Recurrence

C1. Student Training on the Issue

This is where evidence is filed establishing whether the alleged perpetrator was trained in relation to the behavior under investigation and should have known better.

- Class records verifying training received on relevant topics go here, including anti-bullying modules, sexual harassment training, conflict resolution sessions, communication training, tolerance programs, and so on.
- If the alleged perpetrator attended a class or assembly on a relevant topic, include a copy of the lesson plan and any handouts or materials.
- If a video was shown, include information about the video—its title, release date, run time, and content.

C2. Extenuating/Aggravating Circumstances

In this section, you look more broadly. Include any documentation regarding the life circumstances of the alleged perpetrator—cultural differences, language difficulties, disability, health issues, family problems, and so on. This is information that would be relevant contextually but does not establish the facts of the case.

This evidence is used to determine whether other circumstances lessen the egregiousness of the behavior or compound it. For example, if it is determined that a student had just experienced the death of a parent and then came to school and slugged another kid, it would be important to consider that child's actions in the context of his or her entire life. On the other hand, if it were determined that a student had been extorting lunch money daily from another student and threatening to break his arm if he told anyone, that is information that compounds the seriousness of the events.

C3. Prior Help Given

If there have been prior incidents, find out what remedial action was taken.

This section should include:

- Records of prior complaints and how they were resolved
- Documentation of counseling received, memos written, disciplinary action taken, and so on

C4. Efforts to Correct

If there were prior incidents, find out what the alleged perpetrator did to correct his or her behavior. In a situation in which you told someone to modify his or her behavior, did the student attempt to correct? How do you know? Who followed up on the situation? When? What did he or she observe? If you required that the student attend a class to learn more about the issue, did she or he go?

C5. Likelihood of Recurrence

This is where you analyze everything from the previous sections and determine whether there is a pattern. If there were prior occurrences, reference them here (the prior incidents should be described in the Facts section as history of the issue, and analyzed in this section to determine whether there is a pattern) and state whether, added together, they constitute a pattern of behavior.

Action

This section is for the decision maker to fill out, who may or may not be the investigator.

Make six tabbed dividers for the Action section:

A1. Pinpoint Areas for Correction

A2. Recommendations for Accomplishing Correction

A3. Resources Available

A4. Measure(s) of Improvement

A5. Schedule of Follow-Up

A6. Right to Respond

A1. Pinpoint Areas for Correction

In this section, the decision maker pinpoints areas of conduct that are unacceptable, if there are any, and identifies any areas where allegations of misconduct were unproven.

A2. Recommendations for Accomplishing Correction

Here the decision maker lists possible means to accomplish the necessary behavioral correction:

- What needs to change here and how will you foster that change?
- What should be provided to the alleged (or proven) perpetrator?
- What action should be taken to change the environment?
- What additional training should be given to the whole school or whole class?
- What should be monitored and who will be accountable for monitoring it?

A3. Resources Available

Identify resources that can be provided to the perpetrator, victim, and community to support the changes in behavior and to remediate the situation. This could include classes; videotapes; professional development programs; books; and coaching, counseling, or psychological services. Resources may also include sanctions or discipline.

A4. Measure(s) of Improvement

How will you know that your intervention is working? When you follow up, what will you look for? It needs to be something specific and measurable—something that you can see, hear, touch, taste, or smell, and something you can count. Pick measures that don't reopen a wound. You might interview a cross-section of students in the environment. If what you hear in all the interviews is "Yes, I feel safe," then that is a measure of improvement.

You could measure the number of complaints received regarding this student, school site, or classroom over a particular time period. Have the complaints decreased? Establish not only what you are measuring, but also what an acceptable statistic will be. When measuring further complaints about a perpetrator, the acceptable statistic may be zero.

A5. Schedule of Follow-Up

Set up a schedule and determine who will do the follow up. How? When? The follow-up schedule should be linked to your measures. The person who follows up will be measuring improvement at those times.

A6. Right to Respond

If your final report will be placed in a student cumulative file or discipline file, it is a good practice to include a statement indicating the student had an opportunity to respond to the contents of the report in writing, if he or she chose to do so.

A Legally Fit and Educationally Sound Report

This is the complete McGrath Template III. Creating the Final Report using this model will ensure that you are legally fit and educationally sound throughout the entire investigation and in the final result you arrive at through use of the model. The legal principles of due process, just cause, and other legal criteria are built into the instrument. Should litigation ensue, the investigator and the school district will be in an impeccable position to establish all that was done to safeguard the welfare of the students and to respect the rights of all parties.

The McGrath Template III is not a difficult process to follow. And the more you use it, the easier it gets. It simply takes a conscientious approach to matters that require a Level III investigative response. You just need to fill in each section of the template succinctly and in consecutive order. Do not write your report first and then try to fit it into the McGrath Template III format. Do it the other way around. Fill in the template format step by step, and it will guide you to having a legally fit and educationally sound report. Trust the instrument and the process it is guiding you through, and surrender to its format.

In truth, the McGrath Template III is an outstanding model to use with all matters that come to the attention of the administration. With practice, this instrument can become second nature and ensure that all of your complex communications are done at a legally fit and educationally sound level. A McGrath Template III Report Form is available in Resource A.

See pages 157–159 for an annotated Template III followed by a Level III Investigation Report. Each Template section is identified in the text. Study this document and become familiar with the elements as they appear in a real case.

Figure 9.5 McGrath Template III: Annotated for Bullying Investigation Report

---

SYNOPSIS (Complete This Section Last)

(1) Summary of evidence: allegations and investigation steps taken.

(2) Conclusions regarding the facts.

(3) Recommendations to stop any inappropriate behavior in the workplace/school setting (by final decision maker).

F. FACTS

1. Timeliness of investigation

Investigation and reporting must be completed in a timely manner.

Investigation needs to begin immediately following a complaint.

Investigation should be conducted even if complainant delays in coming forward. Delay should be noted along with complainant's explanation for delay.

2. Authority What laws, policies, rules, regulations, job descriptions, performance standards, handbook provisions, prior directives, and/or guidelines are pertinent?

Investigation includes a review of board policies, regulations, and statutes with respect to bullying and harassment. Inspect "chat file," cumulative and discipline records, for prior directives.

3. Facts Who? What? Where? When? How do you know? Be specific! (State current, then past occurrences.)

Investigation gathers the facts from alleged victim(s), alleged perpetrator(s), and witnesses. Summarize the pertinent facts from interview notes that will be attached to the report.

I. IMPACT

1. Impact of Conduct on victims, others in school environment including students, teachers, staff, administration, community, and parents.

Investigation considers impact of conduct from input from interviews with alleged victim(s) and witnesses.

(Continued)

Figure 9.5 (Continued)

2. **Notoriety of Conduct** Comments from coworkers, faculty, the administration, the community, students, and parents.

> Investigation identifies the notoriety of conduct from interviews with witnesses.

3. **Motive for Conduct** List employees'/students' statements or conduct reflecting attitude.

> Record any information given regarding motive for conduct from interview with alleged perpetrator(s). In some instances, this is also elicited from interviews with alleged victim(s), witnesses, or administrator(s).

4. **Personal vs. Group Interests** Consider any inhibiting effect on personal or civil rights of alleged perpetrator balanced against the rights of people who may be harmed by the conduct.

C. CONTEXT (PRIOR INCIDENTS AND PRIOR INTERVENTION)

1. **Student Training on the Issue**

> Investigation considers and reviews information of previous training given alleged perpetrator(s) regarding appropriate conduct in school setting.This may be documented in district policies, training records, discipline, or cumulative files.

2. **Extenuating/Aggravating Circumstances** surrounding conduct

> Investigation identifies if there are any extenuating circumstances from interviews with alleged perpetrator(s), victim(s), administrators, witnesses.

3. **Prior Help Given** to remediate issue (if any)

> Investigation determines prior incidents and prior remediation assistance from personnel or student records and interviews with administrators.

4. **Alleged Perpetrator's Efforts to Correct**

> Investigation may reveal alleged perpetrator's efforts to correct previous issue.

Figure 9.5 (Continued)

5. **Likelihood of Recurrence** State if there is a continuous pattern of conduct.

> Investigation will state finding regarding the likelihood of recurrence, based upon whether an established pattern of conduct appears to exist.

A. ACTION (If investigation determines that unacceptable conduct has occurred, decision maker completes this final section.)

1. **Pinpoint Areas for Correction**

> Final report will specify the necessary areas for changed behavior in the school environment.

2. **Recommendations for Accomplishing Change**

> Final report will identify specific recommendations and directives for changes in behavior, environment, and monitoring.

3. **Resources Available to Student**

> Final report will identify suggested resources to be utilized for corrective action and to support the changed behavior.

4. **Measure(s) of Improvement to Be Applied**

> Final report will list steps and measures to assist in stopping and changing the behavior.

5. **Schedule of Follow-Up by Investigator and/or Principal**

> Final report will specify the follow-up measures necessary: what, when (at what intervals), and how.

6. **Right to Respond**

Note: Schools have their own uniquely adopted procedures for disciplining students that are designed to afford the accused with due process rights. It is important to adhere to these policies and procedures, particularly in the cases where suspension or expulsion may be recommended.

McGRATH TEMPLATE III
Sample Final Investigation Report

SYNOPSIS (Complete this section last.)

1. Brief recap of allegations and investigation steps taken

On Tuesday, March 11, 2008, at approximately 8:45 a.m., an incident occurred involving CP and another student. While standing near one of the portable classrooms on the playground, CP grabbed MR, put him in a headlock and threw him to the ground.

During this school year, CP has had 13 disciplinary referrals for behaviors which include kicking others; sexual harassment/name calling; obscene gestures, pushing and shoving; insubordination, threats; grabbing, classroom disruption; fighting/assault.

Principal Krumpet interviewed witnesses to this latest incident as well as Mrs. Connelly, CP's teacher. CP's student record was reviewed and a Discipline Referral Summary Report for 2004 through 2008 was compiled.

Because City police were contacted and CP was issued a citation for assault, the police are also conducting an investigation of the incident on March 11.

2. Conclusions regarding the facts

CP displays a pattern of aggression that is unacceptable in the school setting. He instills fear in his classmates. Teachers and staff express frustration with his behavior and lack of progress. This behavior is likely to persist without intervention.

3. Recommendations to stop any inappropriate behavior in the school setting or school-related activities (by final decision maker)

[Left blank for final decision maker.]

FACTS
1. Timeliness of investigation

On Tuesday, March 11, 2008, at approximately 8:45 a.m., an incident occurred involving CP and another student. This final investigation report is being submitted on March 21, 2008.

2. Authority (relevant rules, policies, statutes, etc.)

For the most recent incident, CP was assigned to the district Suspension Lab for a period of five days, as provided by Board of Trustees policy and Administrative Regulation. City police were contacted and CP was issued a citation for assault. He is scheduled to appear soon before a juvenile court judge. This was the second incident in this school year that resulted in CP being assigned to the district Suspension Lab.

3. Facts (Who? What? Where? When? How do you know?)

While standing near one of the portable classrooms on the playground, CP grabbed MR, put him in a headlock and threw him to the ground. MR struck his head on the ice, causing him to lose consciousness and to sustain a concussion. MR was taken to the hospital, treated, and released. During this school year, CP has had 13 disciplinary referrals for behaviors which include kicking others; sexual harassment/name calling; obscene gestures, pushing and shoving; insubordination, threats; grabbing, classroom disruption; fighting/assault.

IMPACT
1. Impact of Conduct

CP's behavior has created a climate of fear, specifically with MR, the student who was assaulted, and generally with other students at the school.

2. Notoriety of Conduct

Mrs. Connelly, his teacher, and other staff have expressed frustration with his lack of academic progress and the further deterioration of his behavior. Discipline referrals come from a variety of sources including playground monitors, teachers, substitute teachers, and classroom teaching assistants.

3. Motive for Conduct

Based on his behaviors (crying, sullenness, sadness, anger), Mrs. Connelly states that CP appears to be frustrated by his lack of behavioral control.

4. Personal vs. Group Interests

CP is eligible for special education services under a learning disability. Though he is a special needs student, the needs of the other students must be considered as well in the school setting.

CONTEXT: PRIOR INCIDENTS AND PRIOR INTERVENTION

1. Student Training Related to Behavior

Interventions at the school level have addressed bullying and harassing behavior, and CP participates in weekly social skills studies with his classmates.

2. Extenuating/Aggravating Circumstances Surrounding the Conduct

Since October, we have communicated on numerous occasions with CP's mother, requesting that she have him re-evaluated by a family physician to determine whether he should resume his medication for Attention Deficit Hyperactivity Disorder. Thus far, she has not followed through with that request.

In the fall of 2005, CP went to live with his father when his mother was sent to prison for illegal drug use and distribution. His father was willing to have him evaluated by a physician, who then diagnosed CP with Attention Deficit Hyperactivity Disorder and placed him on Ritalin. The medication was effective; his father provided a stable home environment and CP's behavior was very appropriate with NO discipline referrals during his third-grade school year. In late 2007, when CP was in fourth grade, his mother was released from prison, and CP and his sisters resumed living with her while his father worked out of town driving a truck.

3. Prior Help Given to Remediate Issue (if any)

CP receives daily classroom support and instruction from special education staff in reading and written language. CP has participated in numerous Social Skills interventions and regularly sees the school counselor to help him deal with anger and aggression issues.

4. Alleged Perpetrator's Efforts to Correct

These interventions appear to be unsuccessful in changing his behavior.

5. Likelihood of Recurrence

During the 2006–2007 school year, CP had 12 discipline referrals for the following behaviors: class disruptions, profanity, fighting, insubordination, name calling, and physical aggression. During the current school year, he has had 13 referrals to date for the behaviors listed in Action 1 on page 163. Given this pattern, the conduct is likely to persist without some other intervention.

ACTION

1. Pinpoint Areas of Conduct That Are Unacceptable

Areas of unacceptable conduct include kicking others; sexual harassment/name calling; obscene gestures, pushing and shoving; insubordination, threats; grabbing, classroom disruption; fighting/assault.

2. Recommendations/Directives for Change

The IEP (Individualized Education Plan) Team will convene within 10 business days to decide whether to conduct a multi-disciplinary assessment to determine whether CP may also have an emotional disability.

3. Resources Available to Student

We will work closely with the Department of Family Services and the Multi-Disciplinary Team to develop a case plan that continues to meet the needs of CP, his siblings, and parents.

4. Measure(s) of Improvement to Be Applied

The test of our effectiveness will be whether CP's behavior improves and he is no longer receiving referrals to the office.

5. Schedule of Follow-Up by Investigator and/or Principal

I have asked Mrs. Chambers, school psychologist, to contact Ima Helper, CP's Case Manager at the Department of Family Services, to obtain input and establish a date and time for a meeting.

Right to Respond

Interested parties are invited to contact Mrs. Hoffman, school social worker, or me if they have questions or concerns we should address.

Signed: Herman T. Krumpet

Name (Please Print): Herman T. Krumpet

Title: Principal, Wagon Ho Elementary School

Date: March 21, 2008

Attachment: Discipline Referral Summary Report for 2004 through 2008

SUMMARY

Complaint intake and investigation from Level I through the Level III Final Report has now been covered. In this chapter, the players were identified as well as each of their roles in the process. The five phases of a Level III investigation were reviewed, together with the types of evidence that may be introduced, the elements of the Case and Report Organizer, and the evidence that pertains to each element.

The McGrath Template III and its parallel Case and Report Organizer may seem daunting. Readers may be tempted to avoid these tools, claiming they are too much work and take too much time. However, it is critical that Level III incidents are investigated in exactly this manner. The law is the law, and it is not optional to only follow some of it. Both the legal integrity and reputation of the school district as well as the welfare of students demand that investigations are executed completely. *The best approach is to surrender to the process.* Let the Case and Report Organizer guide your investigation, then write your report one element at a time.

Do not skip anything. There is no unnecessary element in the McGrath Template III. This is actually good news. Investigators who follow the McGrath Template III know up front everything that will be asked of them later should the matter go to litigation. The McGrath Template III contains exactly what districts will confront in any fair hearing, student expulsion, governing board review of your work, OCR compliance review, or lawsuit. Be prepared, or take the gamble on not ending up in court.

10

Conclusion

This book has been a labor of love for me. I have laid out everything that a school administrator and educator needs to know both to navigate the legal waters surrounding bullying and harassment in schools and to put principled thinking, speaking, and listening into action with students.

At the end of this book, you will find a collection of useful Resources including REport forms, a Law Case Digest, a Model Bullying Policy, Sample State Anti-bullying Legislation, a 360-Degree Anti-Bullying Training Plan, a Glossary, and a Bibliography. I have also included URLs for a variety of related Web sites, including links to free, downloadable 8½" × 11" McGrath report forms for your personal use. If you have a suggestion for future publications, please feel free to contact me at mjmbullybook@mcgrathinc.com. My intention is that you will have everything you need to implement the McGrath SUCCEED System with bullying and harassment matters.

The heart of the matter—who to be while taking all of the suggested actions—is the subject of Chapter 7. If you are guided by the four McGrath FICA Standard principles of Trust, Respect, Understanding, and Growth, you will find yourself handling bullying and harassment as a Level I or Level II matter, for the most part. Do not, however, avoid using the McGrath Template III for those matters for which it is needed. This instrument will put you out in front, meeting legal requirements and responsibilities in a timely fashion.

Most important, *you lead with your heart while using your head*—both at the same time! This is the mantra of the McGrath SUCCEED System. Without this approach, you may easily become (or at least add to) the problem. Integrating the system into your daily routines and interactions keeps you present to the possibility and vision of boldly bringing forth greatness and fulfillment in your students.

There is an old story about a man who was on a pilgrimage. As he traveled down the road, one day he came upon three stonecutters working in the hot sun. When asked about their work, the first replied, "Why do you ask?

Isn't it obvious? I am simply cutting stone." The second stonecutter said, "I'm earning a living, which makes my family comfortable." Then the third man stood and spoke, "What am I doing? Why, I am building a cathedral."

When you get up in the morning, look at yourself in the mirror and ask, *What am I building today?* Anyone who has the courage and commitment to work in education is definitely building greatness.

Be unforgettable to your students. Be the one who makes the difference.

PART IV

Resources

Resource A: Forms

McGrath Incident Report Side 1

Record of Concern about Possible Bullying Incident(s) by Students or Staff

Instructions

1. This form should be used only to identify a possible incident of bullying as defined in school policy.
2. It is designed to assist a school staff member who may receive a complaint about possible bullying from a student.
3. The complaining student/staff does not complete this form; the staff who receives the complaint completes this form.
4. The form is then to be forwarded to the site and central office personnel (if appropriate) who are designated to receive such complaints involving possible bullying according to school policy/procedures.
5. DO NOT INTERVIEW THE STUDENT OR STAFF UNLESS SCHOOL POLICY PROCEDURES CALL FOR SUCH INTERVIEWS TO BE CONDUCTED.
6. Use the appropriate category(ies) below to record the information volunteered by the person.

Bullying behavior, according to school policy, involves repeated and/or systematic abuse and/or harassment of a person by another or others.

On _____ I talked with _____
              (Date)   (Alleged Victim)

about an incident with _____
                                          (Alleged Perpetrator)

Category Description: Physical Incident(s)	Mark All That Apply	Comments
Was pushed/shoved		
Was pinched/kicked		
Had clothing removed		
Was punched/hit		
Was denied access to location (where?)		
Gestures were made toward him/her (which?)		
Had possessions taken (what?)		
Had money taken		
Other:		

McGrath Incident Report - Side 2

Category Description: Physical Incident(s)	Mark All That Apply	Comments
Had general put downs, taunting, teasing directed toward her/him		
Had insults directed toward her/his race, gender, ethnic group membership, disability, home language, national origin, religion, sexual orientation		
Had rumors spread about her/him		
Was isolated, intentionally excluded		
Was threatened / intimidated		
Other:		

How this incident came to my attention:

Signature: _____

Date: _____

Position: _____

Site: _____

Complaint of Alleged Bullying or Illegal Harassment

Complainant's Name: _____ Date: _____

Address: _____
                  Street   City   Zip Code

Home Telephone Number: _____

Any other number where you can be reached during the day: _____

I wish to complain against: _____
                                              Name(s) of person(s)

Address or location* of person(s): _____

(*Location may include a specific class, school building, department, residence hall, etc.)

What alleged bullying or illegal harassment action was taken against you to cause you to file this complaint? (What happened? Where did it happen? Who was involved? Who witnessed the behavior?) _____

_____

_____

Date(s) of alleged bullying or illegal harassment: _____
What informal steps have you taken to stop the bullying or harassing behavior?

_____

_____

_____

Is there anyone who could provide more information regarding this complaint? Please list names, addresses, and telephone numbers of these people below.

Name   Address   Telephone

_____

_____

Remedy sought: _____

_____

_____

I certify that this information is correct to the best of my knowledge.

_____   _____
    Signature of Complainant   Signature of Translator

Please use the back of this page if you need more room to write.

McGrath Investigation Checklist

		Date Completed
1.	Complaint received from victim or third party.	_____
2.	Review any written complaint.	_____
3.	Review board policy/regulations and collective bargaining agreement.	_____
4.	Review the student files/cumulative records of alleged victim and perpetrator.	_____
5.	Review proposed investigation plan with legal counsel.	_____
6.	Interview complainant.	_____
7.	Interview the teachers/supervisor of the alleged victim and alleged perpetrator.	_____
8.	Interview witnesses.	_____
9.	Interview the alleged perpetrator.	_____
10.	Re-interview the complainant and the alleged perpetrator after all other witnesses.	_____
11.	Evaluate the case to determine existence of bullying and/or illegal harassment.	_____
12.	Generate investigation report.	_____
13.	Submit report/interviews to designated district administrator.	_____
14.	Place in student file (if warranted).	_____
15.	Formally process any discipline that has been recommended/approved.	_____
16.	Notify complainant and alleged perpetrator as to the conclusion of the investigation.	_____
17.	Continue to monitor the situation and setting.	_____

McGrath Template III

Format for Final Investigation Report

SYNOPSIS (Complete this section last)

1. Summary of Evidence: allegations and investigation steps _____

_____

_____

_____

2. Conclusions regarding the facts _____

_____

_____

_____

3. Recommendations to stop any inappropriate behavior in the school setting or school-related activities (by final decision maker)

_____

_____

_____

F. FACTS

1. Timeliness of Investigation _____

_____

_____

_____

2. Authority (Relevant rules, policies, statutes, etc.) _____

_____

_____

_____

3. Facts (Who? What? Where? When? How do you know?) _____

_____

_____

_____

McGrath Template III

Format for Final Investigation Report (page _____ of _____)

3. Facts (continued) _____

_____

_____

_____

_____

_____

_____

_____

_____

_____

_____

_____

_____

_____

_____

I. IMPACT

1. Impact of Conduct _____

_____

_____

_____

_____

2. Notoriety of Conduct _____

_____

_____

_____

_____

McGrath Template III

Format for Final Investigation Report (page _____ of _____)

3. Motive for Conduct _____

_____

_____

_____

4. Personal vs. Group Interests _____

_____

_____

_____

C. CONTEXT: PRIOR INCIDENTS AND PRIOR INTERVENTION

1. Student Training on the Issue _____

_____

_____

_____

2. Extenuating/Aggravating Circumstances Surrounding the Conduct _____

_____

_____

_____

3. Prior Help Given to Remediate Issue (if any) _____

_____

_____

_____

McGrath Template III

Format for Final Investigation Report (page _____ of _____)

4. Alleged Perpetrator's Efforts to Correct _____

_____

_____

_____

_____

5. Likelihood of Recurrence _____

_____

_____

_____

_____

A. ACTION

1. Pinpoint Areas for Correction _____

_____

_____

_____

_____

2. Recommendations for Accomplishing Correction _____

_____

_____

_____

_____

_____

_____

McGrath Template III

Format for Final Investigation Report (page _____ of _____)

3. Resources Available to Student _____

_____

_____

_____

4. Measure(s) of Improvement to be Applied _____

_____

_____

_____

5. Schedule of Follow-Up by Investigator and/or Principal _____

_____

_____

_____

6. Right to Respond _____

_____

_____

_____

_____

Signed: _____

Name (Please Print): _____

Title: _____

Date: _____

Resource B:
Laws and Policies

LAW CASE DIGEST: A SAMPLER

Failure to Take Preventative Action

STATE Themes & Incidents	CASE DESCRIPTION
Alaska Suicide	Attempted suicide case. Anchorage School District and insurance company paid $4.5 million to settle lawsuit. Family charged that school employees did not do enough to stop the bullying. There was irreversible brain damage.
California Threats of Violence	*Leger v. Stockton Unified School District,* 202 Cal. App. 3d 1448, 249 Cal. Rptr. 688, 689 [47 Ed. Law Rep. [1093]] (Cal. App. 3 Dist. 1988). School authorities who know of threats of violence that they believe are well-founded may not refrain from taking reasonable preventive measures simply because violence has not yet occurred.
California Supervision	*Iverson v. Muroc Unified School Dist.* (App. 5 Dist. 1995). 38 Cal. Rptr. 2d 35, 32 Cal. App. 4th 218. School district and its employees have general duty to supervise conduct of children on grounds during school sessions, school activities, recesses, and lunch periods.
California Safe Environment	*In re William G.,* 709 P. 2d 1287, 1295 (Cal. 1985). "Teaching and learning cannot take place without the physical and mental well-being of the students. The school premises, in short, must be safe and welcoming."
Colorado Suicide Bullying	Girl commits suicide after bullying. She was teased about her weight, clothes, and ethnicity. There were acts of physical assault. Family says principal "shrugged . . . off" harassment complaints. Parents also allege that they were denied critical information. The girl told a counselor she was suicidal. Article highlights high rates of suicide among United States' youth.
Florida Threats of Violence After School Hours	*Ruiz v. Broward County School Board,* 493 So.2d 474 [34 Ed. Law Rep. [1263]] (Fla.App.4Dist.1986). Prior acts of violence between students on school grounds, even though

(Continued)

Failure to Take Preventative Action (Continued)

STATE *Themes & Incidents*	*CASE DESCRIPTION*
	occurring during school hours, would be relevant to whether acts of violence may be expected immediately after school hours while students are still on grounds, for purpose of determining duty to supervise.
Florida Hiring Practices Supervision Retention	*School Board of Orange County v. Coffey,* 524 So. 2d 1052 [46 Ed. Law Rep. [1301]] (Fla. App. 5Dist 1988). School Board has common-law duty to protect others from result of negligent hiring, supervision, or retention, which duty is identical to duty upon private employers who hire, retain, or supervise employees whose negligence or intentional acts in positions of employment can foreseeably cause injures to third parties.
Maryland Suicide	*Eisel v. Board of Education of Montgomery County,* 324 Md. 376, 597 A. 2d 447 [70 Ed. Law Rep. [544]] (1991). School counselors have a duty to use reasonable means to attempt to prevent suicide when they are on notice of a child's or an adolescent's suicidal intent.
New Hampshire Title IX Student-to-Student Sexual Harassment	*Doe v. Londonderry Sch. Dist.,* 970 F. Supp. 64 (D.N.H. 1997). Three male classmates harassed a girl. The school district did not have a formal Title IX policy and procedure, a Title IX Coordinator, or a Title IX grievance procedure. The court found that a school district's failure to end peer-to-peer sexual harassment is actionable under Title IX if the plaintiff can show the following: (1) plaintiff was a student in an educational program or activity receiving federal financial assistance within the coverage of Title IX; (2) plaintiff was subjected to unwelcome sexual harassment while a participant in the program; (3) the harassment was sufficiently severe or pervasive that it altered the conditions of the plaintiff's education and created a hostile or abusive educational environment; and (4) the school district knew of the harassment and intentionally failed to take proper remedial action. Requirement for liability of school district under Title IX for failure to curtail peer sexual harassment, that violation was "intentional," means that district must have intended to create hostile educational environment for plaintiff.
New Hampshire Sexual Harassment Title IX	*Snelling and Snelling v. Fall Mountain Regional School District,* et al., No. CIV. 99-448-JD (D.N.H. March 21, 2001). Two brothers brought a lawsuit against the school district and various individuals for the sexual harassment the boys experienced in high school. Although the boys complained to the principal and the superintendent, the harassment persisted. The court held that the school district had notice of the harassment and that the harassment rose to the level of being sufficiently severe, pervasive, and objectively offensive to be actionable under Title IX. Additionally, the court held that harassment based on sex-based stereotypes of masculinity is also actionable under Title IX.

STATE Themes & Incidents	CASE DESCRIPTION
New Hampshire Sexual Harassment	Doe v. Oyster River Cooperative Sch. Dist., 992 F.Supp. 467 (D.N.H.1997). Two girls complained of sexual harassment by a male classmate on several occasions. The guidance counselor warned the students not to mention the harassment to others as it might bring on lawsuits to the district. The court found the school did not respond to the harassment complaints in a timely manner and did not take remedial steps to end the harassment. However, the girls could not seek punitive damages from the school district because the school's response was not so egregious that punitive damages would be permitted.
New Jersey Anti-Gay	New Jersey school told to toughen policies against gay harassment. State's Civil Rights Director believed that School District allowed a "hostile school environment" to develop.
Oregon Physical Assault Bullying (Case Pending)	Lawsuit seeks damages and attempts to force the district to institute anti-bullying policies. A camera on the parked bus recorded the incident. Boy alleges he was regularly attacked. Additionally, the suit alleges the boy named the attackers but the district failed to prevent continuing assaults.
Texas Physical Assault	Downing v. Brown, 925 S.W. 2d 316 [111 Ed. Law Rep. [560]] (Tex. App. Amarillo 1996). Student assaulted by a classmate. The same perpetrator and friends then attacked the victim again. The victim withdrew from school and filed suit against the district. The teacher and principal were cited for negligence and violation of state constitutional rights. Court granted summary judgment for district and employees; student appealed to Court of Appeals. Court of Appeals agreed with trial court that there was no liability because the district had no special duty to protect one student from a classmate. However, summary judgment on the negligence claim was ruled improper because district plan required all teachers to develop and implement classroom discipline plan.

Deliberate Indifference

STATE Themes & Incidents	CASE DESCRIPTION
Leading Supreme Court Case Adult-to-Student Sexual Harassment	Alida Star Gebser v. Lago Vista Independent School District, 524 U.S. 274 (1998). Supreme Court held that damages may not be recovered for teacher-student sexual harassment unless a school district official, who at a minimum has authority to institute corrective measures on the district's behalf, has actual notice of the harassment and is deliberately indifferent to the teacher's misconduct. In cases where teachers or other educational staff sexually harassed students, the Supreme Court limited the availability of money

(Continued)

Deliberate Indifference (Continued)

STATE Themes & Incidents	CASE DESCRIPTION
	damages by requiring plaintiffs to prove that the school administrators with authority to take corrective action had prior knowledge of the harassment and acted with "deliberate indifference" in addressing the issue.
Leading Supreme Court Case Student-to-Student Title IX Sexual Harassment	*Davis v. Monroe County Board of Education,* 119 S. Ct. 1661 (1999). Supreme Court found peer-to-peer sexual harassment under Title IX. Supreme Court held that a private Title IX damage action may lie against a school district in cases of student-to-student harassment with the following circumstances: when the funding recipient is deliberately indifferent to sexual harassment of which he or she has actual knowledge, and when that harassment is so severe, pervasive, and objectively offensive that it can be said to deprive the student of the access to the educational opportunities or benefits provided by the school.
California Anti-Gay Verbal Harassment Bullying	*Flores v. Morgan Hill Unified School District,* 324 F.3d 1130 (9th Cir. 2003). Anti-gay harassment case ends in $1.1 million settlement to six plaintiffs. Plaintiffs alleged a pattern of indifference to anti-gay harassment. One boy was beaten up in full view of a bus driver. The students detailed constant taunting slurs and sexual jokes. Settlement included model anti-harassment program. The model may help schools that want to comply with California's school nondiscrimination law (AB537). 9th Circuit unanimously ruled that Constitution's guarantee of equal protection to gay and lesbian students was unambiguous; therefore, administrators were not immune from lawsuit.
New York Notice	*Mirand v. City of New York,* 84 N.Y 2d 44, 49 (1994). *Mirand* held that actual or constructive notice of "prior similar conduct" is generally required; however, other courts have set forth a lower standard. See *Brownwell,* a California court of appeals held "foreseeability is determined in light of all circumstances and does not require prior identical or even similar events." *Brownwell,* 5 Cal. Rptr. 2d at 762.
Texas Deliberate Indifference	*Johnson v. Dallas Impendent Sch. Dist.,* 38 F. 3d 198 [95 Ed. Law Rep. [68]] (5 Cir.1994). In order to prevail in a § 1983 case, the plaintiff must document the violation of a constitutional right because of deliberate actions of a government actor.
Washington Racial	School District will pay $7.5 million and make administrative and curriculum changes to encourage racial diversity in order to settle a two-year civil rights suit. The District was accused of tolerating a racially hostile environment.

Negligent Supervision

STATE Themes & Incidents	CASE DESCRIPTION
California Sexual Harassment Verbal and Physical (Case Pending)	Parents say their 14-year-old daughter was tied up with duct tape and stripped. Civil law suit alleges sexual assault, physical and verbal abuse. Lawsuit alleges negligent supervision.
California Physical Assault	*M.W. v. Panama Buena Vista Union School Dist.* (App. 5 Dist. 2003) 1 Cal. Rptr. 3d 673, 110 Cal. App. 4th 508. Student who committed assault had been subject of complaints by minor and had been disciplined for numerous serious infractions. Student may recover for injuries proximately caused by a breach of a school district's duty to supervise.
California Physical Assault	*Daily v. Los Angeles Unified Sch. Dist.* (1970) 2 Cal. 3d 741, 747. School district liable because school authorities failed to supervise students who engaged in 10-minute "slap fight." School authorities have duty to supervise at all times the conduct of children on school grounds and to enforce those rules and regulations necessary for their protection. Supervision during recess and lunch is required. "Such regulation is necessarily precise because of the commonly known tendency of students to engage in aggressive and impulsive behavior which exposes them and their peers to the risk of serious physical harm."
California Physical Assault	*Lucas v. Fresno Unified School Dist.* (1993) 14 Cal. App. 4th 866, 871-872. School district could be held liable for breach of duty to protect a student from injury by a dirt clod thrown by another student.
California Physical Assault	*Forgone v. Salvador U.E. School Dist.* (1940) 41 Cal. App 2d 423, 426. School district could be held liable for breach of duty to protect a student injured when another student twisted her arm.
California Physical Assault	*Charonnat v. San Francisco Unified School Dist.* (App. 1 Dist. 1943) 56 Cal. App. 2d 840, 133 P. 2d. 643. A school district could not escape liability to a 11-year-old pupil whose leg was broken by fellow student in school yard during recess on grounds that district was not liable for willful misconduct of pupil, where evidence supported inference that there was negligent omission to provide adequate supervision, and that had the supervisor assigned seen the fight, serious injury would have been anticipated.
Minnesota Physical Assault	*Sheehan v. St. Peter's Catholic School,* 291 Minn. 1, 188 N.W. 2d 868 (1971). In order to recover damages from school for loss of eye by student who was struck by pebble after rocks were thrown at her for several minutes by other students during recess, it was necessary only to prove that a general danger was foreseeable and that supervision would have prevented the accident.
New York Physical Assault	*Ferraro v. Board of Education of the City of New York,* 32 Misc. 2d 563, 212 N.Y.S. 2d 615 (1961). There was evidence to support findings that principal was negligent in failing to warn substitute teacher regarding aggressive behavior of child who assaulted plaintiff child.

Lawsuit Pending

STATE Themes & Incidents	CASE DESCRIPTION
Indiana Bullying	Parents seek $1.5 million over alleged bullying of children. The tort claim notice stipulates that an attack this January resulted in Seiwert's eldest daughter suffering a broken nose, mild concussion, and lacerations. It claims bullying and harassment in December resulted in son leaving school for a month on doctor's orders. New anti-bullying policy has not been enforced.
Iowa Verbal Harassment Anti-Gay	Boy teased for being gay. Says teacher criticized him for speaking out.
Kansas Verbal Harassment Anti-Gay	Boy teased for being gay.
Louisiana Verbal Harassment	Girl teased because of national origin and eye stigma. Says the hurt she suffered has never really gone away.
Michigan Hazing and Assault	Detroit student files $5 million suit over alleged band hazing. Boy says band members beat him at the direction of band teacher as part of a hazing to join a secret band fraternity. His aunt crashed a vehicle into a tree trying to escape an assault.
Minnesota Title IX Verbal and Sexual	Harassment suit against school in federal court for verbal and sexual harassment. Under Title IX and Section 1983 based on violation of the Equal Protection Clause. Pelican Rapids did not take actions when female student was harassed on daily basis. Teachers not entitled to immunity.
New York Hazing	Military Academy cadet sues for hazing. Police say boy was beaten by fellow classmates at a private boarding school. Parents say school failed to protect son. During a hazing incident known as "blanket party," boy was beaten, causing head injuries and the loss of a tooth.
Pennsylvania Retaliation Bullying	Student with Tourette's Syndrome and obsessive-compulsive disorder "snapped" after two years of bullying and threatened violence. Parents seek damages because school failed to protect boy from harassment.
Pennsylvania Hazing	Alleged hazing incident in which student was assaulted on a team bus returning from a school-sponsored football camp. Part of the state law describes hazing as forced conduct that could result in extreme embarrassment, or that could affect mental health or dignity of the individual.

Other Cases of Note

STATE Themes & Incidents	CASE DESCRIPTION
Leading Supreme Court Case School Board Liable Constitutional Rights	*Wood v. Strickland*, 420 U.S. 308, 322 (1975). A school board may be a defendant in certain circumstances. In the specific context of school discipline, a school board member is not immune from liability for damages under § 1983 if he reasonably should have known that his official action "would violate the constitutional rights of the student affected, or if he took the action with the malicious intention to cause a deprivation of constitutional rights or other injury to the student."
Ohio Retaliation Bullying	Boy kills three students after bullying and teasing.
Washington Bullying Disability Discrimination	Judge awards $310,000. From fifth through eighth grade, Taya Haugstad said a classmate taunted and bullied her. Haugstad, who has cerebral palsy, was tormented by a boy who used insults like "retard," blocked her as she tried to pass in her wheelchair, and rammed her into walls. Haunted by recurring nightmares, she desperately tried to get out of going to school. The boy's family settled the case in April for an undisclosed sum. But the school district, which has denied the allegations, went to trial. By the time the students were in eighth grade, the harassment had become physical. The boy would grab the joystick that controlled Haugstad's wheelchair and ram her into a wall while screaming obscenities, she said. The jury ordered the school district to pay Haugstad $300,000 for infliction of emotional distress, and her parents $10,000 for the impact on their relationship with their daughter.
Washington Civil Rights Bullying	Three students expelled from Catholic schools for harassment and bullying. The school said behavior was contrary to school policy in student handbook regarding harassment and bullying. Victim's family questioned staff competency in handling diverse population.

MODEL BULLYING POLICY

General Policy Statement

It is the policy of this School District to maintain a learning and working environment that is free from bullying based on a person's race, color, sex, national origin, disability, sexual orientation, and economic status. The School District prohibits any and all forms of bullying because it violates the basic right of students and staff to be in a safe, orderly learning environment. This policy seeks to promote positive interpersonal relationships between all members of the school community. It shall be a violation of this policy for any student or staff member to bully another while attending school or school-sponsored events. It shall also be violation of this policy for any school staff member to tolerate bullying during school or at school-sponsored events.

For the purposes of this policy, the term "school staff" includes board members, school employees, agents, volunteers, contractors, or other persons subject to the supervision and control of the District.

The School District will promptly and thoroughly investigate reports of bullying, whether of a physical or a nonphysical form. If it determines that bullying has occurred, it will act appropriately within the discipline codes of the District and will take reasonable action to end the bullying.

Definition of Bullying

For the purpose of this policy, bullying consists of repeated systematic abuse and harassment of a person or persons by another.* Bullying is characterized by seven elements:

1. A desire to hurt or harm motivates the perpetrator.

2. This desire to hurt or harm results in hurtful or harmful action(s) taken by the perpetrator.

3. A formal or informal power imbalance exists between the perpetrator and the victim.

4. The action(s) taken by the perpetrator are manifestations of the unjust use of power.

5. The perpetrator enjoys carrying out the action(s).

6. The victim has a sense of being oppressed.

7. The perpetrator typically repeats the hurtful or harmful actions against the victim.

Examples of Bullying**

Bullying may be either physical or nonphysical acts. It may, or may not, involve criminal behavior. If criminal acts, or suspected criminal acts, have occurred, staff must contact the appropriate criminal authorities as required in law and policy.

Physical acts may include, but are not limited to, the following:

- Assault with a weapon
- Biting
- Grievous bodily harm
- Hair pulling/Shoving
- Seriously threatening to kill or cause harm
- Hitting/Punching/Scratching
- Serious theft
- Kicking
- Abuse/Sexual abuse
- Spitting
- Locking a person in a room
- Pinching/Grabbing
- Damage to victim's property

Nonphysical acts may include, but are not limited to, the following:

- Abusive language
- Mean faces
- Extorting of money or possessions
- Rude gestures
- Intimidation/threats
- Systematically exclusion
- Name calling
- Isolating
- Cruel remarks
- Sending scary/intimidating notes
- Spreading false/mean rumors
- Mean, gender-based pictures
- Gender-based put-downs
- Social scheming

Note: Sexualized bullying is considered to be sexual harassment. See the District policy and procedures that define sexual harassment and that provide procedures for handling it.

Bullying is distinguishable from roughhousing or friendly teasing in that bullying is intentionally hurtful and motivated by the desire to harm the victim.

Duty to Act

Students who experience bullying are encouraged to report it to any adult employee of the District. Any employee of the District who observes bullying or receives reports of it is required to act immediately to protect the alleged victim and to immediately forward an Incident Report to the Principal for prompt investigation as required in site procedures. Staff who fail to protect alleged victims and/or to immediately submit an Incident Report to the

Principal according to site procedures are subject to disciplinary measures, up to and including termination.

Sanctions for Bullying

Once an investigation has concluded, if bullying has occurred, sanctions may be taken against the perpetrator. For students, these sanction(s) must be appropriate to the seriousness of the incident(s) and may include suspension and/or expulsion or other discipline in accordance with accepted common sense application of the district discipline policies. For staff, sanction(s) must be appropriate to the seriousness of the incident(s) and may include termination or other common sense discipline in accordance with contract provisions or other policies of the district.

Retaliation Prohibited

Retaliation or reprisal against any person who reports bullying incident(s) is strictly prohibited. Retaliation includes, but is not limited to, any form of intimidation, reprisal, or harassment used against a person who reports incident(s) of bullying in good faith. Disciplinary action against any person who retaliates or engages in reprisal for reporting such behavior(s) may include sanctions up to and including expulsion/suspension for students and termination for staff engaging in such prohibited conduct.

False Reporting

Students and staff are prohibited from knowingly or willfully falsely accusing one another of bullying. Disciplinary action up to and including expulsion/suspension for students and termination for staff shall be taken if they make such knowingly false reports.

*It is vital to understand that a single incident may meet this definition if it is egregious, violates criminal law, or involves unreasonable harm to the victim.

** Adapted from Sullivan (2000).

SAMPLE STATE ANTI-BULLYING LEGISLATION

SHB 1444
Washington State

BE IT ENACTED BY THE LEGISLATURE OF THE STATE OF WASHINGTON:

(Note: Italicized section headers added by www.bullypolice.org)

Sec. 1. The legislature declares that a safe and civil environment in school is necessary for students to learn and achieve high academic standards. The legislature finds that harassment, intimidation, or bullying, like other disruptive or violent behavior, is conduct that disrupts both a student's ability to learn and a school's ability to educate its students in a safe environment. Furthermore, the legislature finds that students learn by example. The legislature commends school administrators, faculty, staff, and volunteers for demonstrating appropriate behavior, treating others with civility and respect, and refusing to tolerate harassment, intimidation, or bullying.

Dates that Requirements take effect

Sec. 2. (1) By August 1, 2003, each school district shall adopt or amend if necessary a policy, within the scope of its authority, that prohibits the harassment, intimidation, or bullying of any student. It is the responsibility of each school district to share this policy with parents or guardians, students, volunteers, and school employees.

Definitions of bullying and harassment

(2) "Harassment, intimidation, or bullying" means any intentional written, verbal, or physical act, including, but not limited to, one shown to be motivated either by any characteristic in RCW 9A.36.080(3), or other distinguishing characteristics, when the intentional written, verbal, or physical act (a) physically harms a student or damages the student's property; or (b) has the effect of substantially interfering with a student's education; or (c) is so severe, persistent, or pervasive that it creates an intimidating or threatening educational environment; or (d) has the effect of substantially disrupting the orderly operation of the school.

Recommendations about how to make policy—Inclusion

(3) It is recommended that the policy be adopted or amended through a process that includes representation of parents or guardians, school employees, volunteers, students, administrators, and community representatives. It is recommended that each such policy emphasize positive character traits and values, including the importance of civil and respectful speech and conduct, and the responsibility of students to comply with the district's policy prohibiting harassment, intimidation, or bullying.

Date policy is due and duties of the State Superintendent's office

(4) By August 1, 2002, the superintendent of public instruction, in consultation with representatives of parents, school personnel, and other interested parties, shall provide to school districts and educational service districts a model harassment, intimidation, and bullying prevention policy and training materials on the components that should be included in any district policy. Training materials shall be disseminated in a variety of ways, including workshops and other staff developmental activities, and through the office of the superintendent of public instruction's Web site, with a link to the safety center Web page.   On the Web site (a) The office of the superintendent of public instruction shall post its model policy, recommended training materials, and instructional materials; (b) The office of the superintendent of public instruction has the authority to update with new technologies access to this information in the safety center, to the extent resources are made available; and (c) Individual school districts shall have direct access to the safety center Web site to post a brief summary of their policies, programs, partnerships, vendors, and instructional and training materials, and to provide a link to the school district's Web site for further information.

Accountability to the Superintendent—Report to Lawmakers

Sec. 3. A new section is added to chapter 28A.320 RCW to read as follows: Beginning with the 2002-2003 school year, each school district shall report to the superintendent of public instruction by January 31st of each year all incidents (*resulting in disciplinary action*) involving harassment, intimidation, or bullying, (*that result in a short or long-term suspension or*) expulsion on school premises or on transportation systems used by schools, in the year preceding the report.   The superintendent shall compile the data and report it to the appropriate committees of the house of representatives and the senate.

Protection against reprisal, retaliation, or false accusation

4.   A new section is added to chapter 28A.600 RCW to read as follows: (1) No school employee, student, or volunteer may engage in reprisal, retaliation, or false accusation against a victim, witness, or one with reliable information about an act of harassment, intimidation, or bullying. (2) A school employee, student, or volunteer who has witnessed, or has reliable information that a student has been subjected to harassment, intimidation, or bullying, whether verbal or physical, is encouraged to report such incident to an appropriate school official.

Protection against lawsuits upon compliance with policies

(3) A school employee, student, or volunteer who promptly reports an incident of harassment, intimidation, or bullying to an appropriate school official, and who makes this report in compliance with the procedures in the district's policy prohibiting bullying, harassment, or intimidation, is immune from a cause of action for damages arising from any failure to remedy the reported incident.

Resource C: Suggested 360-Degree Anti-Bullying Training Plan

Suggested 360-Degree Anti-Bullying Training Plan, Page 1

 Who?   In What?   Frequency?   Trainers

 Teachers, Classified Staff, Athletic Directors and Coaches (full time or seasonal), Monitors and Chaperones of Extracurricular Activities and Field Trips

- ✓ What constitutes bullying and what the school district's anti-bullying policy contains
- ✓ The difference between bullying and conflict (so that inappropriate referrals are not made)
- ✓ The behaviors that constitute various forms of illegal harassment based on race/national origin, gender, sex, sexual orientation, or disability
- ✓ Their duty to provide a safe learning environment for students and what the district may be liable for should they fail in this duty
- ✓ The signs and symptoms that a child is a target of bullying behavior
- ✓ Classroom or playground interventions and disciplinary actions that they can implement
- ✓ How to respond in a legally sound manner should a student report bullying or harassment (do not dismiss as tattling, do not promise confidentiality, be compassionate and nonjudgmental, do not blame the victim)
- ✓ That the school district administration is serious about these issues and considers it their job to intervene in ALL instances of bullying and harassment that occur
- ✓ Knowing the student code of conduct and procedures and consequences for violations
- ✓ How and when to document and report incidents
- ✓ What matters to refer to site administrators

At least annually; throughout the school year, any new staff and substitutes must be oriented on this subject as well.

 Bring in a specialist to conduct a district-wide program. Site administrators should be trained to provide follow-up training and development and review sessions via a **training of trainers model.**

 This type of training is also **available online.** An advantage to this format is that the district has secure records of the training, including pre- and post-test scores, for every user who completes the course.

For **athletic directors and coaches,** anti-bullying and harassment may be one topic in a **full-day athletic liability workshop.** Particular attention should be given to hazing prevention. Given the risks involved in athletics, annual training by an expert in athletic liability is recommended.

Suggested 360-Degree Anti-Bullying Training Plan, Page 2

 School Site Administrators, Title IX Officers, School Psychologists and Counselors, District-Level Administrators, Investigators

 ✓ Bullying and harassment complaint management, intake and investigation (all the information in this book)

Note: You want this group to know it all right through Level III. Even if they never end up conducting a full-blown Level III investigation, knowing the steps in the process will inform them in their handling of all complaints that they encounter. Knowing what is ahead, they will be able to analyze the situation and make appropriate referrals.

 Annually

 After first year, train new people in the basics; others should receive a review and advanced training.

Bring in a professional. The trainer must be an expert in the law as it pertains to bullying and harassment, not just an expert on socioemotional aspects of this behavior. Warning: The law is complex and ever evolving. Do not attempt to use this book to train others on your own. The cost of getting it wrong is too high.

Self-paced online training is also available for this topic.

 Students at Every Grade Level, Male and Female

 ✓ Bullying and harassment awareness: How it looks and feels

✓ Student rights & responsibilities

✓ What to do if you experience or observe bullying or harassing behavior

✓ How to report

✓ Standing up for others

✓ School District policy including consequences (in age-appropriate language)

 At least annually; build modules into health and citizenship classes

 This is a sensitive topic and program delivery requires quality preparation and a high degree of sensitivity to children's emotions and possible trauma that may be triggered. School counselors are the ideal group to deliver the training. They should be trained by a bullying and harassment professional via a **training of trainers model.**

Suggested 360-Degree Anti-Bullying Training Plan, Page 3

  Parents

- ✓ The School District's commitment to a learning environment free from bullying and harassment
- ✓ Bullying and harassment awareness: How it looks and feels
- ✓ Rights & responsibilities of parents and students
- ✓ How to report a complaint
- ✓ Signs and symptoms that your child is being bullied
- ✓ Signs and symptoms that your child is bullying others
- ✓ School District anti-bullying policy and Code of Conduct, including consequences
- ✓ Demonstrate any videos or other training materials being used as part of the district's anti-bullying effort

 Annually

 School officials can conduct a meeting; district legal counsel, school counselors, student trainers, and others involved in implementation of the district's anti-bullying effort should be on hand to answer questions. If a specialist is being consulted, invite that person to present at a parent meeting.

For more on training, go to www.mcgrathinc.com

Resource D: Glossary

Accusation.   A formal charge that a person is guilty of a punishable offense.

Action.   Right action is derived from understanding the whole of a situation and having a strong commitment to the growth and development of the people affected. Action that is based on transformative thinking, listening, and speaking evolves both the people involved and their environment.

Administrative law.   Policies and procedures adopted by an administrative agency (e.g., a school district governing board) that carry the full weight of law and govern the agency in exercising its authority over others.

Administrative policies and procedures (school).   Binding rules and regulations established by the governing board of a school, school district, military academy, community college district, or university.

Administrative proceeding.   A proceeding that takes place before an administrative agency rather than in a court of law.

Admissible evidence.   Evidence permitted to be introduced during a trial or hearing.

Advocate.   One who argues for a cause; a supporter or defender. One who pleads in another's behalf; an intercessor. A lawyer.

Affirmative defense.   A defense that does not deny the truth of the allegations against the defendant, but gives some other reason (such as insanity, assumption of risk, or expiration of the statute of limitations) why the defendant cannot be held liable. (Note: The defendant bears the burden of proof of affirmative defenses.)

Age of consent.   The age at which a person can exercise all normal legal rights, including contracting and voting. In the United States, the age of *sexual consent* is regulated by local statute and varies from state to state. A person may also be considered legally incapable of consent if he or she has diminished mental capacity or is intoxicated. (Note: Some state, local, or administrative laws governing school employees supersede local age of sexual consent laws, prohibiting sexual relations by employees with students regardless of age.)

Antecedent.   A thing or event that existed before or logically precedes another in time.

Armed robbery.   A robbery by one who carries a lethal weapon, thus threatening bodily harm to the victim.

Assault. A threat or attempt to inflict offensive physical contact or bodily harm on a person that puts the person in danger or apprehension of such harm or contact.

Authority. Jurisdiction; power. The power to enforce laws, exact obedience, command, determine, or judge. One who is invested with this power, especially a government or government officials. Power assigned to another; authorization. A public agency or corporation with administrative powers in a specified field. An accepted source of expert information or advice.

Balance. When looking through the lens of Balance, you are determining whether the action you are proposing fits with what you have learned through the use of the McGrath FICA Standard. Are you making your decisions using a thorough understanding and application of the Formula (Facts + Impact) × Context = Action?

Battery. Physical violence inflicted upon someone without his or her consent; unlawful injury to someone's body.

Beneficence. Active kindness; doing good; helping others. In ethics: principle of preventing and alleviating others' suffering; meeting the needs of the most vulnerable; promoting others' happiness.

Bias. A preference or an inclination, especially one that inhibits impartial judgment. An unfair act or policy stemming from prejudice.

Binding. Obligatory; required.

Blog (or Weblog). An online journal available to the public (see Technobullying).

Buddy list. A list of friends' online screen names that an Internet user can instant message by clicking on the name (see Technobullying).

Bully. A person who perpetrates bullying behavior against another or others.

Bullying. Behavior toward another in which (1) harm or hurt is intended; (2) a power imbalance exists; (3) the perpetrator enjoys carrying out the action; (4) the perpetrator repeats the behavior, often in a systematic way; and (5) the victim has a sense of being persecuted or oppressed and is hurt physically and/or psychologically. The law as found in state statutes defines bullying as not just the flagrant incidents of physical violence and verbal abuse between peers but also the everyday meanness and disrespect that permeates our K–12 campuses.

Bully–victim. A person who is both a victim and a perpetrator of bullying behavior.

Bully–victim relationship. In this third and final phase of the bullying pattern, the victim sees no way out. The victim has a growing sense of hopelessness and despair. The bullying behavior is now persistent and pervasive.

Bystander. A person who is present at an event or incident but does not take part; an observer; an onlooker; a witness.

Campaign phase.   The second phase in the bully-victim relationship, in which the perpetrator escalates the behavior. The victim is still hoping for relief and trying to fit in. He experiences guilt, self-blame, and shame at not being able to stop the behavior or stand up for himself. Bullying becomes more frequent and more pervasive. The bully will often enlist the cooperation of bystanders. This phase includes threats and intimidation should the victim "tattle."

Case law.   The law on a particular subject based upon a group of similar issues decided by other courts. Case law is not based upon statutes, but upon rulings in similar situations in other actions.

Chatroom.   A Web page on the Internet where two or more people can have typewritten conversations. Some chatrooms are private and by invitation only; others are public and may be joined at will (see Technobullying).

Child neglect.   Lack of care and failure to carry out one's duties or obligations regarding the protection of a child.

Child Protective Services.   The Department of Children and Family Services in your state provides child protection services. The goal of the department's child protection program is outlined in each state's Child Abuse and Neglect Reporting Act. Here is an example: "The Department of Children and Family Services shall, upon receiving reports made under this Act, protect the best interest of the child, offer protective services in order to prevent any further harm to the child and to other children in the family, stabilize the home environment and preserve family life whenever possible." More than 65% of all child abuse/neglect reports are made by doctors, teachers, and others mandated by law to report suspected cases.

Child sexual abuse.   "There is no universal definition of child sexual abuse. However, a central characteristic of any abuse is the dominant position of an adult that allows him or her to force or coerce a child into sexual activity. Child sexual abuse may include fondling a child's genitals, masturbation, oral-genital contact, digital penetration, and vaginal and anal intercourse. Child sexual abuse is not solely restricted to physical contact; such abuse could include non-contact abuse, such as exposure, voyeurism, and child pornography. Abuse by peers also occurs" (APA Online, 2001). Definitions and ages of majority vary by jurisdiction. Check your local and state laws.

Chronic trauma.   A long-term, repetitive, and insidious accumulation of everyday insults to one's integrity and sense of safety as a human being, distinct from time-limited events that result in trauma, such as rape, natural disasters, and car accidents.

Civil action.   A suit entered into for the purpose of enforcing a civil or personal right. Not a criminal action. Civil actions are proceedings in which one party sues another party for a legal wrong or for the prevention of a wrong.

Civil law.   Written law. Law prevailing as the result of acts or statutes. Law dealing with civil rather than criminal matters.

Civil Rights Act of 1871, § 1983.   Found in Title 42, § 1983 of the United States Code and commonly referred to as "section 1983." Creates liability for anyone acting on behalf of a state who causes the deprivation of any rights, privileges, or immunities secured by the United States Constitution and federal laws, if the person acts in an official capacity with deliberate indifference.

Civil rights laws.   Those laws passed by Congress to implement the guarantees in the United States Constitution and its Amendments. Civil rights laws guarantee equal protection to all people regardless of race, color, national origin, creed, gender, age, or disability.

Common law.   Law declared by judges functioning in areas not controlled by governmental regulations, ordinances, or statutes. Law originating from usage and custom rather than from written statutes.

Complex Post-Traumatic Stress Disorder.   A suggested diagnosis that describes the psychological harm that may result from severe, repeated trauma that continues over months or years. Complex PTSD is associated with situations in which the victim is under the control of the perpetrator and experiences being unable to flee. Symptoms include alterations in the following: (1) emotional regulation, (2) consciousness, (3) self-perception, (4) perception of the perpetrator, (5) relations with others, and (6) one's system of meanings (Herman, 1997; see Post-Traumatic Stress Disorder).

Confidentiality.   Done or communicated in confidence. The quality of being confidential, privileged, or secret.

Conflict of interest.   A conflict between the private interests and the public obligations of a person in an official position.

Consent.   A voluntary agreement to another's proposition by a person legally capable of consenting (see Age of consent).

Constructive notice.   A presumption that a person received notice even though actual notice was not personally delivered to him or her; notice that one exercising ordinary care and diligence as a matter of duty would possess. The law may provide that constructive notice is a substitute for actual notice in certain circumstances. For example, allowing service (legal delivery of a legal notice) by publication in an approved newspaper when a spouse has left the state to avoid service in a divorce action; the legal advertisement is treated as constructive notice, just as if the summons and petition had been served personally.

Contemporaneous.   Taking place at the same time as another occurrence.

Context.   The circumstances in which an event occurs; a setting. The part of a text or statement that surrounds a particular word or passage and determines its meaning.

Corroborative evidence.   Evidence that strengthens, adds to, or confirms already existing evidence.

Credibility.   The quality, capability, or power to elicit belief.

Crime.   A breaking of the law; either a misdemeanor or a felony.

Criminal action.   A lawsuit that provides for bringing an offender to justice. Not a civil action.

Criminal law.   The branch of law that deals with crimes and their punishment. This branch of law concerns itself with public wrongs such as homicide, robbery, rape, assault, battery, and child sexual abuse.

Damages.   Compensation that the law awards to someone who has been injured or has suffered a loss because of the action of another.

Decision.   A judgment or decree issued by a judge or jury; the deciding of a lawsuit; findings of a court.

Defendant.   The party who refutes a claim made in a lawsuit. The person accused in a lawsuit.

Deliberate indifference.   A practice, custom, or policy of disregarding, dismissing, concealing, and/or discouraging complaints of misconduct.

Denial.   An unconscious defense mechanism characterized by refusal to acknowledge painful realities, thoughts, or feelings. A way of avoiding being painfully connected to something emotionally unacceptable.

Deposition.   Testimony under oath, especially a statement by a witness that is written down or recorded for use in court at a later date.

Direct evidence.   Testimony and proof that relate directly to the issue at hand; proof that requires no other evidence; testimony that arises from the witness's own information and knowledge.

Discipline.   A series of principles and practices that we study, master, and integrate into our lives (Senge, 1990).

Discovery.   The phase of a legal action in which both sides are compelled to answer questions put to them and to produce all documents relative to the case. Each party has a right of discovery in obtaining facts from his or her adversary.

Discretionary act.   An act in accordance with one's own discretion or judgment.

Discrimination.   The denial of equal protection of laws; the failure to treat all people alike despite differences in race, color, age, creed, sex, or social position.

Due process.   The regular course of events in the administration of justice, respecting the rights of every person, giving him or her the time and the right to defend himself or herself without interference and without the fear that the law will be unfair to him or her.

Duty.   A legal obligation.

Equal Employment Opportunity Commission (EEOC).   The EEOC coordinates all federal equal employment opportunity regulations, practices, and policies. The Commission interprets employment discrimination laws, monitors the federal sector employment discrimination program, provides funding and support to state and local Fair Employment Practices Agencies (FEPAs), and sponsors outreach and technical assistance programs. The EEOC enforces the following federal statutes: Title VII of the Civil Rights Act of 1964, as amended; the Age Discrimination in Employment Act (ADEA) of 1967, as amended; the Equal Pay Act (EPA) of 1963; Title I and Title V of the Americans with Disabilities Act (ADA) of 1990; Section 501 and 505 of the Rehabilitation Act of 1973; and the Civil Rights Act of 1991.

Any individual who believes he or she has been discriminated against in employment may file an administrative charge with the EEOC. After investigating the charge, the EEOC determines if there is reasonable cause to believe discrimination has occurred. If reasonable cause is found, the EEOC attempts to conciliate the charge by reaching a voluntary resolution between the charging party and the respondent. If conciliation is not successful, the Commission may bring suit in federal court. As part of the administrative process, the EEOC may also issue a Right-to-Sue Notice to the charging party, allowing the charging party to file an individual action in court without the Agency's involvement.

Evidence.   Everything that is brought into court in a trial in an attempt to prove or disprove alleged facts. Evidence includes the introduction of exhibits, records, documents, objects, and so on, plus the testimony of witnesses.

Exclusion.   Isolation from and by one's peer group; being shut out; a type of relational bullying.

Extort.   To compel against one's wishes; to coerce. To extort money, such as in blackmail, is to make someone give it against his own wishes for fear of exposure.

Fact.   Something that took place; an act; something actual and real; an incident that occurred; an event. Information presented as objectively real.

Fairness.   The state of being just or appropriate to the circumstances; conformity or consistency with rules, logic, ethics, or standards; the ability to make judgments free from discrimination or dishonesty.

Family Educational Rights And Privacy Act (FERPA).   The Family Educational Rights and Privacy Act of 1974, as amended (also referred to as the Buckley Amendment), is a federal law regarding the privacy of student records and the obligations of an educational institution, primarily in the areas of release of student records and the access provided to these records. Any educational institution that receives funds under any program administered by the U.S. Secretary of Education is bound by FERPA requirements. Institutions that fail to comply with FERPA may have funds withheld by the Secretary of Education.

FERPA gives students the following rights: (1) the right to inspect and review education records, (2) the right to seek amendment of education records, (3) the right to consent to disclosure of education records, (4) the right to obtain a copy of the school's Student Records policy, and (5) the right to file a complaint with the FERPA Office in Washington, DC.

Fifth Amendment.   Grants the privilege against self-incrimination, whereby a person is privileged to refuse to answer a question or give testimony that might subject him or her to a criminal conviction.

Five point criterion for determining actionable bullying.   The behavior complained about must (1) be intended to harm; (2) be unwelcome or unwanted; (3) be severe or persistent, or pervasive; (4) substantially interfere with work or study; (5) meet the subjective and objective tests or standards related to its level of interference with work or study.

Five-point criterion for determining illegal harassment.   The behavior complained about must (1) be related to a protected classification; (2) be unwelcome or unwanted; (3) be severe or persistent, or pervasive; (4) substantially interfere with work or study; (5) meet the subjective and objective tests or standards related to its level of interference with work or study.

Foreseeability.   The ability to be foreseen, predicted, or reasonably anticipated.

Freedom of Information Act (FOIA).   Federal agencies are required under the FOIA to disclose records requested in writing by any person. However, agencies may withhold information pursuant to nine exemptions and three exclusions contained in the statute. The FOIA applies only to federal agencies and does not create a right of access to records held by Congress, the courts, or by state or local government agencies. Each state has its own public access laws that should be consulted for access to state and local records.

Free speech.   Guarantees, contained in the First and Fourteenth Amendments to the United States Constitution, of the right of people to speak what they please without government regulations or restriction, limited only by abuse of the right.

Governmental immunity.   The doctrine from English common law providing that no governmental body can be sued unless it gives permission. The Federal Tort Claims Act, which removed the power of the federal government to claim immunity from a lawsuit for damages due to negligent or intentional injury by a federal employee in the scope of his or her work for the government, negated this rule. The tort liability of local and state governments is now the subject of statute and varies from state to state.

Hazing.   Humiliating and sometimes dangerous initiation rituals forced upon underclassmen or new members of a team, club, fraternity or sorority, military unit, or other group.

Health Insurance Portability and Accountability Act of 1996 (HIPAA). HIPAA is a set of rules, to be followed by doctors, hospitals, and other health care providers, which took effect on April 14, 2003. HIPAA ensures that all medical records, medical billing, and patient accounts meet certain consistent standards with regard to documentation, handling, and privacy. In addition, HIPAA requires that all patients be able to access their own medical records to correct errors or omissions, be informed as to how personal information is shared, and notified of privacy procedures to be used.

Hearing.   A procedure during which evidence is taken to determine an issue of fact and come to a decision based on that evidence. A hearing may take place out of court, but it must be presided over by someone with judicial authority.

Hearsay.   Something not heard or witnessed personally, but which is based upon what was heard or witnessed.

Although only some school health records (e.g., records that derive from school-based health centers) fall directly under HIPAA jurisdiction, all schools need to exchange information with health providers, clinics, hospitals, and other entities required to adhere to HIPAA. As such, "release of information" forms used by schools to notify health agencies that student information is being sought must now comply with HIPAA regulations if they are to serve their purpose.

The handling of private information described in HIPAA is particularly relevant to schools. The flow of protected health information within the school system needs to be analyzed and addressed for compliance, for example, how items such as phone logs, records of students visiting the school nurse, students visiting the school psychologist or counselor, and lists of students with health problems are utilized and who has access to them. This confidentiality applies to written, oral, and electronic forms of information.

Hearsay evidence.   Secondhand evidence; evidence that derives its value not directly from the testifying witness but from the believability of another person who has given information to the witness. Such evidence is often ruled to be inadmissible in criminal proceedings, but may be used in administrative proceedings within certain guidelines.

Hostile environment sexual harassment.   Any unwelcome sexually oriented conduct or atmosphere that is so severe or pervasive that it is intimidating or offensive to a "reasonable person similarly situated" to the victim.

Hyperactive bully/anxious bully.   A member of a subgroup of bullies, characterized as a student who struggles academically, has poor social skills and low self-esteem, and does not read social cues accurately. Reacts aggressively to others' innocent actions; blames others.

Impact.   The section of the McGrath FICA Standard that refers to the consequences or repercussions of a person's actions. Impact tells us why the situation is important. Impact questions include: Who was hurt or may be hurt by this behavior? How were they hurt? Who else was impacted and how? There is a direct, cause-effect correlation between Facts and Impact.

IEP Team.   The team of educators and specialists who plan and implement the Individual Education Plan (IEP) for a special education student in K–12 schools. For adults with disabilities receiving special services, the team develops an Individual Program Plan (IPP).

In loco parentis.   Latin term meaning "in place of a parent."

Inquiry.   An examination, exploration, or analysis. Implemented when a situation meets the criteria for informal resolution on page 127 (as distinct from an investigation, which is implemented when a situations meets the criteria for formal resolution).

Instant messaging.   Through this service, Internet users can see which of their buddies (see Buddy list) are online and send messages, photos, or other content instantly. The onscreen representation is a two-way "chat," with each party typing their side of the conversation. Onlookers who are physically present with either party can see the conversation on screen. It is also possible to copy the contents of an instant message, paste it into an e-mail, and send it to someone else's computer.

Intent.   The determination or resolve to do a certain thing, or the state of mind with which something is done. Mental desire and will to act in a particular way, including wishing not to participate. Intent is a crucial element in determining whether behavior constitutes bullying. It is not a criterion for determining illegal sexual harassment, which is based not upon the intent of the perpetrator but how the victim perceives the behavior.

Interrogatories.   A set of written questions presented to a witness in order to obtain his written testimony while under oath to tell the truth. They often take place prior to the trial.

Intimidation.   An expression of the intent to hurt or punish another. The act of making timid; filling with fear; coercion; inhibiting another by or as if by threats; frightening into submission, compliance, or acquiescence.

Investigation.   Careful, intensive examination of circumstances and situations to discover facts; questioning concerned parties; a legal inquiry.

Just cause.   A legal and fair cause for carrying out an action.

Justice.   The quality of being fair or reasonable; integrity in the dealings of people with each other; equity; equality; the principle of moral rightness.

Larceny.   An intent or plan to steal.

Leading questions.   Questions in which the interviewer suggests the answer that the witness might give. This is putting the words in the person's mouth and is problematic in legal proceedings and interviews. For example, "When he came into the room, did he frighten you?"

Liability.   Legal responsibility; the obligation to do or not do something; an obligation to pay a debt; the responsibility to behave in a certain manner.

Listening.   The ability to clear your mind of preconceptions so you can hear what is being said, whether or not you agree with it. Enhanced listening includes the ability to understand the *entire* situation in a holistic manner.

Minimization.   A psychological defense mechanism whereby the person relates to the impact of an event as minimal, unimportant, or "no big deal" in order to cope with pain, injury, or trauma.

Molestation.   The act of harassing or annoying someone. The term is often used to describe the conduct of an adult who makes physical advances toward, or otherwise annoys, a child.

Monitor.   To systematically keep track of something with the intent of collecting information. To test or sample on a regular or ongoing basis. To keep close watch over; supervise. To direct.

Moral negotiation.   Resolution of a disagreement in which there is a difference in values. During adolescence, human beings are challenged by the need to differentiate themselves from others and the process of self-understanding that need entails. In the process, adolescents grapple with moral vocabulary that is unfamiliar or new to them. They are resolving the question *What do I* *think about that?* This shows up in social interactions as both disagreements and gossip among peers. Experts on social aggression (see Underwood, 2003) speculate that the role of gossip at this age may not always have malicious intent, but rather may be part of how adolescents figure out where they stand on an issue. Even well-meaning adolescents talk about others' behavior loosely. They lack the maturity and sensitivity to protect the identity of the person whose behavior is in question. This can lead to harm, intended or not.

"Need-to-know" basis.   Information is only given to individuals who are directly involved in an investigation, and then only that information which they need to know in order to get their job done. In the case of the accused, the person is usually given details of the accusation(s) and the name of the complainant and due process is followed. In the case of the complainant, the person is kept apprised of the progress of the investigation and told what action is being taken to remedy the situation, unless that action is not disclosable under a collective bargaining agreement. Should a civil or criminal action be initiated, rules of discovery then apply.

Negligence.   Failure to do what a reasonable, careful, conscientious person is expected to do; doing something that a reasonable, careful, conscientious person would not do.

No Child Left Behind Act of 2001 (NCLB).   Reauthorized the Elementary and Secondary Education Act (ESEA), the main federal law affecting education from kindergarten through high school. Passed into law by the U.S. Congress on January 8, 2002, NCLB is built on four principles: accountability for results, more choices for parents, greater local control and flexibility, and an emphasis on doing what works based on scientific research.

Nonmaleficence.   Avoiding inflicting suffering and hardship on others. In ethics: The principle of doing no harm.

Obligation.   Something a person is bound to do or bound not to do; moral or legal duty. Penalties may be imposed upon people who fail in their obligations.

OCR: Office for Civil Rights, U.S. Department of Education.   The mission of the Office for Civil Rights is to ensure equal access to education and to promote educational excellence throughout the United States through vigorous enforcement of civil rights. The Office for Civil Rights enforces five federal statutes that prohibit discrimination in education programs and activities that receive federal financial assistance.

Open-ended questions.   Questions that do not elicit a "yes" or "no" answer, allowing for spontaneous, unstructured responses.

Paradigm.   An example that serves as a pattern or model. An assumed frame of reference. A context.

Passive victim.   A victim of bullying who does nothing that could be considered provocative toward the person or group instigating the bullying behavior.

Persistent.   Refusing to give up or let go. Persevering obstinately. Insistently repetitive or continuous.

Personal space.   The area surrounding a person, which he considers his domain or territory and into which other people are not welcome. If someone enters this regions, the resulting "boundary violation" will feel uncomfortable and he may move away to increase the distance. This is because closeness lends a sense of intimacy that is at odds with his relationship to the other individual. (The exceptions are family members, close friends, and romantic relationships.) The distance required for comfort is highly variable, affected by factors such as culture, gender, and ethnicity.

Pervasive.   Present throughout the environment; permeating.

Plaintiff.   The party who is bringing a lawsuit against a defendant. The person who is suing.

Policy.   A course of action to be followed or avoided. The programs and aims of a government (or governing board) in caring for those it serves.

Post Traumatic Stress Disorder (PTSD).   "A psychiatric disorder that can occur following the experience or witnessing of life-threatening events such as military combat, natural disasters, terrorist incidents, serious accidents, or violent personal assaults like rape. Most survivors of trauma return to normal given a little time. However, some people will have stress reactions that do not go away on their own, or may even get worse over time. These individuals may develop PTSD. People who suffer from PTSD often relive the experience through nightmares and flashbacks, have difficulty sleeping, and feel detached or estranged, and these symptoms can be severe enough and last long enough to significantly impair the person's daily life.

"Most likely to develop PTSD: (1) Those who experience greater stressor magnitude and intensity, unpredictability, uncontrollability, sexual (as opposed to nonsexual) victimization, real or perceived responsibility, and betrayal; (2) Those with prior vulnerability factors such as genetics, early age of onset and longer-lasting childhood trauma, lack of functional social support, and concurrent stressful life events; (3) Those who report greater perceived threat or danger, suffering, upset, terror, and horror or fear; (4) Those with a social environment that produces shame, guilt, stigmatization, or self-hatred" (National Center for PTSD, n.d.).

Power imbalance.   Circumstance in which there is an imbalance of physical, psychological, and/or social power of the perpetrator(s) over the target(s).

Practices.   What you do.

Prejudice.   A negative bias or dislike of a group of people because they belong to a particular group one dislikes. The group is often an ethnic, racial, or other social category.

Preponderance.   Weight, superiority, credibility.

Principles.   Guiding ideas and insights.

Preponderance of evidence.   A standard of proof wherein 51% or more of the evidence establishes a fact.

Probable cause.   A reasonable cause; one that has a good chance of being true; a good ground for suspicion that a crime has been committed.

Procedure.   *Legal usage:* Rules governing the conduct of a lawsuit, including the presentation of evidence, the making of motions, pleadings, and so on. It is the method of proceeding in order to prove a legal right. *Common usage:* A manner of proceeding; a way of performing or effecting something. A series of steps taken to accomplish an end. A set of established forms or methods for conducting the affairs of a business.

Proof.   The establishment of truth through evidence; the effect of evidence; a conviction of the mind that a certain fact in issue has been established as true.

Protected classification.   A classification of people protected against discrimination by civil rights laws. Protected classes include race, color, national origin, creed, gender, age, and disability. In some locales, sexual orientation is also protected.

Provocative victim.   A victim who behaves in a way that seems to provoke the bullying behavior directed toward him or her. These victims often have behavioral problems and/or attention deficits and engage in behaviors that others find irritating.

Proximate cause.   The immediate cause of an injury or accident; the legal cause; the real cause; a direct cause.

Quality.   The quality of your communication is directly correlated with your ability to identify and eliminate opinion from the factual foundation.

Quid pro quo.   Latin for "this for that." A form of sexual harassment that entails abuse of supervisory power involving a tangible employment or educational action.

Rape.   The forcing of sexual relations by a man upon a woman against her will. Several courts have also ruled that rape exists when a woman forces sexual relations upon a man against his will or, in some instances, when a female has relations with a male who is under the age of consent, even if he is a voluntary and willing participant in the sexual act. Rape also can take place between two people of the same sex.

Rapport.   Relationship, especially one of mutual trust or emotional affinity.

Reasonable doubt.   A lack of sufficient certainty from the evidence that an accused person is actually guilty of a particular crime; a fair doubt based on rational, sensible thinking.

Reasonable suspicion.   *Reasonable:* Governed by or being in accordance with reason or sound thinking. Not excessive or extreme. *Suspicion:* The act of suspecting something, especially something wrong, on little evidence or without proof.

Relational bullying.   Harm to another through damage (or the threat of damage) to relationships or to feelings of acceptance, friendship, or group inclusion. The most difficult type of bullying to detect from the outside, relational bullying is often unseen and can be hard to identify. It is most prominent among middle and high school children because it thrives in a climate that separates and classifies young people into cliques. It is not exclusive to girls but is more common among girls than boys (see Social scheming).

Remediable.   Capable of being corrected, rectified, or redressed.

Remediation.   The act or process of correcting a fault or deficiency.

Remedy.   The means employed by the law to correct injuries or to enforce legal rights.

Respect.   Due regard for the feelings, wishes, rights, or traditions of others. Esteem, admiration, deference or honor. The principle underlying the Impact section of the McGrath FICA Standard.

Respondeat superior.   Latin for "let the master answer," a key doctrine in the law of agency, which provides that a principal (employer) is responsible for the actions of his/her/its agent (employee) in the "course of employment." Thus, an agent who signs an agreement to purchase goods for his employer in the name of the employer can create a binding contract between the seller and the employer.

Sanction.   A penalty imposed for the purpose of obtaining compliance and obedience to the law.

Severe.   Very serious; grave or grievous. Causing sharp discomfort or distress; extremely violent or intense. In the context of hostile environment sexual harassment: Generally, for the behavior to be considered severe, it violates criminal law.

Sex discrimination.   Treating people differently based on their gender.

Social networking Web site.   A complex web of friends connected online by a common interest, for example, MySpace.com or Friendster.com (see Technobullying).

Social scheming.   Attacking another in circuitous ways such as indirect signaling (e.g., "dirty looks" or turning away), deception, changing alliances, plotting, backbiting, spreading gossip intended to ruin the victim's reputation, shunning, or ostracizing the victim. Also known as indirect aggression, this type of bullying is more common among girls than boys and is viewed as hurtful because it harms the intimate relationships that girls value (see Three-way calling attacks).

Speaking.   Transformative communication is more than words coming out of your mouth. It is a way to put masterful, holistic thinking and listening into action. When speaking is objective and fair, it can be more easily received and makes a difference.

Statute.   A law passed by the legislative branch of a government. Includes federal law, state law, and local laws, for example, the Education Code in your state.

Statutory rape.   In certain states, it is statutory rape when an adult male or female has sexual relations with a female or male who is under the age of consent, even if she or he is a voluntary and willing participant in the sexual act.

Structure.   Analyzing a McGrath FICA Standard communication for structure is very straightforward. You are looking for all four parts—Facts, Impact, Context, and Action—in that exact order. Are they in the F.I.C.A. sequence? Is anything muddled or out of place?

Superseding cause.   An act that interrupts a chain of events so that it severs the connection between the chain of events and the outcome, thus becoming the proximate cause.

Systematic abuse.   Planned, methodical cruelty or violence toward another.

Tacit authorization.   Authority or permission implied by or inferred from actions or statements. Authorization arising by operation of the law rather than through direct expression.

Tangible employment action.   An action resulting in a significant change in employment or academic status. There are three characteristics: (1) It is the means by which a supervisor brings the official power of the employer or school to bear on subordinates; (2) It usually inflicts direct economic or academic consequences; and (3) In most cases, it can only be taken by a supervisor or another person acting with authority granted by the employer or school.

Taunt.   To provoke with insulting remarks. The context of "taunting" is that intimidation, denigration, and/or humiliation are experienced by the recipient and intended by the perpetrator. Taunting behavior is usually persistent in nature, happening over and over again. It often involves jeering—intentionally provocative, mocking, insulting, and/or intimidating comments. The behavior is unwelcome to the recipient.

Tease.   To make fun of someone in a playful way, in which harm is neither intended by the speaker nor felt by the recipient.

Technobullying.   Bullying behavior that involves the use of electronic equipment such as computers, mobile telephones, pagers, and handheld devices to send or post messages or commentary intended to hurt another (see Blog, Buddy list, Chatroom, Social networking Web sites and Text messaging).

Testimony.   Evidence given under oath by a witness, as distinguished from evidence derived from written documents.

Text messaging.   The practice of sending typed messages to someone's cell phone, pager, or e-mail address from a computer, PDA, or cell phone (see Technobullying).

Theft.   Stealing property.

Thinking.   To see things clearly, and assess and reflect them honestly, without opinion.

Thinking errors.   Errors of logic that become habituated. Faulty assumptions and misconceptions. Cognitive therapists use this term to define errors in thinking that can lead to faulty conclusions about causal responsibility, justifiability for actions taken, wrongdoing, or all of the above, for example, blaming, excuse making, lying, minimizing, or maximizing.

Three-way calling attacks.   A type of social scheming in which a deception is perpetrated on an unsuspecting victim via telephone. The objective is to get one child on the phone (A), then conference in another child (B). B doesn't know that A is on the line. The originator of the call then traps B into saying something mean about A.

Title IX, Education Amendments of 1972.   A federal law prohibiting sex discrimination, including sexual harassment, against students and employees of educational institutions. Title IX states: "No person in the United States shall, on the basis of sex, be excluded from participation in, or denied the benefits of, or be subjected to discrimination under any educational program or activity receiving federal assistance." Under this law, males and females are expected to receive fair and equal treatment in all arenas of public schooling: recruitment, admissions, educational programs and activities, course offerings and access, counseling, financial aid, employment assistance, facilities and housing, health and insurance benefits, marital and parental status, scholarships, and athletics.

Tone.   Tone is the character, effect, or atmosphere of the communication. It is the relationship factor.

Tort.   A wrong committed by one person against another; a civil rather than a criminal wrong. A violation of a legal duty that one person has toward another. (Negligence and libel are torts.) Every tort is composed of a legal obligation, a breach of that obligation, and damage as the result of the breach of the obligation.

Train.   To coach in or accustom to a mode of behavior or performance. To make proficient with specialized instruction and practice.

Trauma.   An emotional wound or shock that creates substantial, lasting damage to the psychological development of a person.

Trolling.   The first stage of the bully-victim relationship, trolling behavior is characterized by single, subtle acts of bullying behavior aimed at different individuals. The perpetrator is looking for easy targets and will test potential victims' boundaries by invading their personal space and test their reactions with quick comments, threats, or taunts.

Witness.   One who can give a firsthand account of something seen, heard, or experienced. One who furnishes evidence. An individual who testifies under oath at a trial, a hearing, or before a legislative body.

Resource E:
Useful Web Sites

McGrath Bullying Resources Download Page

www.mcgrathinc.com/bullyresources.htm
Download 8½" × 11" reproducible McGrath Anti-Bullying Forms
Links to articles, white papers, and Internet resources

McGrath CyberSchool

www.mcgrathcyberschool.com
Distance learning courses include:
Sexual Harassment and Abuse Awareness for School Personnel and
Complaint Management and Investigation for Administrators
New online courses added annually

McGrath Training Systems

www.mcgrathinc.com
Articles, links, free demos
Information about Mary Jo McGrath and McGrath Training Systems' onsite
programs, videos, and CyberSchool courses

ANTI-BULLYING SITES
(ENGLISH-SPEAKING COUNTRIES)

These sites contain a wealth of resources for kids, teens, parents, and
educators.

Anti-Bullying Centre (Ireland)	www.abc.tcd.ie
Anti-Bullying Network (Scotland)	www.antibullying.net
Bullying Online (United Kingdom)	www.bullying.co.uk/
Colorado Anti-Bullying Project (USA)	www.no-bully.com
No Bully (New Zealand)	www.police.govt.nz/service/ yes/nobully

| Teaching Tolerance (USA) | www.tolerance.org |
| www.bullying.org (Canada) | www.bullying.org |

BULLYING AND DISABILITY

Bullying No Way!   www.bullyingnoway.com.au
Go to "The Issues" → "Deeper Issues" → "Disability"

Muscular Dystrophy Association   www.mdausa.org/publications
Search in upper right for "Beating the Bully Problem"

National Center on Secondary   www.ncset.org
Education & Transition

"Publications" → "Issue Briefs" → "Bullying and Teasing of Youth With Disabilities: Creating Positive School Environments for Effective Inclusion"

"Teleconferences" → "Transcripts of Past Teleconference Calls" → "Bullying, Teasing, Youth Violence, and Prevention: Addressing the Needs of Youth with Disabilities"

BULLYING AND SEXUAL ORIENTATION

Gay Lesbian Straight   www.glsen.org
Education Network
Human Rights Campaign   www.hrc.org
National Mental Health Association www.nmha.org

"About Us" → "NMHA Programs" → "What Does Gay Mean?" → "Bullying and Gay Youth" → "Bullying in Schools: Harassment Puts Gay Youth At Risk"

Parents, Families & Friends of   www.pflag.org
Lesbians & Gays

TECHNOBULLYING AND INTERNET SAFETY

Center for Safety &	
Responsible Internet Use	www.csriu.org
Cyberbullying.org	www.cyberbullying.org
WiredSafety.net	www.wiredsafety.net
STOP Cyberbullying	www.stopcyberbullying.org
StopTextBullying.org	www.stoptextbully.org
Take Charge	www.cox.com/takecharge/

GOVERNMENT PUBLICATIONS

Department for Education and Skills   www.dfes.gov.uk/bullying

"Don't Suffer in Silence" Project, United Kingdom

DFES Anti-Bullying Pack

Anti-Bullying Postcards for students (in pdf) available in English, Albanian, Arabic, Dutch, French, Kurdish, Mandarin, Russian, Somali, Swahili, Tamil, and Turkish

Kentucky School Boards Association   www.ksba.org/legalhipaa.htm

In association with Kentucky Department of Education

Local School Districts' Responsibilities Under HIPAA

Model HIPAA Authorization Form

National Center for Education Statistics   http://nces.ed.gov

"Publications and Products" → Search: "Guide to Protecting the Privacy of Student Information: State and Local Education Agencies (NCES 2004-330)"

"Annual Reports" → "Indicators of School Crime and Safety" (report updated annually)

National Mental Health   www.mentalhealth.samhsa.gov
Information Center

Search "The School Bully Can Take a Toll on Your Child's Mental Health"

National Youth Violence Prevention   www.safeyouth.org
Resource Center

Keyword search "bullying" brings up downloadable publications

U.S. Department of Education   www.ed.gov

"Offices" → "Office for Civil Rights"

"Prevention" → "Sexual Harassment Resources" → "Revised Sexual Harassment Guidance: Harassment of Students by School Employees, Other Students, or Third Parties, Title IX, January, 2001"

"Reports and Resources" → "Database of ED Publications in ERIC"→ "basic search form" → search database → "Protecting Students from Harassment and Hate Crime: A Guide for Schools"

U.S. Department of Health &   www.stopbullyingnow.hrsa.gov
Human Services

Stop Bullying Now Resource Kit: "What Adults Can Do" → "Additional Resources" → "Order the campaign Resource Kit online"

"What Adults Can Do" → "Tip Sheets and Resources" → "Bullying Among Children and Youth With Disabilities and Special Needs" (Tip Sheet #24)

United States Secret Service   www.treas.gov/usss/ntac
                                              .shtml

National Threat Assessment Center Safe Schools Initiative

The Final Report and Findings of the Safe School Initiative: Implications for the Prevention of School Attacks in the United States

Threat Assessment in Schools: A Guide to Managing Threatening Situations and Creating Safe School Climates

PROFESSIONAL ASSOCIATIONS

American Medical Association   www.ama-assn.org

Search in top right for "Educational Forum on Adolescent Health: Youth Bullying"

National Education Association   www.nea.org/schoolsafety
National Bullying Awareness Campaign

STUDIES ONLINE

Nickelodeon/Kaiser Family Foundation   www.kff.org/kaiserpolls

Search "Talking with Kids About Tough Issues: A National Survey of Parents and Kids"

The Pew Internet and American   www.pewinternet.org/
Life Project

The Pew Internet & American Life Project produces 15–20 reports a year that explore the impact of the Internet on families, communities, work and home, daily life, education, health care, and civic and political life.

For other studies referenced in this book, please see the Bibliography.

Bibliography

Academy School District 20. (2005). *School accountability reports.* Retrieved March 31, 2006, from http://www.d20.co.edu/schools/menu.html

Alsaker, F. D., & Valkanover, S. (2001). Early diagnosis and prevention of victimization in kindergarten. In J. Juvonen & S. Graham (Eds.), *Peer harassment in school: The plight of the vulnerable and victimized* (pp. 175–195). New York: Guilford Press.

Anderson, M., Kaufman, J., Simon, T. R., Barrios, L., Paulozzi, L., Ryan, G., Hammond, R., Modzeleski, W., Feucht, T., Potter, L., & School-Associated Violent Deaths Study Group. (2001). School-associated violent deaths in the United States, 1994–1999. *Journal of the American Medical Association, 286*(21), 2695–2702.

APA Online (2001). Understanding child sexual abuse: Education, prevention, and recovery. Retrieved March 20, 2006, from http://www.apa.org/releases/sexabuse/

Argyris, C. (1991, May/June). Teaching smart people how to learn. *Harvard Business Review,* 99–109, Reprint 91301, 5–15.

Argyris, C. (1994, July/August). Good communication that blocks learning. *Harvard Business Review, 72*(4), 77–86, Reprint 94401, 77–85.

Askew, S. (1989). Aggressive behavior in boys: To what extent is it institutionalized? In D. Tattum & D. Lane (Eds.), *Bullying in schools* (pp. 59–72). Stoke-on-Trent, UK: Trentham Books.

Associated Press. (2005, December 24). Bullied Kansas teen wins $440,000 settlement from school district. *Detroit News.* Retrieved March 24, 2006, from http://www.detnews.com/apps/pbcs.dll/article?AID=/20051224/SCHOOLS/512240428/1026/METRO

Atlas, R. S., & Pepler, D. J. (1998). Observations of bullying in the classroom. *The Journal of Educational Research, 92*(2), 86–99.

Beaudoin, M. N., & Taylor, M. (2004). *Breaking the culture of bullying and disrespect, grades K–8.* Thousand Oaks, CA: Corwin Press.

Brownstein, A. (2002). The bully pulpit: Post-Columbine, harassment victims take school to court. *Trial, 38*(12), 12–17, 62.

Carnell, L. (2006). *Staying safe in cyberspace.* Retrieved March 24, 2006, from http://www.bullying.co.uk/children/internet_safety.htm

Centers for Disease Control and Prevention. (1998, August 14). Youth risk behavior surveillance—United States, 1997. *CDC Surveillance Summaries,* MMWR 1998, 47, p. 8 (No. SS–3). Atlanta, GA: U.S. Department of Health and Human Services.

Change and healing in Chile. (2006, January 17). *Chicago Tribune.* Retrieved March 28, 2006, from http://www.opctj.org/articles/editorial-staff-02-02-106-224549.html

Coloroso, B. (2003). *The bully, the bullied and the bystander* (pp. 11, 18–21). New York: Harper-Resource.

Conn, K. (2002). *The internet and the law: What educators need to know* (pp. 20–23). *Alexandria, VA: Association for Supervision and Curriculum Development.*

Conn, K. (2004). *Bullying and harassment: A legal guide for educators* (p. 164). *Alexandria, VA: Association for Supervision and Curriculum Development.*

Craig, W. M., & Pepler, D. J. (1997). Observations of bullying and victimization in the school yard. *Canadian Journal of School Psychology, 13*, 41–59.

Crick, N. R., Nelson, D. A., Morales, J. R., Cullerton-Sen, C., Casas, J. F., & Hickman, S. E. (2001). Relational victimization in childhood and adolescence: I hurt you through the grapevine. In J. Juvonen & S. Graham (Eds.), *Peer harassment in school: The plight of the vulnerable and victimized* (pp. 196–214). New York: Guilford Press.

Davis, S. (2004). *Schools where everyone belongs: Practical strategies for reducing bullying* (p. 10). Wayne, ME: Stop Bullying Now.

Davis v. Monroe County Board of Education. 526 US 629 (1999).

de Souza Guedes, D. (2002, December 9). District settles hazing lawsuit. *Clinton Herald.*

Doyle, Sir A. C. (1887). *A study in scarlet* (p. 15). New York: Sears & Co.

Egale Canada. (2005, April 21). *B.C. Court of Appeal supports bullied student: Egale Canada calls on all school boards to build safe learning environments* [Press release]. Retrieved March 24, 2006, from http://www.egale.ca/index.asp?lang=E&menu=20&item=1158

Fein, R., Vossekull, B., Pollack, W. S., Borum, R., Modzelski, W., & Reddy, M. (2002). *Threat assessment in schools: A guide to managing threatening situations and creating safe school climates.* Washington, DC: U.S. Secret Service & U.S. Department of Education. Retrieved March 18, 2006, from http://www.treas.gov/usss/ntac/ssi_guide.pdf

Firn, G. (2005). *Culture and climate* (pp. 1, 4–5). Milford, CT: Milford Community Schools.

Garabino, J., & deLara, E. (2002). *And words can hurt forever: How to protect adolescents from bullying, harassment and emotional violence.* New York: The Free Press.

Gebser v. Lago Vista Independent School District. 524 US 274 (1998).

Graham, S., & Juvonen, J. (2001). An attributional approach to peer victimization. In J. Juvonen & S. Graham (Eds.), *Peer harassment in school: The plight of the vulnerable and victimized* (pp. 49–72). New York: Guilford Press.

Gravitz, H. L. (2004). *Unlocking the doors to triumph* (pp. 134–135). Santa Barbara, CA: Healing Visions Press.

Halligan, J. (2004). *The effects of cyber bullying: Teen takes his own life.* Carlsbad, CA: i-Safe America. Retrieved March 22, 2006, from http://www.isafe.org/imgs/pdf/education/CyberBullying.pdf

Harmon, A. (2004, August 26). Internet gives teenage bullies weapons to wound from afar. *New York Times*, p. A1.

Havel, V. (1990, September 27). On Kafka (P. Wilson, Trans.). *New York Review of Books, 37*(14). Retrieved March 22, 2006, from http://www.nybooks.com

Herbert, C. (1996). *Stop the bullying.* Cambridge, UK: Carrie Herbert Press.

Herman, J. (1997). *Trauma and recovery: The aftermath of violence—from domestic abuse to political terror* (pp. 74, 120–121). New York: Basic Books.

Holt, J. C. (1982). *How children fail.* Reading, MA: Perseus Books.

Houston, P. D., & Sokolow, S. L. (2006). *The spiritual dimension of leadership: 8 key principles to leading more effectively* (pp. 104–105). Thousand Oaks, CA: Corwin Press.

Intrator, S. M., & Scribner, M. (Eds.). (2003). *Teaching with fire.* San Francisco: Jossey-Bass.

i-Safe America. (2004). *Beware of the cyber bully.* Retrieved March 22, 2006, from http://www.isafe.org/imgs/pdf/education/CyberBullying.pdf

Jackson, C. (2006, Spring). e-Bully. *Teaching Tolerance*, 50–54.

Kaeufer, K., Scharmer, C. O., & Versteegen, U. (2003). Breathing life into a dying system: Recreating healthcare from within. *Reflections, 5*(3), 3–10. Retrieved March 31, 2006, from http://www.dialogonleadership.org/Breathing%20Life.pdf

Kentucky School Boards Association & Kentucky Department of Education. (2004). *Advisory on local school districts' responsibilities under HIPAA.* Retrieved March 22, 2006, from http://www.ksba.org/legalhipaa.htm (Note: Web page includes a Model HIPAA Authorization Form.)

Kohn, A. (2000). The case against standardized testing: Raising the scores, ruining the schools. In F. Sennett (Ed.), *400 quotable quotes from the world's leading educators* (p. 57). Thousand Oaks, CA: Corwin Press.

Kuhn, T. S. (1996). *The structure of scientific revolution* (3rd ed.). Chicago: University of Chicago Press.

Lee, C. (2004). *Preventing bullying in schools: A guide for teachers and other professionals.* London: Paul Chapman, Sage.

Lenhart, A., & Madden, M. (2005, November 2). *Teen content creators and consumers.* Washington, DC: Pew Internet and American Life Project. Retrieved March 23, 2006, from http://www.pewinternet.org/pdfs/PIP_Teens_Content_Creation.pdf

Marshall, S. P. (2006). *The power to transform: Leadership that brings learning and schooling to life* (p. 64). San Francisco: Jossey-Bass.

McGrath, M. J. (1994). The psychodynamics of school sexual abuse investigations. *The School Administrator, 51*(9), 28–30, 32–34.

McGrath, M. J. (1996a). Video 1: Pay attention: What is sexual harassment? (for ages 11–19). *Student sexual harassment: Minimize the risk* [Videotape and curriculum guide]. Santa Barbara, CA: McGrath Training Systems.

McGrath, M. J. (1996b). Video 2: Pay attention: Don't be a victim! (for ages 11–19). *Student sexual harassment: Minimize the risk* [Videotape and curriculum guide]. Santa Barbara, CA: McGrath Training Systems.

McGrath, M. J. (1996c). Video 3: Avoid harm and liability (for teachers & staff). *Student sexual harassment: Minimize the risk* [Videotape and curriculum guide]. Santa Barbara, CA: McGrath Training Systems.

McGrath, M. J. (1996d). Video 4: Investigation template & techniques (for administrators). *Student sexual harassment: Minimize the risk* [Videotape and curriculum guide]. Santa Barbara, CA: McGrath Training Systems.

McGrath, M. J. (1996e). Video 5: Vital do's and don'ts (for administrators). *Student sexual harassment: Minimize the risk* [Videotape and curriculum guide]. Santa Barbara, CA: McGrath Training Systems.

McGrath, M. J. (1996f). Video 6: In our schools (for parents). *Student sexual harassment: Minimize the risk* [Videotape and curriculum guide]. Santa Barbara, CA: McGrath Training Systems.

McGrath, M. J. (1998a). Video 1: Show and tell: The movie! *The early faces of violence: From schoolyard bullying and ridicule to sexual harassment* [Videotape and curriculum guide]. Santa Barbara, CA: McGrath Training Systems.

McGrath, M. J. (1998b). Video 2: You and me (for ages 4–6). *The early faces of violence: From schoolyard bullying and ridicule to sexual harassment* [Videotape and curriculum guide]. Santa Barbara, CA: McGrath Training Systems.

McGrath, M. J. (1998c). Video 3: Learning the game (for ages 7–9). *The early faces of violence: From schoolyard bullying and ridicule to sexual harassment* [Videotape and curriculum guide]. Santa Barbara, CA: McGrath Training Systems.

McGrath, M. J. (1998d). Video 4: Max's magical machine (for ages 10–12). *The early faces of violence: From schoolyard bullying and ridicule to sexual harassment* [Videotape and curriculum guide]. Santa Barbara, CA: McGrath Training Systems.

McGrath, M. J. (1998e). Video 5: A culture of cruelty (for teachers & staff). *The early faces of violence: From schoolyard bullying and ridicule to sexual harassment* [Videotape and curriculum guide]. Santa Barbara, CA: McGrath Training Systems.

McGrath, M. J. (1998f). Video 6: Just the facts, ma'am (for administrators). *The early faces of violence: From schoolyard bullying and ridicule to sexual harassment* [Videotape and curriculum guide]. Santa Barbara, CA: McGrath Training Systems.

McGrath, M. J. (1998g). Video 7: You and your school (for parents). *The early faces of violence: From schoolyard bullying and ridicule to sexual harassment* [Videotape and curriculum guide]. Santa Barbara, CA: McGrath Training Systems.

McGrath, M. J. (2000). The human dynamics of personnel evaluation. *The School Administrator, 57*(9), 34–38.

McGrath, M. J. (2003a). Video 1: Principles, practices and the legal framework. *McGrath SUCCEED with communication, supervision, evaluation and leadership video education series.* Santa Barbara, CA: McGrath Training Systems.

McGrath, M. J. (2003b). Video 2: The human dynamics of leading and supervising people. *McGrath SUCCEED with communication, supervision, evaluation and leadership video education series.* Santa Barbara, CA: McGrath Training Systems.

McGrath, M. J. (2003c). Video 3: Whole-person based leadership and supervision: Why it works. *McGrath SUCCEED with communication, supervision, evaluation and leadership video education series.* Santa Barbara, CA: McGrath Training Systems.

McGrath, M. J. (2003d). Video 4: Building relationships: A continuum of communication and supervision. *McGrath SUCCEED with communication, supervision, evaluation and leadership video education series.* Santa Barbara, CA: McGrath Training Systems.

McGrath, M. J. (2003e). Video 5: Stepping into the powertools of constructive supervision and evaluation *McGrath SUCCEED with communication, supervision, evaluation and leadership video education series.* Santa Barbara, CA: McGrath Training Systems.

McGrath, M. J. (2003f). Video 6: SUCCEED facilitator video. *McGrath SUCCEED with communication, supervision, evaluation and leadership video education series.* Santa Barbara, CA: McGrath Training Systems.

McGrath, M. J. (2005a). *McGrath SUCCEED with communication, supervision, evaluation and leadership instructor manual.* Santa Barbara, CA: McGrath Training Systems.

McGrath, M. J. (2005b). *McGrath SUCCEED with communication, supervision, evaluation and leadership participant training manual* (Version 5.1). Santa Barbara, CA: McGrath Training Systems.

McGrath, M. J. (2005c). *McGrath SUCCEED with communication, supervision, evaluation and leadership video education series facilitator guide* (Version 5.1). Santa Barbara, CA: McGrath Training Systems.

McGrath, M. J. (2006a). Awareness training for school employees. *Sexual harassment and abuse: Minimize the risk distance learning series.* Santa Barbara, CA: McGrath CyberSchool.

McGrath, M. J. (2006b). *Case study: The impact of student and staff training on the incidence of bullying and harassment complaints in a large U.S. school district.* Santa Barbara, CA: McGrath Training Systems.

McGrath, M. J. (2006c). Complaint management and investigation training for school administrators. *Sexual harassment and abuse: Minimize the risk distance learning series.* Santa Barbara, CA: McGrath CyberSchool.

McGrath, M. J. (2006d). *McGrath athletic liability: Minimize the risk training manual.* Santa Barbara, CA: McGrath Training Systems.

McGrath, M. J. (2006e). *McGrath bullying and harassment investigation training manual* (Rev. Ed.). Santa Barbara, CA: McGrath Training Systems.

McGrath, M. J. (2006f). *McGrath bullying and harassment training of trainers manual, staff training.* Santa Barbara, CA: McGrath Training Systems.

McGrath, M. J. (2006g). *McGrath bullying and harassment training of trainers manual, student training, grades pre-K–6.* Santa Barbara, CA: McGrath Training Systems.

McGrath, M. J. (2006h). *McGrath bullying and harassment training of trainers manual, student training, grades 7–12.* Santa Barbara, CA: McGrath Training Systems.

McGrath, M. J. (2006i). *McGrath sexual harassment staff and teacher awareness training manual* (Rev. Ed.). Santa Barbara, CA: McGrath Training Systems.

McGrath, M. J. (2006j). *McGrath sexual harassment investigation manual* (Rev. Ed.). Santa Barbara, CA: McGrath Training Systems.

McGrath, M. J. (2006k). *McGrath vulnerable educators liability: Minimize the risk training manual.* Santa Barbara, CA: McGrath Training Systems.

McGrath, M. J. (2006l). *McGrath workplace investigation training manual* (Rev. Ed.). Santa Barbara, CA: McGrath Training Systems.

Monroe, S. (2006, January). *Letter to educators.* Retrieved March 22, 2006, from http://www.mcgrathinc.com/ocr/EFlashOCR.htm#readmore

Moran, G. (2002, August 16). Teen's explanation given in interviews with psychiatrist. *San Diego Union-Tribune,* Retrieved March 22, 2006, from http://www.signonsandiego.com/news/metro/santana/20020816-9999_1n16psych.html

Morse, J., Barnes, E., & Rivera, E. (2001, March 19). Girlhoods interrupted. *Time, 157*(11), 28.

Mynard, H., Joseph, S., & Alexander, J. (2000). Peer-victimisation and posttraumatic stress in adolescents. *Personality and Individual Difference, 29*(5), 815–882.

Nansel, T. R., Overpeck, M., Pilla, R. S., Ruan, W. J., Simmons-Morton, B., & Scheidt, P. (2001). Bullying behavior among U.S. youth: Prevalence and association with psychosocial adjustment. *Journal of the American Medical Association, 285,* 2094–2100.

National Center for Education Statistics. (2004). *Guide to protecting the privacy of student information: State and local education agencies* (NCES 2004–330). Washington, DC: NCES. Retrieved March 22, 2006, from http://nces.ed.gov/pubsearch/pubsinfo.asp? pubid=2004330

National Center for Education Statistics. (2005a). *Indicators of school crime and safety 2005. Indicator 12: Bullying at school.* Retrieved March 17, 2006, from http://nces.ed.gov/programs/crimeindicators/Indicators.asp?PubPageNumber=12

National Center for Education Statistics. (2005b). *Indicators of school crime and safety 2005. Indicator 17: Students' perceptions of personal safety at school and away from school.* Retrieved March 17, 2006, from http://nces.ed.gov/programs/crimeindicators/Indicators.asp?PubPageNumber=17

National Center for PTSD. (n.d.). *What is posttraumatic stress disorder?* Washington, DC: U.S. Department of Veteran's Affairs. Retrieved March 22, 2006, from http://www.ncptsd.va.gov/facts/general/fs_what_is_ptsd.html

Nickelodeon & Kaiser Family Foundation. (2001). *Talking with kids about tough issues: A national survey of parents and kids.* Menlo Park, CA: Kaiser Family Foundation. Retrieved March 17, 2006, from www.kff.org/kaiserpolls

Nishina, A., & Juvonen, J. (2005a, March 28). *Bullying among sixth graders a daily occurrence, UCLA study finds* [Press Release, pp. 1–2]. Los Angeles: UCLA.

Nishina, A., & Juvonen, J. (2005b). Daily reports of witnessing and experiencing peer harassment in middle school. *Child Development, 76*(2), 435–450.

Nishina, A., Juvonen, J., & Witkow, M. (2005). Sticks and stones may break my bones, but names will make me feel sick: The psychosocial, somatic, and scholastic consequences of peer harassment. *Journal of Clinical Child & Adolescent Psychology, 34*(1), 37–48.

Office for Civil Rights. (2001, January 19). *Revised sexual harassment guidance: Harassment of students by school employees, other students or third parties, Title IX* (p. 38). Washington, DC: U.S. Department of Education.

Olweus, D. (1993). *Bullying at school: What we know and what we can do* (pp. 24–25, 32–35, 54–58) Oxford, UK: Blackwell.

Olweus, D. (2001). Peer harassment: A critical analysis and some important issues. In J. Juvonen & S. Graham (Eds.), *Peer harassment in school: The plight of the vulnerable and victimized* (pp. 3–20). New York: Guilford Press.

O'Moore, A. M., & Minton, S. J. (2004). Ireland: The Donegal primary schools' anti-bullying project. In P. K. Smith, D. Pepler, & K. Rigby (Eds.), *Bullying in schools: How successful can interventions be?* (pp. 275–287). Cambridge, UK: Cambridge University Press.

Oncale v. Sundowner Offshore Services, Inc. 523 US 75 (1998).

Owens, L., Slee, P., & Shute, R. (2001). Victimization among teenage girls: What can be done about indirect harassment? In J. Juvonen & S. Graham (Eds.), *Peer harassment in school: The plight of the vulnerable and victimized* (pp. 215–241). New York: Guilford Press.

Paulson, A. (2006, February 2). Schools grapple with policing students' online journals. *Christian Science Monitor.* Retrieved March 9, 2006, from http://www.csmonitor.com/2006/0202/p01s04-stct.html

Pepler, D. J., & Craig, W. (2000). *Report #60: Making a difference in bullying.* Retrieved March 18, 2006, from http://netscaffold.bullying.org/external/documents/making_a_difference_in_bullying.pdf

Pesznecker, K. (2004, July 1). District settled suit for millions. *Anchorage Daily News.* Retrieved March 22, 2006, from http://www.adn.com/front/story/5251643p-5187093c.html

Rigby, K. (1996). *Bullying in schools: And what to do about it.* Melbourne: Australian Council for Educational Research.

Rigby, K. (2001). Health consequences of bullying and its prevention in schools. In J. Juvonen & S. Graham (Eds.), *Peer harassment in school: The plight of the vulnerable and victimized* (pp. 310–331). New York: Guilford Press.

Roth, A. (2001, September 6). Dad says bullying drove son to act. *San Diego Union-Tribune,* Retrieved March 21, 2006, from http://www.signonsandiego.com/news/metro/santana/20010906-9999_1n6andy.html

Salmivalli, C. (2001). Group view on victimization: Empirical findings and their implications. In J. Juvonen & S. Graham (Eds.), *Peer harassment in school: The plight of the vulnerable and victimized* (pp. 398–419). New York: Guilford Press.

Science Daily. (2003). *New research dispels popular myth that a bully's words will never hurt you* [Press release]. Retrieved March 18, 2006, from http://www.sciencedaily.com/releases/2003/04/030417080610.htm

Seamons v. Snow. No. 1:94-CV-04-ST (D. Utah Mar. 23, 2001).

Senge, P. M. (1990). *The fifth discipline: The art & practice of the learning organization* (pp. 90, 139, 142, 373) New York: Doubleday.

Senge, P. M., Scharmer, C. O., Jaworski, J., & Flowers, B. S. (2005). *Presence: An exploration of profound change in people, organizations, and society* (p. 6). New York: Doubleday.

Shaw, G. B. (1903). *Man and superman: A comedy and a philosophy* (p. 29). Cambridge, MA: University Press.

Shaw, G.B. (n.d). *George Bernard Shaw quotes*. Retrieved May 5, 2006, from http://en.thinkexist.com/quotation

Shimkus, J. (2005). *H.R. 284: To amend the Safe and Drug-Free Schools and Communities Act to include bullying and harassment prevention programs*. Washington, DC: United States House of Representatives. Retrieved March 25, 2006, from http://www.govtrack.us/congress/bill.xpd?bill=h109-284

Sickmund, M., Snyder, H. N., & Poe-Yamagata, E. (1997). *Juvenile offenders and victims: 1997 update on violence*. Washington, DC: U.S. Department of Justice, Office of Juvenile Justice and Delinquency Prevention.

Simmons, R. (2002). *Odd girl out* (p. 3). San Diego, CA: Harcourt.

Smith, P. K., Pepler, D., & Rigby, K. (Eds.). (2004). *Bullying in schools: How successful can interventions be?* (pp. 2–5). Cambridge, UK: Cambridge University Press.

Spitalli, S. J. (2003). Breaking the code of silence: How students can help keep schools—and each other—safe. *American School Board Journal, 190*(9), 56–59.

Steinberger, E. D. (1995). Margaret Wheatley on leadership for change. *The School Administrator, 52*(1), 16–20.

Stout, M. (2005). *The sociopath next door: The ruthless versus the rest of us* (pp. 7, 9, 11, 46, 49–50). New York: Broadway Books.

Sullivan, K. (2000). *The anti-bullying handbook* (pp. 22, 25–28, 30–31, 36–38). Oxford, UK: Oxford University Press.

Sullivan, K., Cleary, M., & Sullivan, G. (2004). *Bullying in secondary schools* (pp. 15–16, 19–20, 112). Thousand Oaks, CA: Corwin Press.

Tolle, E. (2005). *A new earth: Awakening to your life's purpose.* New York: Penguin.

Underwood, M. K. (2003). *Social aggression among girls* (pp. 9, 16, 65, 93, 134, 183, 186). New York: Guilford Press.

U.S. Centers for Disease Control. (2002, June 28). *Centers for Disease Control and Prevention surveillance summaries* (MMWR 2002:51 No. 22–4). Washington, DC: Author.

U.S. Department of Education Office for Civil Rights & National Association of Attorneys General. (1999, January). *Protecting students from harassment and hate crime: A guide for schools*. Washington, DC: U.S. Department of Education. Retrieved March 22, 2006, from http://www.ed.gov/offices/OCR/archives/Harassment/index.html

U.S. Department of Health and Human Services. (2004). *Stop bullying now resource kit*. Washington, DC: Author. Retrieved March 20, 2006, from http://www.stopbullyingnow.hrsa.gov

Vossekull, B., Fein, R., Reddy, M., Borum, R., & Modzelski, W. (2002). *The final report and findings of the safe school initiative: Implications for the prevention of school attacks in the United States*. Washington, DC: U.S. Secret Service & U.S. Department of Education. Retrieved March 18, 2006, from http://www.treas.gov/usss/ntac/ssi_final_report .pdf

Washington State School Directors' Association. (1999). *Using common sense, safety and civility in our schools*. Seattle, WA: WSSDA.

Wiseman, R. (2002). *Queen bees and wannabes: Helping your daughter survive cliques, gossip, boyfriends, and other realities of adolescence*. New York: Three Rivers Press.

Wright, J. L. (2002). Panelist remarks in American Medical Association. *Proceedings: Educational forum on adolescent health: Youth bullying*. Chicago: AMA.

Ziegler, S., & Pepler, D. J. (1993). Bullying at school: Pervasive and persistent. *Orbit, 24,* 29–31.

Index

**CORWIN
PRESS**

The Corwin Press logo—a raven striding across an open book—represents the union of courage and learning. Corwin Press is committed to improving education for all learners by publishing books and other professional development resources for those serving the field of PreK–12 education. By providing practical, hands-on materials, Corwin Press continues to carry out the promise of its motto: **"Helping Educators Do Their Work Better."**